YOU *had me at* COWBOY

JENNIE MARTS

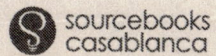

Copyright © 2018 by Jennie Marts
Cover and internal design © 2018 by Sourcebooks, Inc.
Cover design by Dawn Adams/Sourcebooks, Inc.
Cover image © Rob Lang
Internal images by ibrandify/Freepik

Sourcebooks and the colophon are registered trademarks of Sourcebooks, Inc.

All rights reserved. No part of this book may be reproduced in any form or by any electronic or mechanical means including information storage and retrieval systems—except in the case of brief quotations embodied in critical articles or reviews—without permission in writing from its publisher, Sourcebooks, Inc.

The characters and events portrayed in this book are fictitious or are used fictitiously. Any similarity to real persons, living or dead, is purely coincidental and not intended by the author.

All brand names and product names used in this book are trademarks, registered trademarks, or trade names of their respective holders. Sourcebooks, Inc., is not associated with any product or vendor in this book.

Published by Sourcebooks Casablanca, an imprint of Sourcebooks, Inc.
P.O. Box 4410, Naperville, Illinois 60567-4410
(630) 961-3900
Fax: (630) 961-2168
sourcebooks.com

Printed and bound in the United States of America.
OPM 10 9 8 7 6 5 4 3 2 1

Also by Jennie Marts

COWBOYS OF CREEDENCE

Caught Up in a Cowboy

*This book is dedicated to my grandmothers,
Jeanne Bryant and Helen Haring—
two women who taught me
the meaning of hard work and dedication,
of love and loyalty to faith and family,
who loved to laugh and were quick to hug
and always believed in good grammar
and that I could do and be anything I set my mind to.*

Chapter 1

TESSA KANE PACED THE STEPS OF THE LODGE AND CHECKED her watch. Again.

She could hear the laughter of the party going on inside and catch the scent of grilled meat every time someone opened the front door.

She was ignoring the growling of her stomach—she knew she should have eaten something on the drive up the pass, but she'd been too nervous. This was the first date she'd been on in over a year. It should have been no big deal, a simple setup with her friend's brother whose girlfriend had dumped him and left him dateless for an important weekend of wedding events.

Except that her friend's brother just happened to be a professional hockey player, and the wedding was for his Colorado Summit teammate, the notorious bad-boy bachelor Rockford James.

Why had she agreed to this stupid idea anyway? She had enough on her plate right now without adding the stress of going out with a man she didn't know to an event full of celebrities, supermodels, and professional athletes.

Shielding her eyes against the bright Colorado sun, she stepped into the shade of an aspen and peered down the road, searching for Mick's car. A bead of sweat rolled down her back, and she tugged at the too-tight waistband of her skirt, another reminder that she had no business being here. Apparently, trading dating for ice cream and Netflix had added a few pounds to her already tall and curvy frame.

It had taken her over an hour just to find a suitable—which was another word for *still fits*—outfit for this party, and she had brought three spares and a comfortable pair of jeans, in case she'd gotten the first look of a black pencil skirt and burgundy silk top completely wrong.

She'd traversed the depths of her closet like an explorer searching for gold in the Mayan ruins to find the box with the matching burgundy party shoes. The expensive pumps were in pristine condition, which just went to show how long it had been since she'd gone to an actual party.

Her phone vibrated in her pocket.

That better be Mick, and he'd better be on his way.

She pulled the phone free and checked the display. *Not Mick*. "Hi, Mimi."

"Hi, honey," her grandmother said. "I was hoping you could grab some of those marshmallow cookies while you're at the store."

Tess rolled her eyes. "I'm not *at* the store. I'm on a date. I told you that."

"Oh. I thought you were kidding."

"Thanks," she muttered as her shoulders slumped forward. "And even if I were at the store, you know we can't afford luxuries like cookies." They couldn't afford anything—not since The Scam.

"I know." Her grandmother's voice held the tone of an insolent child. "And I know it's all my fault."

"It's not *all* your fault, Gram," Tess reassured her. "It's the fault of those bastard scam artists who swindled you out of all your money." And out of all hers too, since Tess had given her grandmother every single dime she had after Mimi had sent thousands of dollars in money orders and gift cards to someone who'd said that they were in *dire need* of her help.

Well, now Mimi was in *dire* need, because she was about to lose her house. Which would be equally bad for Tess, since she lived there too.

That was why she should be home right now, working on a great story that would garner them some much-needed moolah instead of standing outside the Masonic Lodge in the tiny mountain town of Creedence, sweating through the band of her bra and waiting for some guy to take her to a fancy party that she had no real interest in attending.

"I really thought he was a prince," her grandmother was saying for the hundredth time.

"Listen, Mimi, we'll come up with something." Tess softened her tone. It really wasn't Mimi's fault that she had a compassionate heart and wanted to help someone in need. "I think I'm just going to come home. This guy hasn't shown up, and I have an idea for a story to work on." On the hour's drive up from Denver, she'd been mulling over an idea to pitch to her boss at *Colorado In-Depth*.

"No. No. NO. This is the first time you've been on a date in years."

Well, one year actually, but who's counting?

"You stay and have fun, and I'll figure something out. We have another week or so to come up with the money, and I'm working on a few ideas."

Tess would bet she was. But who knew what kind

of harebrained scheme her grandmother would come up with next? Her last idea of a "spiked" lemonade stand had almost gotten them kicked out of the neighborhood.

Her phone buzzed.

"I gotta go, Mimi. I'll call you later. Don't wait up."

She clicked off, but her heart sank as she read the text message displayed on the screen. Sorry, baby. Can't make it. Have fun without me.

Seriously?

Was this really happening? The first time she'd finally put herself out there and agreed to a date, and Mick—the dick—had stood her up.

Well, Mick, she *would* have fun. At home. In her pajamas. Even without cookies.

She took a step forward just as a wet splat hit the front of her silk shirt. A gag filled her throat as she looked down at the greenish-yellow gob of bird turd that was running down her boob.

Could this fracking day get any worse?

Her party shoes were already digging painfully into the sides of her ankles as she trudged across the parking lot to her crappy, ancient car. The '89 Ford Taurus was older than she was. It had been her grandmother's car, but Tess couldn't complain too much. She kept reminding herself that having a free car to drive when she needed it beat out the cost of her pride any day.

Her phone buzzed again, but this time the screen showed an unknown number. Maybe it was Mick calling to apologize and say he was showing up after all.

"Hello?"

"Tessa, this is Gordon. We need to talk." Again—*not* Mick. Gordon was her boss, and in her experience, no conversation that started with the words *We need to talk* ever ended well.

She climbed into the car and started the engine, praying that the air-conditioning fairies had miraculously shown up and fixed hers. No such luck. Her car was like an oven, and a blast of hot air blew her bangs across her sweat-dampened forehead. "What's up?"

"Listen, Tess. I like you. You're a nice person, but you're just not the kind of writer that we need here at *In-Depth*. I'm going to have to let you go."

Apparently, the worst thing to do in the middle of a crappy day was to throw down a threat to the "bad day" gods. But was he really *firing* her? Not that she liked this job that much anyway, but it was the only job she had, and she couldn't afford to lose it. Not now.

"But why?"

"I told you two weeks ago that you needed to take the hard line on your next piece, to really get in there and dig for the good stuff. I even gave you something easy, an assignment covering the problems with the homeless population downtown."

"And that's what I wrote about."

"You wrote about a homeless woman who rescued a kitten from the sewer and made her out to be some kind of damned hero."

Tess huffed. "Well, that sounds like a hero in my book. You should have seen that kitten."

She heard him groan. "I don't give two shits about the kitten. It's not the kind of story we cover. It's just not working out, Tess."

"Can't you just give me one more chance? I need this job. And I've seriously had the worst day. I just got stood up on the first date I've gone out on in a year, a bird pooped on me, and now I have to drive all the way back down the pass."

"Down the pass? What kind of date were you on?"

"A terrible one. I was supposed to go to a fancy-pants prewedding party for Rockford James, but instead, I'm just going home to sulk at a pity party for one."

"Wait a minute. *The* Rockford James? The hockey-playing cowboy who was on everyone's most eligible bachelor list?"

"I guess."

"Everybody's talking about the NHL's infamous bad boy who was a player on the ice and off and what happened to make him suddenly settle down with a quickie wedding." Her editor's voice fairly crackled with excitement. "You want to keep your job, Tess? Go in there and get me *that* story."

"You want me to go spy on the bride and groom at their own party?"

"That's exactly what I want you to do. Go in there and mingle... Talk to the family, the guests, find the dirt."

"But that's not the kind of story I write."

"It is now. It is if you want to keep your job."

She chewed at her bottom lip, knowing she had no choice. She couldn't let her grandmother down—not after everything Mimi had done for her. Tess didn't *want* to keep the job, but she *needed* to keep the job. Needed it enough to go into that party and motherfinking mingle for the muck on Rockford James.

It seemed she had no other choice.

"Okay, I'll do it. On one condition," she said, knowing she was pressing her luck but not caring. Heck, she'd already been fired and pooped on. What could it hurt to try?

"Do you really think you're in a place to ask for conditions?" Gordon asked.

"Do you want the story or not?"

"Fine. What's your condition?"

"If I get the story this weekend, you pay me a bonus, like the one you gave Steve Larson for that piece he did on the political scandal, and you pay me *in cash* when I turn it in." She'd heard the rumors about Steve's bonus and knew it was enough to pay two of the delinquent house payments.

"You get me that story in time for next week's edition, and I'll pay you *half* what I gave Steve. But you can have it in cash."

Her heart leapt in her poop-plastered chest. That was good enough for her. "Deal."

They spent another few minutes on the phone, with Gordon telling her what he knew about Rockford and what he could quickly google—the names of the bride and the members of Rock's family, and a few details about the family ranch where he'd grown up. "Oh, and from everything I've ever heard, the guy hates reporters, like freaking *loathes* them. So you need to be crafty about finding a way to talk to him."

Great. No problem. She could be crafty. If by crafty, Gordon meant good with a glue gun. "Thanks for the warning. Although you could have told me that before."

"I never said it would be easy."

She let out a sigh. She'd come up with something. Mick had told her that the party would go all afternoon and into the evening, so she still had plenty of time. "Talk to you Monday."

She turned off the engine and unzipped the bag sitting in her passenger seat. Rummaging through it, she searched for the white blouse she'd pulled from the dryer that morning. It wasn't as fancy as the silk one, but it was clean, fairly unwrinkled, and better than what she had on. She grabbed the shirt, then slung her purse over her shoulder as she climbed out of the car, automatically pushing the lock down as she rehearsed ways to approach the bride and groom.

Already nervous about going into the party alone, she absently let the door swing shut behind her, realizing she'd just locked it at the same moment she spied the keys still hanging from the ignition.

"A toast," Mason James proclaimed, holding up his glass. "To my brother Rock and his beautiful bride, Quinn."

He looked around the room at the mix of family, friends, and Rock's teammates who filled the lodge. It had been his mom's idea to host a party for the team several days before the wedding. She'd thought it might help ease the pain when Rock didn't invite the whole Colorado Summit hockey team to his actual wedding.

It had to be rough to be that popular. But that was his brother.

He turned to Rock and had to smile. He just looked so dang happy.

Mason raised his voice above the noise of the crowded room.

"I might be the best man at this wedding, but Rock is the real best man, and he's getting the best girl." He smiled at his brother's fiancée. "I feel like I've known Quinn and her brother, Logan, all my life. Our ranches are across the field from each other, and even though our families have been feuding for as long as we can remember, us kids never cared a whit about that. We grew up together, swimming in the pond in the summer and playing hockey on the ice in the winter."

He stopped, clearing his throat against the emotion suddenly filling it, but keeping his gaze trained on Quinn. "Rock has loved you since he was old enough to understand what love is. And Colt and I have always loved you just like you were our sister, so on behalf of my mom, Colt, and myself, we couldn't be happier to welcome you into the family."

He raised his glass higher. "To Rock and Quinn, may your life be full of love and laughter, and may all your dreams come true. Including the one about winning the Stanley Cup next year."

The crowd cheered, and the sound of laughter and clinking glasses filled the hall. The town of Creedence, Colorado, might be small—in fact, the population of twelve hundred people would barely fill a hockey arena—but they were die-hard fans of their hometown boy and the team he played for.

Rockford stood and threw his arm around Mason's shoulders. "Thanks, Brother."

Colt stood on his other side. The three of them clinked their glasses, then all took a swig of beer.

Quinn pushed back her chair and squeezed between them. "Thanks, Mace. That was a great toast." She gave him a warm hug and spoke softly into his ear. "And your dream girl is out there. You just haven't met her yet. But I know you're going to be someone's *best* man too."

He squeezed his almost sister-in-law and winced as he looked over her shoulder at Leanne Perkins, her maid of honor and the girl he'd once had plenty of dreams about. Leanne's eyes were red and tearstained, and he wondered if her tears were for the touching words of his toast or for the fact that Rockford James was now good and truly off the market.

They got along fine now, but he and Leanne had a history he'd rather forget. He'd had the worst crush on her in high school and thought himself the luckiest guy around when she'd agreed to go to prom with him junior year. Then he'd found out her real interest was in Rockford, and she'd only been dating him to get to his older brother.

She hadn't been the last woman who had burned him with that particular stunt.

He hated being used and couldn't stand liars. And he'd learned quickly that when it came to Rock, some people of the female persuasion couldn't be trusted. He'd also learned that his bullshit detector wasn't always accurate, and it was easier to keep a healthy distance than to open himself up to getting hurt again. So despite Quinn's encouraging words, he wasn't planning on finding the woman of his dreams any day soon.

Finished with his best man duties, he escaped the table and circled around to the back of the room, giving high fives and handshakes as he passed Rock's teammates.

The town's ancient librarian, Lola Carter, patted him on the arm as he approached the buffet table. "Don't worry, honey. The right girl is out there for you. I'm sure we'll be celebrating your wedding next."

He tried to smile through his grimace.

He *wasn't* worried. In fact, the only thing he *was* worried about was that he might strangle the next person who told him he was next or that a special girl was out there waiting for him. He knew Lola meant well. Just like the multiple other well-meaning neighbors, friends, and various elderly women who had told him essentially the same thing over the course of the party. But dang, he was so tired of hearing the same old racket.

"I'm sure you're right, Miss Lola," he said, patting the papery-thin skin of her small hand.

"I usually am." She gave him a small chuckle and a wink. "And don't forget about my niece, Kara. She's still single too. I can give you her number."

Seriously? All he wanted was a chocolate chip cookie. "That's mighty kind of you, ma'am. But I'm okay for now."

She shrugged and turned her attention to the food. "You know where to find me."

He snagged a couple of cookies and made his escape. Letting out a sigh, he dropped into the seat next to his great-aunt Sassy. "How you doing, beautiful?"

Her real name was Cassandra, but he and his brothers had called her Aunt Sassy from the time they were little, and it was a well-earned nickname. She was his grandmother's sister and had always been important in their lives. She didn't take bullshit from anyone—or offer it either. That was one of the things Mason loved about her.

"I've been better, but I've been worse," Sassy said.

"My joints are killing me, and my girdle must have shrunk in the dryer 'cause it's digging into my gut. But your brother doesn't look like anything is killing him. I don't think I've ever seen him look so happy." His aunt winked at Mason. "And I thought you gave a real fine toast."

He offered her a shrug and a murmured, "Thanks."

She held up a tiny square of bread. "Speaking of toast, who in the hell decided a piece of cucumber and a sliver of nut constituted a sandwich? Your mother probably paid top dollar for these. In my day, a sandwich was ham or bologna on white bread. And if we wanted to get fancy, we'd slap on some Miracle Whip and maybe cut the crust off."

He grinned. There were a lot of things they'd done differently in her day. "Don't worry. Those are only the appetizers. Mom's got plenty of barbecue coming out, and you know she'll have all the fixin's to go with it."

His mother, Vivienne James, would make sure every detail was attended to. She'd successfully run the Triple J Ranch and raised three boys on her own. She could easily handle a shindig for a few hundred people—especially with Rock's bank account funding the whole thing.

"You need anything?" He gestured to Sassy's half-empty glass of iced tea, its condensation leaving a dark ring on the teal-blue tablecloth. "You want me to get you some more tea?"

"Nah. I'm fine, honey. I'm getting ready to switch to beer anyway." She pointed toward the drink table. "But you might want to try to find a mop. That penis ice sculpture is melting all over the floor."

Mason choked on his swallow of tea. "That what?"

Her wrinkled finger stabbed at the air. "I might be an old woman, but I do remember what they look like." She shook her head and added a couple of *tsk*'s for effect. "Personally, I think it's in poor taste, and I'm surprised your mother allowed it, but who am I to say?"

He tilted his head at the sculpture, then stifled a laugh. "Aunt Sass, it's supposed to be a hockey stick and a couple of pucks."

She squinted her eyes. "Ah. I thought it was weird to have the centerpiece symbolizing an erection. But it is a men's hockey team, and you never know these days."

He let out a chuckle. "Yeah, I can see how you might think that." He could also see the puddles forming on the floor where the ice was melting. "I'll go find a mop."

Tessa slipped into the back door of the lodge, clutching the clean shirt to her waist. She spied the ladies' room door at the end of the hall and hurried toward it, but the door wouldn't budge.

Dang it.

She waited a few seconds, then checked the other doors in the hallway. The first one was locked, but the second opened into an odd combination coat closet and storeroom, and she slipped inside. One half of the small room was carpeted and had a rod of hangers along part of the wall, while the other side was tiled and had a tall shelf that held assorted books and cleaning supplies.

The door didn't have a lock, but it would work in a pinch, and she wouldn't need long to change.

She quickly unbuttoned the stained silk blouse and let it fall to the floor, her mind preoccupied with how she was going to get into the party without Mick. This wasn't how her day was supposed to go—especially the part about locking her keys in the car—but after a quick round of cussing followed by a swift bout of self-pity, she'd rallied, giving herself the kind of pep talk she imagined Mimi would have offered.

This might not have been the original plan for the day, but she was improvising and moving on to plan B.

Shoving her arms into the sleeves, she noticed the shirt felt odd but didn't realize what the problem was until she tried to pull the lapels together. *What the heck?*

She pulled at the sides again and felt the material stretch across her back.

No. I couldn't have.

She looked closer at the shirt, and her shoulders fell.

I did. She'd grabbed the wrong white shirt from the dryer. Instead of removing her roomy, stretch-cotton shirt, she'd taken her grandmother's blouse. Her petite, five-foot-nothing grandmother.

Well, shit. She wanted to weep as she looked down and realized there was no way she was squeezing her ample chest into that blouse.

Plan B ruined by a double-D cup!

Dammit.

Please fit, she prayed as she tried again, squashing her chest and working to squeeze the small button into the opposite hole. She cursed the extra weight she'd put on, knowing this wasn't the first time lately she'd tried to squeeze into apparel that was just a smidge too small.

She let out a tiny shriek as the door to the utility closet suddenly opened, then froze as she took in the ridiculously handsome cowboy who filled its frame. The hinges of his chiseled jaw must've been broken because his mouth dropped open and his eyes went wide at the sight of her.

Par for the course of her day, the button on her shirt picked that horribly inopportune moment to work free, and her shirt popped open like a can of biscuits.

"Oh dang. Sorry," the cowboy muttered, his eyes widening further as his gaze dropped to the black lacy bra for just a moment before he turned his back and shimmied out of his suit jacket. He passed it back to her. "You all right there, miss?"

No, she was not all right. She was *definitely* not all right.

She wanted to cry and stamp her feet and run home to Mimi's house to curl up on her grandmother's outdated chintz sofa and stuff her face with marshmallow cookies.

But that wasn't an option because Mimi's cupboards were bare, and she may not have her house—or the chintz sofa—for much longer. Tess held back a sigh as she slid her arms into the sleeves of the jacket, careful not to damage the red rose pinned to the lapel.

It was time to admit defeat. To give up on this stupid plan and try to come up with another way to raise the money. She wasn't cut out for this kind of stress. Maybe she should rethink Mimi's lemonade-stand idea or see if she could get a job as a waitress.

"I'm fine. Mostly. Except that a bird pooped on my shirt, and the one I was trying to change into must have shrunk in the dryer." She couldn't believe she'd just blurted out the bird-turd fiasco, and she couldn't bring herself to admit the added stupid mistake of grabbing the wrong blouse. "I just need a minute."

"I'll leave you to it then," he answered, turning his head slightly and offering her a tip of his hat. She noticed a grin tugging at the corners of his lips as he backed away from the door.

She pulled one side of the coat over the other, thankful the suit jacket covered her exposed chest.

Hmmm. She skimmed the satiny petals of the rose. Boutonnieres were typically reserved for the bridal party. This guy must be one of the groomsmen.

"Wait," she called as the cute cowboy started to walk away.

Plan B had just turned into plan C.

Chapter 2

TESS SUCKED HER BOTTOM LIP UNDER HER FRONT TEETH and tried for her best damsel-in-distress voice. "I realize you don't know me, but I could really use your help."

The cowboy turned back and arched an eyebrow before glancing down at her now-covered chest. "It seems like we've passed formal introductions. I may not know your name, but I feel like we've already made it to second base." His tone was teasing, and he offered her an impish grin. "Which is further than I got on my last date."

She doubted that.

He was the epitome of tall, dark, and handsome. Lean and broad shouldered, with jet-black hair and traces of a five-o'clock shadow already smudged across his jaw, he couldn't have to work that hard to get dates. And with that panty-melting grin, she suspected women would be lined up to not just get to second base, but also to slide into home with this charmer.

She grinned back—dang it, she couldn't help it; he was just so cute—and held out her hand. "I'm Tessa Kane, but you can call me Tess."

"Mason." He reached for her hand, and the feel of his warm, callused palm against her skin sent a shiver of heat down her back. His voice was deep and rich and melted over her like butter on a pancake.

She couldn't seem to stop smiling. "Nice to meet you, Mason."

Forget the damsel-in-distress ruse. Hell, forget about the stupid story. She should just say "Screw it" to this terrible day and pull this cowboy into the closet with her. She was already halfway to undressed—all it would take would be to drop his jacket and step out of her skirt and painful party pumps.

Or, on second thought, she could leave the heels on and just step out of her skirt. What came next would be worth the pain.

His eyes narrowed, almost as if he could read her thoughts, and a slow smile turned up the edges of his lips. Dang, he had great lips too.

He seemed to have a great everything. Even his jacket smelled amazing—like expensive aftershave with hints of musk—and she wanted to lift it to her face and inhale his scent.

But she couldn't because she couldn't move, could barely breathe as she stood frozen, captured by the heat of his stare. She swallowed, her mouth suddenly dry, as his gaze dipped to her lips.

The air around them fairly sizzled with energy. Neither of them spoke. He seemed to drink her in, as if feasting on her with his eyes, and her body heated with the intensity of his gaze.

What the heck was happening?

Was she seriously considering yanking this guy into the closet and having her way with him? Her body tingled at the thought, even as the heat of a blush warmed her neck.

But there was something about this man—maybe the way he'd chivalrously offered her his jacket, the deep timbre of his voice, or just the fact that he was a ridiculously hot cowboy. Whatever it was, it was turning her brain to mush and robbing her of all sane thought.

It wouldn't be the first time she'd done something reckless and foolish, and her inner vixen was cheering her on.

Do it. It's a wedding. And he's a hot cowboy named Mason. What could go wrong?

Wait.

Mason?

Her inner vixen sighed as her brain suddenly reengaged. And she remembered Mason was the name of Rockford James's younger brother.

Maybe it's another Mason, her vixen cajoled. *A seriously hot Mason, with lots of muscles and hard abs and a sexy smile.*

Yeah, right. Another guy named Mason who was so close to Rock that he'd made him one of his groomsmen. Sure, that could happen.

Maybe her luck had turned and this was her chance to get an introduction to Rock.

Dammit. Her inner minx sulked, realizing Tess's luck might have turned but their chances of actually *getting lucky* had just faded away.

Oh well. There were more important things she needed to be doing than steaming up a utility closet with a cute cowboy.

"Any chance you know where I could find another shirt?" she asked, tamping down her desire. "I have another one, hopefully one that didn't shrink, but it's locked in my car, along with the keys."

He let out a soft chuckle. "Man, you *are* having a bad day."

"You don't know the half of it," she muttered, then looked down at the jacket pulled across her chest. "I do know I can't very well go into the party wearing just this."

His grin widened. "You could, but you might steal the show from the bride-to-be."

A flirty smile pulled at the corners of her lips. "You certainly seemed to enjoy the show."

He let out another low laugh, and she swore she saw a tinge of pink coloring his cheeks. Another flash of heat surged down her spine. Why it seemed ridiculously sexy that she'd just made this cowboy blush was beyond her. But she liked it.

He held up his hands in surrender. "Guilty. But before I get myself into any more trouble, I do think I can help. Stay right there. I'll be back in a minute."

He shut the closet door, and she sagged back against the wall, her feelings warring between the hope that she could actually get her story and despair at the thought that she'd just missed out on something she had a feeling would have been toe-curlingly amazing.

Mason shook his head as he pushed through the back door of the Masonic Lodge and headed toward his truck. What in the heck had just happened?

He blinked against the bright Colorado sun and tried to regain his bearings. He felt like he'd just been through a tornado—a dark-haired, gorgeous, half-naked tornado—and his mind couldn't seem to process the effects of the storm.

He couldn't have been more surprised when he'd opened that closet door in search of a... Hell, he could barely remember what he'd been looking for. But what he'd found had been a curvy woman in a snug skirt and a black lace bra, with legs that seemed to be about a mile long. A woman who had quite literally taken his breath away.

He still didn't feel like he could catch his breath.

Opening the door of his truck, he grabbed the blue button-down shirt he'd taken off earlier when he'd changed into his dress shirt and suit, and headed back to the lodge.

Stopping outside the closet door, he hesitated, wondering for a moment if he'd imagined the whole thing. Imagined the beautiful woman, the suggestive grin, and the feeling that if he had stepped into that closet, he would have walked back out with a big dang smile on his face.

The thought of running his hands over those curves had his heart racing, and he tugged at his collar before reaching for the doorknob.

Please still be there.

A smile broke out on his face as he pulled open the door and saw the dark-haired beauty straighten from where she'd been slumped against the wall. The lapels of his suit coat gaped, and he caught a glimpse of her creamy skin and the sumptuous cleavage spilling over the top of the lacy bra.

He averted his eyes, drawing them up to her face as he handed her the shirt. "Try this. It might be a little big, but it'll cover up your…er… I mean, it will cover you up." Heat flamed his neck as her lips curved into a grin. "You know what I mean."

"I do." She clutched the shirt to her chest. "Thank you. I really appreciate this."

He stood in the doorway, unable to tear his gaze from her, then realized she probably wasn't planning to change in front of him. *Idiot*.

"Well, I'll let you get changed. I'll wait for you out here." He took a step back and closed the door.

A minute later, she stepped out, his shirt buttoned up and tucked into her skirt.

"That shirt looks a heck of a lot better on you than it ever has on me." And it would look even better lying on the floor next to her skirt. Images of her pale skin against black lace filled his head, and a flurry of heat swirled in his gut.

"I doubt that," she said, smoothing the shirt across her waist, then offering him a flirty grin.

Or maybe it was just a grin, and he was hoping it was flirty.

Dang. He hadn't had a woman affect him like this in… He couldn't even remember how long. Maybe that was because he was used to seeing the same women all the time. In a town this small, the dating options were slim. But he didn't think so. There was something about this one. Something that made him notice how long her eyelashes were and the navy-blue color of her eyes.

It made his brain turn to mush, and he couldn't seem to form a reasonable sentence. But he needed to say something. He couldn't just stand there staring at her. Except that he couldn't think of anything to say. She had rendered him speechless.

"Do you think we should head back to the party?" she asked.

"Yeah, sure, of course." *Dang*. One minute he couldn't talk, and the next his tongue was tripping over his words. A sudden thought had his back teeth clenching as he realized she might be anxious to return to the party because someone was waiting for her there.

He cleared his throat. "We should get you back. I'm sure your date is wondering what happened to you." *Smooth, Mace, real smooth.*

She let out an annoyed huff. "More like *I'm* wondering what the heck happened to *him*." She looked down at the strap of her purse and twisted it between her fingers. "My date ditched me. Apparently he had other pressing matters to attend to and didn't bother to show up."

Mason's eyes widened. "What? He's crazy."

She shook her head. "I don't know about that. But he is a conceited jerk. Just because he plays for the NHL doesn't mean he can do whatever he wants."

Her words hit him like a punch in the gut.

The NHL? Of course. Why couldn't he seem to catch a break?

He let out a sigh. "So you're dating a hockey player?"

Tess heard the irritation in Mason's voice as he asked her the question and knew she needed to tread carefully. She may not be the best reporter, but she still had good instincts about people. There was something about either the sport of hockey or the players themselves that had put the contempt in Mason's voice.

"No. I'm *not* dating one. But one did invite me to this party."

Mason's tone remained wary. "But do you *usually* date hockey players?"

Interesting. She sensed there might be more than just

a story on Rockford here. "No. I've never dated one before, and after the way this went, I'm not inclined to try another one."

A small smile tugged at the corner of his lips, and she knew that was the answer he'd wanted to hear.

She figured she might as well try to tip the scales further in her favor. "Which is fine by me because I don't really even like hockey all that much."

His grin widened.

Bingo.

"Sounds like maybe you're better off. And his loss is my gain." He held out his arm. "I'd be glad to escort you to the party."

She arched an eyebrow at him. "What about *your* date? I'm not sure she'll be happy to share."

"It just so happens that I am also dateless at this event. You'd be doing me a favor by keeping me company."

"I guess that's the least I can do after you literally gave me the shirt off your back." She slipped her arm through his and smiled up at him. He was several inches taller than her, and she loved the fact that he made her feel small.

He also made her feel a bit nervous, and suddenly the temperature of the room seemed to rise. Her heart raced a little at the feel of his muscled forearm beneath her fingers. Dang, this guy was built.

She walked with him down the corridor and took a quick breath as they approached the doors to the hall. This was it—her chance to get the in-depth details of Rockford James's wedding. She was actually going to make it inside. And not just inside, but on the arm of the groom-to-be's brother.

Maybe her luck was changing. Pushing back her shoulders, Tess tilted her chin up and hoped Mason didn't feel the slight tremble in her fingers as they entered the reception.

Her breath came out in a soft gasp as they stepped into the crowded room. Laughter flowed as professional athletes with models and actresses on their arms hobnobbed with locals in Wranglers and cowboy hats. Recognizing several famous hockey players, Tess tried to play it cool in front of Mason and not set off his annoyance again.

But she couldn't help letting out a tiny squeak as she recognized a popular actor standing by the buffet table. Her grip tightened on Mason's arm as she leaned closer, then practically swooned from the masculine scent of his aftershave. She kept her voice to a whisper. "Isn't that…?"

"Yep."

"Wasn't he in that new superhero movie?"

"Yep. But apparently he's from Colorado and quite a hockey fan." He nodded at the man's plate as he set another rib on the already toppling mound filling it. "Or else he just likes free barbecue."

She hadn't realized quite how hungry she was. Her stomach must have somehow recognized the scent of the smoked meat filling the air and the sight of the sauce-slathered ribs, because it let out a low growl.

Seriously?

Mason cocked an eyebrow at her. "Sounds like he's not the only one who's hungry."

She pressed a hand against her belly as heat crept up her neck. *Stupid stomach.*

"I guess in the rush to get up here, I may have skipped lunch." *And breakfast.*

"Then we'd better get you something to eat." He slipped his arm around her waist and guided her through the maze of people, which wasn't easy considering half the room wanted to stop and talk to him. But he pressed forward to the buffet table and pushed a plate into her hands. "You missed out on the appetizers, but according to my aunt Sassy, you didn't miss much."

"Did you say Aunt *Sassy*?"

He grinned, and her stomach dipped and swirled, this time more from the way his lips curved than from hunger pains. "Yeah, and she *is* a sassy thing. You'll see when you meet her. She wasn't a huge fan of the watercress sandwiches, but don't worry, there's plenty of meat left."

He wasn't kidding. There was meat—and beef, as in beefcake—everywhere she turned. Tess didn't think she'd ever been in a room full of so many beautiful people. Yet she couldn't seem to take her eyes off the cowboy who was piling ribs onto a plate for her.

She was suddenly aware of how many of those beautiful people were also thin and fit, and if she weren't starving, she'd probably be a little more conscious of her own full curves. But at the moment, she couldn't care less. Her mouth watered as Mason dumped a scoop of creamy macaroni and cheese next to the ribs.

"This is supposed to be my mom's recipe. She gave it to the caterers, and they did their best. It's not quite as good as hers, but it'll do in a pinch."

Somebody needs to pinch me, Tess thought as he led her toward a table. She couldn't believe she'd just walked through a buffet line behind one of her favorite celebrities.

Mason got her settled at a table and signaled for one of the caterers to bring them some drinks. "What are you drinking? Tea? Soda? Wine? It's an open bar, so get whatever you feel like."

"What are you getting?" she asked as she lifted a rib and tore off a bite. A moan escaped her lips. "Oh my gosh. These ribs are amazing."

He chuckled. "I think I'll get a beer. They've got one from a local brewery called Creedence Clearwater, and it's pretty good."

"That does sound good. I'll have one too."

His eyes widened, then a grin covered his face and his voice fell into a deep, low tone, reminding her of a biscuit dipped in thick, rich honey. "Damn, girl, I haven't even known you thirty minutes, and I think you've already won my heart. You drink beer, eat barbecue like a truck driver, and I've already seen you in your bra. I might have just fallen in love."

Chapter 3

TESSA LET LOOSE A BURST OF LAUGHTER, BUT HER STOMACH had dropped at the sound of his words spoken in a slow, sexy drawl.

She'd better be careful, or she might just fall in love herself.

Whoa. Down, girl. Nobody was falling in love with anyone.

She'd already fallen—into a mess of trouble—and the only way she was going to get herself and her grandmother out of it was to forget about the distraction of the cute cowboy and stay focused on the task at hand.

But the task at hand was heading toward the dessert table, and it looked like it would be a while before she'd get a chance to talk to Rock, so she might as well enjoy the food—and the company—while she waited.

Mason took his hat off and set it in the center of the table. It was a small gesture of manners but told her a lot about the kind of man Mason James was.

His hat was black—she couldn't help but wonder at the significance of that detail—but it was also high quality and looked expensive. Obviously, a good hat and not one he donned to work in. A slight hat ring circled his head, a barely noticeable crease in his dark hair, and a shock of his bangs fell across his forehead, giving him an even more rakish look.

The temperature of the room had increased a notch,

or maybe it was just the heat building in her chest as she tried not to squirm in her chair. She clasped her hands tightly in her lap to keep from reaching up and brushing his hair from his forehead.

A petite blond waitress sauntered up to their table and offered Mason two bottles of beer and a suggestive smile.

Grabbing a napkin, Tess wiped the barbecue sauce from her mouth, noting that the perky blond's shirt fit just fine over her chest.

Perky, petite blonds were so lucky. Tess had always felt like an Amazon around them—and not in a warrior princess way, but in a clumsy, too-tall, size-ten clodhopper-shoes way.

Although the heels she wore today were far from clodhoppers. The cute burgundy pumps had cost more than she usually doled out for a pair of shoes, but they'd seemed worth it at the time. But that was *before*. Before she'd stopped attending parties and before her grandmother had started chatting online with a Nigerian prince.

Still, no matter how much her shoes cost or how shiny their finish was, Tess still felt gawky and self-conscious sitting in front of a plate full of half-devoured ribs while the waitress swung her tiny hips and cute ponytail at Mason.

He didn't seem to notice as he took the beers, offered her a polite smile, and turned his attention back to Tess.

Score one for the Amazon.

She took one of the bottles and held it up. "What should we drink to?"

He reached his hand toward her face, and she sucked in her breath as he slowly swiped his thumb across her chin. A dab of barbecue sauce garnished its tip, and he sucked it between his lips. Lord, he had amazing lips.

She couldn't breathe as she watched him lick the tip of his thumb, and she was fairly certain one of her eggs had just dropped.

Swallowing at the dryness in her mouth, she tried to keep from melting right into her chair.

He tipped his bottle toward hers and offered her a cocky grin. "To good barbecue, cold beer, and…"

He hesitated, and she raised an eyebrow as she waited for him to say *lacy bras*.

Instead, he winked and said, "…and new friends."

She let out a chuckle and relaxed her shoulders. She liked this guy. Clinking her bottle against his, she repeated, "…to new friends."

He took a swig, then leaned back in his chair and casually rested his arm on the back of hers, as if they were old friends and totally at ease with each other. And surprisingly, she was at ease with him. Despite her earlier moments of squirming and the heat that seemed to radiate from his body, she was comfortable sitting next to him as they people-watched and casually sipped their beer.

They didn't talk constantly, but he pointed out people of the town, and she laughed as he told her funny stories about growing up in Creedence with his two brothers and all the trouble the three of them had gotten into. She tried to memorize it all, jotting it down in her brain until she could get to her computer. Everything he was telling her was solid-gold information for her article.

Beyond her journalistic interest, she loved listening to him talk, loved the rich, deep baritone of his voice and the way he chuckled softly. Loved the way he talked about his brothers with both respect and admiration.

As an only child, she had no idea what it would be like to grow up with siblings, and she envied the stories he told.

A live band had been setting up in the corner of the room, and one of the band members, an older man in a red vest and a black cowboy hat, picked up the microphone and called for the room to settle down.

He tapped the microphone. "For those of you who don't know me, I'm Buck Richards, and I've been a ranch hand at the Triple J for most of my life. I've watched Rock and his brothers grow up, and I've known this beautiful girl since she was old enough to walk. And once she could walk, her feet usually carried her to the Triple J. She and her brother spent just about as much time on our ranch as the boys did on theirs. It's been my honor and privilege to watch all these fine kids grow up, and I couldn't be prouder and happier to welcome Quinn into the family."

He pulled a red bandanna from his back jeans pocket and dabbed at his eyes. "Now, Rockford, you get your skinny butt over here and bring that gorgeous gal with you."

The crowd cheered, and Mason let out a whoop and applauded as Rock and Quinn made their way to the stage and embraced the older ranch hand.

"We've got a special song for these two to start this shindig off right," he said, grinning at the happy couple. "We didn't write it, but we'll sure try to do it justice as you all get ready to start your lives together. This one's for you."

He nodded to the dance floor as he picked up his guitar and looped the strap around his shoulder. After a few warm-up strums, the band joined in and they sang an old country song that spoke of love and tenderness and building a life together.

Rock pulled Quinn into his arms and was surprisingly graceful for such a big guy. Not that anyone noticed his gracefulness or lack thereof. Instead, the entire room was captured by the way he looked lovingly at his fiancée.

Including Tess.

She was mesmerized as she watched them dance, then let out a soft sigh as Buck announced that the next dance was for the parents of the couple.

She'd googled Rock on her phone and knew his mom was a pretty blond named Vivienne. She hadn't found out anything about their father, but she knew Quinn's dad ran Rivers Gulch, the ranch to the west of the Triple J.

Expecting Hamilton Rivers to look a little country, she glanced around the room, but wasn't prepared for the handsome older cowboy who stood up, a sly grin covering his tan face.

He looked as though he could have been Sam Elliott's younger brother, right down to the thick salt-and pepper-mustache, as he swaggered out onto the floor and pulled Quinn into a fatherly embrace. The music started, and he moved them smoothly around the floor, his cowboy boots gliding across the linoleum as if it were made of glass.

That father-daughter scene was touching enough, but Tess had to blink back the tears as Rock approached his mother and tenderly took her in his arms. She reached up and gently touched his cheek, her eyes shining with the kind of love only a mother knew.

Tessa's heart ached with the memory of her mother looking at her that way. She took a swig of beer to wash back the emotion stinging her throat and focused on the dance floor.

Sneaking a glance at Mason, she thought she might have caught a tear in his eye as well as he watched his mom with his brother.

It was obvious they were a close-knit family. And even though Vivienne James had both beauty and a country elegance, it was evident that she loved her boys with the fierceness of a mother tiger. A tiger who could easily destroy someone possibly using one of her sons to get some dirt on another.

Hopefully, Tess wouldn't be sticking around long enough to see that happen. All she needed was to spend a little time with the bride and groom, listen to them talk and tell a few stories, then feed them a few well-timed questions, and she could get in and out without anyone realizing what she was there to do.

Easy. No complications.

Yeah, right. The biggest and hottest complication was sitting next to her, looking good enough to eat.

She smiled over at him. "Your mom is beautiful."

"Yeah, she is."

"Is your dad here too?"

Mason turned his head and stared out across the room. He blinked his eyes, then swallowed before turning back to her. His voice was quiet as he said, "Yeah, I think he is. But just in spirit. He died when we were kids."

Tess covered her hand with her mouth, cursing Gordon for not delving deeper into the James family history. That would have been good information to know. "I'm so sorry."

Mason shrugged and picked at the seam of his sleeve.

"It was a long time ago. But I do miss him, especially at times like these."

"I understand."

He glanced up at her.

"No, really. I know what it's like. I lost both my parents in a car accident when I was a kid." She pushed back the familiar feelings of guilt that washed through her whenever she talked about that day. Her therapist had spent years trying to convince her the accident wasn't her fault, but she knew the truth—she was to blame.

"That's rough."

"Yeah, it was. But luckily, I have an amazing grandmother who took me in and raised me as her own."

The song ended, and Buck called into the microphone, "Let's bring the bridal party and the rest of the family up here."

Mason stood and held out his hand. "Now it's my turn to ask you a favor. Would you like to dance?"

A battalion of butterflies swirled through her stomach at the idea of being led around the dance floor by him, but she pushed down her nerves and stood up from her chair. "Sure."

He took her hand and led her onto the floor as the band kicked off a new song. The tempo was slow—the opposite of the frantic beating of her heart as she waited for Mason to pull her into the circle of his arms.

Stepping onto the dance floor, he turned and offered her a grin as he slid his hand easily around her waist and flattened his palm against her back. His movements were fluid and smooth as he guided her around the room using just the pressure of his hand against her back.

She could hear him humming along to the tune, feel

the vibration in her body. His skin was tanned, and a faint smudge of dark whiskers was just starting along his jaw. The scent of his aftershave surrounded her, and she wanted to rest her head on his shoulder. Either that or lick his neck. Hell, she wanted to lick his everything.

He was so damn sexy.

He'd taken off his tie and unbuttoned the top few buttons of his shirt, and she could just glimpse the skin of his chest. But she could feel the hard muscles under his shirt and knew he would be as strong as an ox.

In her line of work, she was surrounded by guys in suits who got their strength from working out and eating lean. Mason had told her a little bit about what he did on the ranch, and she could tell his body was toned and muscled not from working out, but from working, period. He had the kind of muscles that came from hard hours of lifting and hauling and working cattle and horses.

And he didn't strike her as the type to eat salads and organic vegan meals—more like a full-on meat-and-potatoes man. Heck, she'd already seen him work his way through a plate of ribs and mac-and-cheese with ease.

She wondered if he was as smooth and skilled in other places as he was on the dance floor, and the thought sent a surge of heat flowing through her veins. She could feel the strength of his hand on her back and the warmth of his breath tickling her skin as he leaned a little closer.

The song ended much too quickly, but the band moved smoothly into the next one, and she and Mason remained on the floor. Buck invited the rest of the guests to join them, and the dance floor quickly filled.

Mason pulled her a little closer as the crowd squeezed

in around them. She sucked in a breath as his knee touched the inside of her leg, the soft fabric of his suit pants whisking against her bare skin. Even though they were surrounded by people, it felt as if they were the only two on the dance floor.

They didn't speak, didn't make stupid small talk. She didn't apologize for clumsily missing the steps, because she didn't feel clumsy. She felt like a princess at the ball where the handsome prince magically glides her around the dance floor until the clock strikes twelve and she makes a run for the pumpkin carriage.

But she didn't feel like making a run for it; she felt like staying here all night.

And her shoe wasn't the only thing she was hoping to lose.

She had a feeling if she got another chance at being alone in a closet—or anywhere—with Mason James, there was a strong possibility she would lose her shirt, her skirt, and any other piece of clothing that might get in the way of pressing naked against his hard, muscled body.

A shock of dark hair fell loose across his forehead, and she again had the urge to brush it back across his brow. His eyes were brown, the color of milk chocolate, with flecks of gold circling the pupils, and she couldn't stop looking into them.

She couldn't stop looking at him, period. She wanted to memorize all his features and pretend this night was a real date, and that there might be future dates, which she knew was unlikely, if not impossible. Especially after the article with her byline came out. But she didn't want to think about that now. She only wanted to focus on him, on the details of his face. A faded scar crossed through his eyebrow, and his cheek dented into the slightest dimple when he grinned.

She'd never understood that bit about a man having a chiseled jaw—until now. Mason's face seemed to be sculpted from a fine block of marble. Marble with a dark stubble of whiskers. And she couldn't help but imagine how those whiskers would feel against the tender skin of her body.

He was staring at her with the same intensity, and she caught her breath as he tilted his head and leaned a little closer. Her lips parted as if offering him an invitation, but her heart thundered in her chest at the idea of him actually kissing her.

She couldn't tear her eyes from his. Her mouth went dry as she saw his gaze dip to her lips and his eyes narrow with desire.

He bent closer still. She could feel the whisper of his breath against her skin.

Her body reacted to his, warming with need and nerves, and she hoped her hand wasn't sweating in his.

Kiss me already, she thought. *Before I die with wanting you.*

Closer still.

Yes.

She swore she felt his lips graze hers right before they were jostled to the side by a red-haired guy in a badly fitting suit who slugged Mason in the arm.

"You'd better get a move on, Mace, if you're gonna catch up to your brother. He's getting a wife *and a kid* in one shot. And you're still hanging around the ranch. I thought you were supposed to be the *best* man. When are you going to get your own ball and chain?"

He laughed hilariously at his own joke, but the short, dark-haired woman he was dancing with, presumably his wife, didn't look as amused.

Mason's jaw tightened for just a moment, then eased back into an easygoing smile. Tess wasn't sure she'd even seen it. It was like a ripple across still water, as if his good-natured mask had slipped for just a second, then popped back into place.

She might have thought she'd imagined it, if it weren't for the way his hand tightened its grip on hers.

"Good one, Dougie. I can only hope to be as happy as you and Kim someday," Mason said, offering the woman a smile before he dropped Tessa's hand and pulled away from her. Turning, he walked off the dance floor and headed back to their chairs.

He may have just been smiling, but the tension in his shoulders was unmistakable as the fabric of his coat tightened across his back. As she followed, Tess reached out her hand to gently touch his arm. Then she pulled it back, the gesture seeming too intimate for someone she had just met, even though a minute and a half ago she'd thought she might die if he didn't kiss her. And an hour ago she had considered taking him against the wall of the utility closet.

He stopped suddenly and turned back to her, and she almost stumbled into him. Reaching for her arm, he cupped her elbow to steady her as he nodded toward the back of the room. "I think I need some air. I'm gonna go for a walk, stretch my legs a little. You want to get out of here?"

No. Of course not. That's a terrible idea. How could she even consider leaving the party? She hadn't even talked to Rock or Quinn. "Yeah, sure. Let's go."

This was a bad idea. She knew it. But really, it couldn't hurt to get a little air, could it? And it wasn't as if Rock and Quinn were going anywhere—it was their party. Right?

Mason grabbed his cowboy hat off the table and jammed it on his head. Pulling her bag from the back of her chair, Tess hoisted it onto her shoulder, then followed Mason out the door.

Surprised to see that it was already dusk, that the afternoon had flown by, she inhaled a deep breath of mountain air. It was cooler up here than it was in Denver, and she let out a little shiver.

Mason shrugged out of his jacket and placed it around her shoulders. His own shoulders visibly relaxed as he turned away from the party. "Come on. There's a stream that runs down the side of town, and it's got a nice path next to it. We can walk up a ways, then come back down."

"Sounds good."

"You ever been to Creedence before?"

"No, but I like it. It's a beautiful town. Did you grow up here?" She already knew the answer, but it seemed like the logical question to ask.

He nodded as he led her onto the path. It was more like a broad sidewalk that meandered along the side of the stream. It was dotted with benches and an occasional light devised to look like an old-fashioned lamppost. With the dusk settling in and the gurgling stream and gorgeous green surroundings, the setting made for a perfect romantic evening stroll.

But I'm not here for romance, she reminded herself. *I'm here to get a story.*

Which meant deceiving this nice, cute guy who was reaching for her hand to help her over a cracked part of the sidewalk.

The touch of his warm, callused hand had the task slipping from her mind. There would be time for the story later.

"Yep, born and raised here," Mason said, responding to her question. "I've lived on the Triple J Ranch my whole life. Which is part of why I feel such responsibility to it. After our dad died, we boys took over the majority of the work of running the ranch. But Rock always had big dreams. He's wanted to play hockey for as long as I can remember. And he had the talent to do it. He was good even as a kid. And if there was something he didn't know how to do, he practiced—for hours on end—until he mastered it. That guy is one of the hardest workers I know."

"Sounds to me like you're a pretty hard worker too, if you've been helping to run a ranch essentially since you were a kid."

He shrugged. "I never really thought about it. I just did it. We all did. That's how our folks raised us. My dad had the strongest work ethic I'd ever seen. That's probably where Rock got it. On a ranch, there's always work to be done, and we needed to make sure things got taken care of. That our mom was taken care of."

"I can't imagine being a widow with three boys and still trying to run a ranch. Your mom seems pretty amazing."

"She is. And she'd probably swat me for saying that we felt like we needed to take care of her. Her pride almost equals her strength, but she's always had our backs." His face broke into a warm smile, and Tessa's heart melted a little in her chest. "She always knew Rock would be a star. We all did. He had the talent and the drive to create a career for himself in professional hockey. My little brother, Colt, had a good chance too. He may have been better than Rock even. His talent came easier, so he didn't have to work so hard. He was just great on the ice and could handle a stick like it was part of his arm, but an injury in high school wrecked that for him."

She liked the way Mason's face shone with pride as he talked about his brothers. "How about you? Did you ever want to play? Professionally?"

"Nah. I mean, I played in high school and in the junior leagues with my brothers, but I didn't love it like they did. And you have to love it to play it like that. Besides, I've always known my place was on the ranch. And I knew the only way Rock had any chance of leaving was if I stepped up and took on that responsibility."

Tess thought she detected a hint of bitterness in his tone, but she couldn't be sure. He spoke of his brother with respect and admiration, but there seemed to be just a whiff of animosity when he spoke about staying behind to run the ranch.

"What would you have done if you hadn't stayed?" she asked, stopping on the path and turning to look at him. "You said your brothers had big dreams of playing hockey. What were your big dreams?"

He stared at her, his eyes narrowing as if he wasn't sure whether she was making polite conversation or really wanted to know. "Nobody's ever asked me that before."

"That doesn't mean you haven't ever thought about the answer."

He grinned, then turned his gaze to the rushing water of the stream. "I don't know. It doesn't matter anyway. Ranching is in my blood. And I'm good at it."

"You're also good at evading the question."

He grinned again, then cocked an eyebrow at her. "You seem to be good at *asking* questions but never answering any yourself. I feel like all we've talked about is me. I barely know anything about you."

Uh-oh. The last thing she wanted, or needed, was for him to start asking questions about her. She hated lying to him—especially after he'd been so frank and already told her so much about his life.

If she could keep the conversation focused on him or, better yet, on Rock, she wouldn't have to lie.

"Me? I'm boring. Your life is much more interesting… running a ranch and having a famous brother. And a wedding coming up this week too. That's exciting. Let's talk about that. How did your brother and Quinn meet?"

There. That ought to do it. Get the focus off her and steer it toward gaining information on Rock.

"Good try. But I'm not falling for it." He picked up a stone and skipped it across the water. "You don't have to tell me your whole life story. We can start with something easy. Like…where do you work, or what do you do for a living?"

Chapter 4

Something easy? Yeah, right. He'd just asked the one question that Tess was trying the hardest to avoid.

Being a reporter often involved subterfuge and investigating the facts. Which meant sometimes pretending to be someone she wasn't. Like an innocent bystander at the scene of the crime, or a clumsy ditz who accidentally spills her wine on a key witness, or a guest at a wedding party of a notorious hockey player.

She hated to lie, but maybe she could fudge her answer a little while trying to keep as close to the truth as possible.

"Um...I'm a writer." There. That wasn't so hard.

Mason raised an eyebrow. "Yeah? That's cool. What do you write?"

Crud. That hadn't worked as well as she'd hoped. She couldn't very well tell him she was currently writing a story on his famous brother and his quickie wedding.

"Stories. About people, sometimes animals," she said, nodding her head and avoiding eye contact as she smoothed out a wrinkle in the front of his jacket.

"Oh yeah? You had anything published? Anything I might have read?"

"Uh...yes. I mean...no." She fumbled for an answer. He'd assumed she was an author, and it was easier to let him think that than to stumble through another fib. "I haven't exactly published a book yet. But the story I'm working on isn't something you'd probably want to read anyway. It's more of a romance."

"Ah."

Time to change the subject, get the focus back on him. "Personally, I love a good mystery. How about you? What do you like to read?"

He shrugged. "I like mysteries and sometimes a little science fiction. I love those old westerns. My dad had a collection of Louis L'Amour books, and I read all of them as a kid."

The corners of her mouth pulled up in a grin. "I've always liked guys who read."

He offered her a flirty smile in return. "Oh yeah? Well then, it might interest you to know that I subscribe to the *Farmers' Almanac* and *Readers Digest* magazines, and I've read through numerous funny pages and comic books. In fact, I read the back of the cereal box just this morning."

"Impressive." She chuckled. "So, it sounds like you really go in for the deep literary stuff."

"Oh yeah, but I draw the line at any type of instruction manuals. I refuse to read that kind of garbage."

Her chuckle turned into a full-out laugh. "Smart. I can tell you're a guy who knows his limits."

"I've actually got a mystery novel sitting on the nightstand next to my bed, if you're interested in checking it out," he teased, giving her a gentle nudge with his elbow.

"Tempting, for sure," she teased back, but the thought of being in his bedroom sent a surge of heat down her spine. She let out a grimace as she stepped over an uneven section of the sidewalk, and her shoe rubbed against the blister that had been forming on her ankle all afternoon.

"You okay?" His teasing expression turned to concern as he took in the angry red welt.

"I'm fine. But my feet are killing me. Apparently these shoes were not the most appropriate footwear for a walk." She stopped and reached out a hand to steady herself as she pulled the heels off.

He held out his arm for support. As her palm gripped his forearm, she tried to focus on kneading her sore arch instead of the hard muscle she was holding on to.

She shoved the heels into her bag. "It's a high price we pay for fashion." Three inches shorter now, she had to tilt her head to look up at him.

"Doesn't seem worth the fee. You look great to me, with or without shoes. I'd bet you could wear flip-flops and a gunnysack, and you'd still look good."

She ducked her head, his praise making her coy. What was that about? She'd had men tell her she looked good before, and her skin hadn't warmed with a blush. But never any men who looked like Mason James or who delivered a compliment in a low, sexy tone.

"How about soaked to the skin?" she asked, shrinking her shoulders against the sudden flash of lightning.

He narrowed his eyes, then gazed slowly up and down her body. "I'd bet you'd look good like that too."

Oh my.

Before she could think of anything reasonably comprehensible to say in return, the sky opened up and let loose a torrent of rain. Letting out a shriek, she ran for cover under the nearest tree. Not that it did much good. She was already soaked by the time she got there, and the tree only offered a little protection.

Mason followed and held out his arms, trying to

block the worst of it with his back as he let out a whoop. "Gotta love a spontaneous Colorado thunderstorm."

She did not, in fact, have to love it at all. Her clothes were drenched, and droplets of rain dripped from her bangs. But this seemed par for the course, considering the way her day had been going.

"You want to try to wait it out or make a run for it?" He didn't seem the least bothered by getting wet.

She tipped her head to glance up at the dark, menacing clouds racing across the sky. "Looks like we could be waiting a long time. Might as well make a run for it." She looked down at her bare feet, now covered in mud.

His gaze followed hers. "I can't have you running in bare feet." He turned his back to her and bent down. "Hop on, and I'll carry you piggyback."

"You've got to be kidding," she said, raising her voice to be heard over the rain. "No way. I am *not* crawling up on your back." Although, just a few minutes ago, she had considered crawling up his front.

"Well, you can't run back down this path in your bare feet. And my guess is those heels are too painful and too nice to put back on and ruin in the rain. So, it's either you let me carry you, or you can stay here and wait while I run down to get my truck, then come back and pick you up."

Neither option sounded like a great choice.

She could wait for him, but who knew what kind of weird transients might show up in the dark to attack her. That scenario didn't seem completely likely, but she did have a writer's imagination, which usually involved thoughts of being attacked in empty stairwells or elevators or deserted paths along a mountain stream.

She equally hated the thought of putting him out by

having him drive up there to pick her up. The idea of him carrying her sounded fun and romantic, but the reality was that she was tall and curvy and would be humiliated when he realized he couldn't carry her two yards, let alone all the way back to the lodge.

Gnawing on her bottom lip, she weighed her options of possibly being assaulted by a serial killer who didn't mind the rain against the inconvenience of making Mason go back to the lodge and get his truck against the humiliation of climbing on his back and risking him falling to the ground under her weight. "I think I'll just take the risk of messing up my feet."

"What? No way. You can't walk back down there in your bare feet. Not with this rain. Just let me carry you."

"I can't."

"Why not?"

She let out a heavy sigh. "You do realize I'm not some cute, little petite thing."

He reared his head back as his eyes widened. "Are you worried I'll drop you? You seriously think I'm not strong enough to carry you back down this path?" He let out a hard laugh. "Darling, I've carried half-grown calves that weigh more than you across my shoulders through acres of fields."

She raised an eyebrow at him, and his laughter died.

"Not that I'm insinuating you weigh as much as a half-grown calf or that you in any way resemble a cow…" he fumbled.

She squeezed her eyes tightly shut, then let out her breath. "Oh, all right. Shut up, and I'll let you haul me down the path on your back."

A grin spread across his face. He pulled off his

cowboy hat and plunked it on her head. "This will help a little." He gestured to her skirt. "I'm not getting fresh, but when I turn around, you're probably gonna have to hike your skirt up a ways."

She swore she could practically see the blush covering his cheeks. But she kind of liked it.

"All right. As long as you're not getting fresh." She couldn't help teasing him a little. Really, who wouldn't want to get fresh with a woman who was barefoot and soaked to the skin, in a borrowed shirt, with mascara running down her face and her hair in a dripping, tangled mess under a too-big cowboy hat? Seriously, she couldn't imagine herself looking any more unattractive than at that minute.

A loud crack of thunder shot through the night as a flash of lightning lit up the sky.

"That was close. Let's go." He turned and bent down a little.

Oh hell. She pushed her arms through the sleeves of his jacket, then heaved her bag higher on her shoulder. After hiking up her skirt, she wrapped her arms around his neck and crawled onto his back piggyback-style.

His muscled arms circled her legs, hoisting her higher onto his back. "You ready?"

No. Not even a little bit.

She had to admit she'd fantasized about having her legs wrapped around his waist, but this wasn't what she'd had in mind. "I'm ready."

"Hey, Tess," he said, turning his head. A trickle of rain dripped from a lock of his dark bangs, and he gave her a roguish grin. "You may not be petite, but I do think you are a cute little thing."

Before she could respond, he stepped out from under the tree and let out a whoop as he jogged down the path. She shrieked as the cold rain pelted her back and gripped his shoulders tighter.

He didn't seem to be buckling under her weight. In fact, he didn't seem to be weighed down by her at all, and she let out a burst of laughter as he splashed through a puddle on the sidewalk.

"What a crazy night," he yelled, and she could feel his shoulders shake as he laughed with her.

They made it off the path and stopped to let a truck pass before they crossed the road. Realizing a second too late what was going to happen, Mason tried to take a step back as the truck hit a giant puddle and sprayed a shower of muddy water across his front.

"Oh no," Tessa cried, letting out another burst of laughter.

"You think that's funny, do you?" He laughed with her, then turned so she was facing the road as another car drove toward the puddle.

Letting out another squeal, she clung to his back, burying her head in his neck as she hunched her shoulders.

But at the last second, he wheeled back around, protecting her with his body and taking the shower of water against his chest. "Hold on." He gripped her legs tighter and made a run for it across the road.

Both of them were hooting with laughter as he yanked open the door to the lodge and stepped inside. The noise of the reception hall receded as everyone seemed to stop talking at once to take in the appearance of a huge, bedraggled, and soaked cowboy with an equally bedraggled and drenched woman clinging to his back.

"You can put me down now," Tess whispered against his ear. He released her legs, and she slid to the floor behind him. She was sure they made quite a sight. Mason's black hair dripped with water, and his soaked white shirt revealed his muscled chest.

But while he looked like an ad for *Hot Cowboy* magazine, she could only guess how she looked. Wearing his too-big jacket and his hat lopsided on her drenched head, she shifted from one bare foot to the other as she tried to pull her skirt back down to an acceptable length above her knees.

Taking a small step back, just so she wasn't pressed against him anymore, she tried to stay behind him, letting his larger body shield her from the stares of the partygoers.

But he didn't seem embarrassed at all. In fact, he let out a loud whoop. "Whew. It's raining cats and dogs out there, folks. Ms. Kane and I have officially tested out the forecast for you though, and we are recommending you stay inside and dance off more of that great barbecue. Isn't that right, Tess?"

He started to step to the side as if giving her a chance to speak, but she grabbed the back of his shirt, gripping it in a tight fist to hold him in place. Her pulse pounded in her throat, sweat formed on her already-damp back, and her mouth went as dry as cotton as she used her other hand to offer a little wave, then continued to cower behind Mason. As much as a five-foot-nine woman could cower.

He gave her a questioning look.

But after she offered the slightest shake of her head, her lips pressed tightly together, he must have gotten the message that she had nothing to say. That, and he might have felt the trembling in her hand as she still held the back of his shirt in a death grip.

"See, she agrees. Now if you'll excuse us, we're going to go find some towels." He ducked his head at the crowd, then signaled for the band to play some music.

Buck and his group headed for the stage, and the noise of the crowd recommenced.

Mason turned to her. "You okay?"

"Yes-s-s," she said, her teeth chattering together.

He wrapped an arm around her and led her down the hallway. "Come on. Let's get you warmed up. They have one of those hand dryers in the bathroom. That should help."

The door marked LADIES' ROOM was on her right, and she stopped in front of it, holding up her hand in case he had any idea of coming in with her. "I'll take it from here. I just need a few minutes." She took off his hat and passed it to him, a trickle of water leaking from its brim. "Sorry."

He chuckled. "It's fine, really. It's not the first time a hat of mine has seen rain."

She suspected from the new look of brushed felt that it was the first time this one had.

"You get cleaned up. I'll try to find you a sweatshirt," he told her.

"I've got dry clothes. They're just locked in my car."

"Okay, I'll work on that too. What kind of car do you have?"

"An old Ford Taurus."

"American made... That's good. Does it have a key fob or just electronic locks?"

She shook her head as she uttered a sarcastic laugh. "Neither. When I said old, I meant it's a *really old* car, an '89. It was my grandmother's, and I don't think electronic locks and key fobs were even invented when that thing rolled off the line."

He chuckled. "The good news is that a car that old should be easier to unlock. I saw one of the county deputies here earlier. I'll see if he's got a slim jim. That should get us right in."

She reached out a hand and rested it on his arm. "Really. You don't have to. You've helped me enough already."

"I'm glad to do it." He offered her a wink, then pushed his hat onto his head and walked back toward the reception hall. He might have been wearing a black hat, but he sure seemed like a white knight to her.

But she was far from being the damsel in distress. Well, she might be in distress, or under duress, but instead of feeling like a damsel, she felt more like a swindler, a fraud, a phony. No better than those con artists who'd tricked her grandmother into giving them all her money.

Okay, maybe she didn't feel quite as bad as that, but she still felt shitty. Shitty that she was tricking this nice guy, using him to get to his brother to get a stupid story. The problem was that she needed that stupid story.

Her shoulders slumped, and she let out a sigh as she pushed through the door of the ladies' room. Her sigh turned into a gasp as she caught a look at herself in the mirror.

Holy Hagsville. She was a wreck. Most of her hair was plastered to the top of her head, except for the pieces that were sticking out in curly, frizzy wings from the side. She looked as if she was preparing for takeoff.

Any traces of her mascara were gone, except the faint trail of a black smudge on one cheek. A smear of dirt covered the edge of her chin.

Her shirt—well, Mason's shirt—was plastered to her skin, and she silently applauded him for not gawking at the definition of her black lace bra that was clearly visible through the soaked blue fabric.

Her bare feet and legs were splattered with mud and bits of gravel, and a long scratch made its way down one of her calves from where she'd brushed her leg against a pine tree as they'd made their way down the path. She had to smile at the thought of how hilarious they must have looked and also of how much fun she'd had with Mason. Her lipstick had faded, but her cheeks held a healthy pink glow. Or maybe that was just the blush of thinking about how it'd felt to be pressed against Mason's muscled back.

Grabbing some paper towels, she tried to wash the dirt and remaining makeup off her face, then cleaned as much mud from her legs as she could.

Thankfully, she carried a huge purse that was fully stocked. In addition to the normal stuff like her wallet, insurance cards, sunglasses, and mints, she also carried a supply of gum, a nail file and clippers, a can of Mace, a hairbrush, hair spray, notebooks, pens, coupons, and way too many lip glosses.

MacGyver would have a field day with her bag.

The items in her bag had saved her more times than she could count. She only wished she'd stuffed in an extra set of clothes.

She did have an emergency makeup kit and took a minute to brush on a little eye shadow and a few swipes of mascara. Mimi had taught her that lipstick was the most important tool in her makeup arsenal, but the dark-berry shade she had chosen to match her ruined shirt seemed a bit too much for her current state. She smoothed on some spearmint-infused gloss instead.

Unfortunately, she'd left her hairbrush and spray on the seat of her car after she'd done a quick hair refresh when she'd arrived in town. Hitting the hand dryer, she turned the nozzle so it pointed at her hair and used her fingers to try to comb through the wet strands.

The bathroom door opened, and Mason's mom came in with a stack of dish towels.

She held them out to Tess. "You poor thing. You're soaked. I raided the lodge's kitchen, but this was the best I could come up with. I'm Vivi, Mason's mom. I saw you all come in, thought you could use a hand."

"That's so nice of you. I'm Tessa. Tess. You can call me Tess. These are great." She didn't know why she was stuttering or why her nerves seemed so jumpy. Just because Vivienne James was a mom didn't mean she'd be able to tell that Tess was there for nefarious reasons. Not every woman had that uncanny mom sense. But for some reason, she thought Mason's mom just might.

Feeling guilty about mussing up the white dish towels, Tess took only one and tried to dry her legs.

"Here. Let me help." Vivi set the stack of towels on the bathroom counter, then grabbed one off the top and pressed the ends of Tess's hair into its folds. "Your hair is gorgeous."

"Thank you. I'm such a mess." Wow. She was killing

it with her conversation skills. This was her chance to learn more about Rock's family, to ask some questions of the matriarch—the woman who knew everything. But instead of asking anything, Tess was unnerved by the motherly attention of a woman helping to dry her hair.

"You all really got caught in it. You've got to be careful with these Colorado thunderstorms. Up here in the mountains, they can come out of nowhere and come on fast. Where are you from, honey?"

"I'm from Denver."

"You and my son sure seemed to be having a good time. How do you two know each other?"

The question came out innocently enough, but Tess wasn't fooled.

Apparently Vivienne was on a bit of a fishing expedition of her own.

Chapter 5

Tessa tried to think of a reasonable response but was saved from having to answer Vivi's question by a loud knock at the door.

"You still in there, Tess?" Mason's voice called through the crack. "I found a sweatshirt for you."

She pulled the door open and watched his eyes widen as he saw her standing there with his mother.

"Hey, Mom."

"Hi, honey. I was just helping out your new friend here."

"I'll bet," he muttered under his breath. "I appreciate that, but she's not really my *new* friend. Tess and I go way back." He offered her a quick grin, then held the door open wider for his mother. "Thanks, Mom, but I got it from here."

His mom held her hands up in surrender. "Just trying to help. Nice to meet you, Tess." She offered Tess a smile as she squeezed past her son, who was still standing in the open doorway.

He glanced toward the two stalls. "Anyone else in here?"

She pushed both doors open. "Nope. Just us."

"Good." He let the bathroom door shut behind him and stepped closer to her as he held out a hooded zip-up sweatshirt and a pair of flip-flops. "This was the best I could do. I found the sweatshirt in my truck, so I can't guarantee it doesn't smell like horses, but at least it's dry. And Quinn had an extra pair of sandals in her car."

"Thank you, really. But you didn't have to do this." She wasn't used to this much attention. First his mom, now Mason.

"I know. But it was my idea to take a walk. We wouldn't have gotten caught in that storm if we'd stayed inside." He pulled a thin metal tool from his back pocket. "I found a slim jim too. So we can get your keys out of your car."

"Thanks. Again." What else could she say? She was standing in her bare feet, shivering in wet clothes. The small bathroom was already crowded enough with her and the tall cowboy; there was no extra room for her pride.

She took the sweatshirt and shoes and set them on the counter, then gestured for him to turn around. "I feel like we've been here before."

"Right?" His eyes narrowed, and his grin went all cocky and flirty. "Seems to me that since this is the second time in one night you've gotten half-naked with me, I should be allowed to watch."

A flash of heat soared up her spine, and her stomach filled with dive-bombing butterflies. She swallowed at the sudden dryness in her mouth and tried to play it cool.

Even though all she felt was hot.

What would happen if she really did let him watch? If she slowly unbuttoned her shirt and let it drop to the floor?

She imagined him shoving the stack of towels off the counter and hoisting her onto it. She could almost feel his lips on hers, imagine the rough scrape of whiskers against her chest as he kissed her neck. Her hands were reaching for the top button of her shirt before she came to her senses.

She knew what would happen. And even though it might be amazing, toe-curling passion, it would still be on a bathroom counter in the Masonic Lodge at his brother's wedding party. Which might be deemed spontaneous and sexy, but also degrading and demeaning. And she'd had enough degrading and demeaning in her life.

A hard fist squeezed around her heart, stealing her breath and tightening her chest.

Pushing those thoughts aside, she tried to breathe and refocus on why she was here. Why spending time with Mason and his family really mattered. She couldn't risk messing up this article. Not this time. She needed to stay sharp. Stay focused.

"Good try, cowboy," she said, planting a hand on her hip. "Now turn around."

His grin widened and he shrugged, then turned his back to her. "You can't blame a guy for trying. Seems like if you're going to keep getting undressed in front of me, I should get a little something out of the deal."

Tess ignored his remark and tried to concentrate on getting out of the wet shirt. But his comment must have affected her more than she wanted to let on, because her fingers trembled as she fumbled to unfasten the buttons and peel the damp fabric from her skin.

The sweatshirt was too big, but it was warm and dry and felt heavenly against her cool skin. She pulled the zipper up to cover her bra, then crossed her arms over her chest and rubbed the dry fabric against her arms.

She dropped the flip-flops to the floor, praying they would fit. The curse of the tall girl. Slipping her feet into them, she let out a sigh of relief that they fit perfectly and sent up a silent thanks that Quinn was tall as well.

Mason's back was still turned. She studied the definition of his broad shoulders and, despite her admonition of a moment before, might have given a moment of appreciation to the way he filled out his suit pants. She could only imagine how he'd look in jeans.

And she *was* imagining it.

Stop it. Focus on the story. Change the subject.

Time to get her mind on something besides how good this man looked in a suit. "So what was all that business with your mom? Why did you tell her we go way back instead of admitting we just met tonight?"

"I was trying to make it easier on both of us," Mason said, leaning a hip against the bathroom counter. "I'm sure the tongues of Creedence are already wagging about the two of us busting through the door of the lodge, soaking wet and laughing like hyenas. I just didn't want to give them any more ammunition. I figured it would be less scandalous if folks thought we were old friends."

He hadn't really given it all that much thought. The comment had just popped out. His subconscious must have tossed it out in a moment of self-preservation.

"Scandalous?" she mused. "I don't know that getting caught in a rainstorm would qualify as all that."

"Then you don't know how small towns work. We might know that it was a piggyback ride in the rain, but by the time it rolls through this town, that account will have turned into a completely different story."

"Gotcha. I appreciate you protecting my reputation."

She picked up the items that lay scattered across the counter and loaded them back into her bag.

"Wow, that's some purse," he said. "It looks like you've got everything but the kitchen sink in there."

"Thanks. I like to be prepared for any situation. And this bag is one of my favorite things. I bought it as a gift to myself when I got my first real job. It was ridiculously expensive, but I love it, and it's been with me through all sorts of adventures. I've had it for over five years now. It's the longest relationship I've held."

The corners of his lips tugged up in a grin as he arched an eyebrow. "Oh yeah? Why's that? Do you have a problem with commitment?"

"No, I just have a tendency to make bad judgment calls, and I have a pretty good thing going with screwing-up-your-life decisions as well." She clamped a hand over her mouth. "That was probably a little too much information. Let's just forget I said that and go back to talking about what a great bag this is."

He chuckled. This woman cracked him up. "I'm sorry it got wet."

The bag was spotted and damp from the rain. "It'll be fine. It's seen worse. Besides, it's leather, and cows get wet all the time, right?"

"Right."

She ran her hands along the fine leather of the bag and fingered the row of teal leather daisies that were stitched around the top. A silver daisy charm that looked like an expensive key chain hung from the side of one strap. "I love daisies. They were my mom's favorite flower, so when I saw this bag, I knew I had to have it. I know it's silly, but sometimes it makes me feel like my mom is with me, helping me carry whatever load of stuff I'm hauling around."

"That's not silly at all." He pointed to the side of the bag where it looked like one daisy had started to come loose and was clinging to the leather by only a few threads. "But it looks like it might need a repair."

"It's on my never-ending list of things to do." She tossed the last item into the bag, then picked up his wet shirt. Folding it as neatly as she could, she set it on the counter next to him and smoothed down the front pocket.

"You don't have to do that," he said, setting his hand on top of hers. He felt her body go still, but he didn't move his hand. He didn't move at all for several seconds, then lightly stroked his thumb across the top of her knuckles.

He heard her quick intake of breath and raised his eyes to her mouth. The woman had a great mouth—full, pink lips that looked just ripe for kissing.

She didn't look at him, didn't take her eyes off their hands, and he felt the slightest tremble of her fingers.

But he couldn't stop staring at her lips.

She sucked her bottom lip under the edge of her top teeth.

Oh dang. He was going to have to kiss her now. There was no stopping it.

No stopping whatever this crazy thing was that was happening between him and this woman he'd just met. Although it didn't feel like they'd just met. It felt like he'd known her forever.

Her hair was still wet and curling on the ends. A stray strand fell across the corner of her eye, and he raised his other hand and brushed it behind her ear.

She closed her eyes and tilted her cheek just the slightest into his hand.

He leaned closer, anticipation swirling in his gut, aching to touch, to taste, to feel her lips against his.

The bathroom door swung open, and Ida May Phillips, his Sunday school teacher from fourth grade, walked in. She stopped in her tracks, letting out a gasp as she pressed her hand to her heart.

"Why, Mason James... You about scared the devil right out of me. What in the world are you doing in the ladies' restroom?"

Seriously? Was he ever going to get to kiss this girl?

He dropped his hand and pushed away from the counter, knowing he probably looked guilty as hell. Thank goodness Ida May couldn't actually read his mind.

If she could, she'd know she wasn't the only one with the devil in her—the thoughts he'd just been having about Tessa Kane were downright sinful. "Sorry, Miss Ida. I was helping out a friend, but we were just leaving. Take care now." He took Tess's hand and saw her grab her bag and his shirt before he pulled her out of the bathroom and toward the front doors of the reception hall.

He smiled as he heard her laughing behind him. Her sandals made loud, slapping noises with each step, but that didn't slow her down. And she didn't let go of his hand.

The rain had stopped, and several of the guests had already left the party. He looked out over the remaining cars. "Which one is yours?"

She offered him a sheepish look as she pointed toward the back of the parking lot. "Do you have to ask?"

He shrugged as they headed toward the light-blue sedan

surrounded by pickups and newer-model cars. "Hey, if it gets you where you want to go, that's all that matters."

"That's what I think. It's not real pretty, but I couldn't beat the price. My grandmother gave it to me as a gift when my car was totaled in an accident last year. It's cheap to insure and does okay on gas, so I can't complain."

"I get it. I've got an old truck like that. An '89 Chevy…belonged to my dad. I've been driving it since I was old enough to reach the pedals. We run that beast all over the farm, back and forth to town, and have hauled tons of stuff in it, and the thing just keeps going. I'm afraid we'll have to bury it in the back pasture if it ever dies, we're all so sentimentally attached to it."

"I'm not that emotionally attached to this car. I'm more like budget-attached. I can't afford a better one right now, so there's no point in letting it get to me. I'm just thankful that Mimi—that's my grandmother—was ready to get something new and let me have this one."

"Like I said, the good news about this car is that it should be a piece of cake to get unlocked. The slim jim should work great." He pulled the tool from his pocket.

"My hero. Again," she said, leaning against the side of the car. "I'm running out of fingers to count the number of times you've saved my bacon today. Including covering for me when we made our grand entrance to the party after our rainy walk. Thanks for not making me talk."

"No problem." He slid the slim jim along the window and down inside the door, shifting it around as he tried to find the lock mechanism. "So what was going on back there anyway? When we came in, I mean. Your face went so pale, you looked like you might pass out."

"I felt like I might pass out." She shook her head, her chest tightening again. "I could *never* do what you did."

"What? Carry a beautiful woman on your back through the rain?"

She nudged his arm. She liked the way he teased her out of her own head. "No. Well, I could probably never do that either. But I meant that thing where you just started chatting to an entire room full of people. Everyone was staring at us, we looked like drowned rats, and you just busted out a speech like you were entertaining friends in your living room."

"What are you talking about? I've known most of those people my whole life."

"You've known those celebrities and supermodels and famous athletes all your life?"

"Well, no. I guess not them. But I didn't really even say anything. It wasn't any big deal."

"It would be to me. I'm deathly afraid of public speaking. We had to take a speech class in college, and I never would have gotten my degree if the professor hadn't felt so sorry for me and given me just enough points to pass her class." There was more to the story than a disastrous college course, but she wasn't going to share that with him.

"Really?"

"Really. I mean, I'm not like a social pariah. I can converse with a small group of people, but when the spotlight is on me, I am terrified. Like, so scared that I can't move. Can't breathe. I just stand stock-still, like I'm frozen."

"Oh no. That must be something to see."

"Oh, it is. Sweat beads on my forehead, and I'm

freezing and overheating at the same time. My hands shake like a nervous Chihuahua, and sometimes I even stutter and ramble nonsensical words and phrases. It's super attractive."

He chuckled. "I'll bet." He raised the slim jim, and the door lock popped up. "Got it."

She let out a sigh of relief. "Thank you so much. I can't believe this day." She was going to fill five pages in her journal later just with the events of the last several hours.

He held open the door and gave her a charming smile. "I don't know. I think it's been a pretty great day."

Her cheeks tinged a soft pink, and she ducked her head.

He liked that he could make her blush.

"I've got a bag of extra stuff in the back seat. I'll get my shoes and take Quinn's sandals back to her."

"Don't worry about it. I can return them."

"No, I've got it. I'd like to thank her myself. Besides, I can't let you do something else for me. You've already done so much. Thanks for everything." She held the damp, crumpled shirt out to him, her earlier efforts at folding it ruined when they made their escape from the bathroom. "It looked so nice, and now I've practically destroyed it."

"You haven't destroyed it at all. It just got wet. I've never seen it look better than when it was on you." He let out a soft laugh and offered her a sideways grin. "Especially when it was wet."

His grin widened as he watched her cheeks flame again, and a smile pulled at the sides of her lips.

"I just wish I could do something to help you," she said.

The sound of a baby crying had him turning his head. A harried-looking couple with a toddler and the crying baby had exited the lodge and were heading toward a minivan.

The father waved at Mason. "See ya, Mace. Great party. Next time, let's hope we're celebrating your wedding."

"Yeah, come on, Mason. Hurry up and get hitched. We want our kids to at least be in school together," the woman called.

"Old classmates of mine," he told her before returning the couple's wave. "Yep, right behind you guys." The muscles of his jaw tightened, and his eye constricted in a tic. "Thanks for comin' out. See you at the wedding."

He kept a smile pasted to his face as he watched them load the minivan and pull out of the parking lot, then he slammed her car door closed and flung the slim jim on the ground.

Enough is enough. Why couldn't these people just leave him alone?

He glared at Tess, his neck hot and his blood boiling under his skin. "You want to know what would help me? What would *really* help me?" he asked, his voice a little too loud. "It would really help me if the people of this town would mind their own damn business and quit looking at me with these pity-filled looks in their eyes as they pat my shoulder and tell me not to worry, that some great girl is out there waiting for me. That there are plenty of fish in the sea and that it's okay that I'm not married yet, when what they really mean is that it's *not* okay."

He shook his head, letting out a huff of frustration as he cut his eyes to the ground.

She didn't say anything for a minute, and he was afraid to look up.

He liked this girl. He didn't have the time or the inclination for a woman in his life right now. But he liked her. And he *hated* feeling embarrassed and humiliated in front of her. She had to think he was an idiot.

"I get it," she said, her voice not sounding disdainful at all. "The same thing happens to me."

"Yeah? So how do you handle it?"

She shrugged. "Very maturely. I simply choose to avoid going out altogether."

He chuckled. "Smart." He raised his head and studied her. Then an idea came to him, a wild thought that surprised even him. "You know, I was happy to help today, and I don't expect anything in return, but maybe there is something you could do for me."

Chapter 6

TESSA RAISED AN EYEBROW. "YOU'VE GOT AN ODD GLEAM in your eye. It's making me nervous. What kind of 'something' did you have in mind?" Was he thinking of asking her to repay him with some kind of kinky sex act? The idea thrilled and disturbed her.

Mason chuckled. "It's nothing too crazy. Well, I don't know. Maybe it is. I was just thinking—since your date didn't show up and all, and since I'm also currently without a date—that maybe, you know, if you want to, you could be my date for the wedding and the activities this weekend."

Oh.

Wait. Was he asking her because he really wanted her to be his date or because he suddenly realized she would be an easy way to keep people off his back about not being married?

Did it matter? This was her chance to spend time with Rock's family, to get the inside scoop. So why did she feel as if she'd just knocked down all the bottles in a carnival booth, expecting to win the big teddy bear, and had been given the cheap substitute prize of a plastic whistle instead?

"Sure, I guess. If it will help you."

His tightened shoulders relaxed. "It would help. And no one would really know that this was our first date. Especially if you show up for all the prewedding activities. This town runs on gossip. If they have something to gossip about, like if we're a new couple or already involved, they might leave me alone, at least until after the wedding activities die down."

She wanted to ask what would happen after this weekend, but he was making it pretty clear that he was just looking for a stand-in date. And it's not like it would matter. He wasn't going to be interested in her after this weekend anyway—not that he was interested now. But after the article came out, he would know what she'd really been doing at the wedding party.

By the time that happened, she'd be gone anyway. She'd have the cash in hand and be one step closer to saving her grandmother's house. But first she had to get the story.

She leaned against the side of the car. "This sounds like a terrible, awful, yet kind of brilliant idea."

He chuckled.

"But I do know what it's like to be single at a wedding and have every busybody in attendance come up and not so gently remind me that I'm still single with well-meaning but ridiculously insulting words of advice."

"Tell me about it."

"So, I think you're right. The best way to nip that in the bud is to have a date. And not just a date, but a date with a whisper of a relationship."

His lips curved into a flirty smile. "You know, Ms. Kane, I believe you're onto something. So, let's give them something to whisper about."

She lifted her shoulders and offered him an impish grin. "I'm game if you are."

A battalion of butterflies swirled through Mason's stomach.

What the hell's that about?

She hadn't agreed to anything beyond being his date for the weekend, but it felt as if they were slinging innuendo around like happy hogs in a pool of mud. The way the corners of her lips pulled up when she'd said *whisper* had his mouth going dry and his pulse beating against his throat.

What was it about this woman? She hadn't even said that she liked him, so maybe she just liked free barbecue. He didn't think that was it. Although she obviously liked barbecue—the way she'd sucked the meat off those ribs earlier had his mind going to dark places—she didn't strike him as a party girl.

She seemed...nice. And maybe that's all this was. Her truly feeling indebted to him for helping her out on a day when everything had gone wrong and she'd been stood up. Maybe she was just doing something nice to help him in return. And it wasn't like he was proposing that they *actually* have a relationship. It was just a whisper, a hint, enough of a murmur to get a little gossip going. Nothing to get his stomach tied in knots over.

So why were his hands suddenly sweaty?

He wiped his palms on his pants and tried to seem casual. *Pull yourself together, man.*

He pushed his hat up and raised his eyebrows in a playful tease. "So, what should we do to get this 'whisper' going?"

She laughed and swatted at his arm. "Not *that*. I'm not doing you that big of a favor."

"Can't blame a guy for trying."

"Yeah, you said that before." She tapped her chin and wrinkled her nose as she thought about it. "I think we've probably already started people talking with that dramatic entrance into the lodge a little bit ago."

"True," he agreed. He was warming to the idea of spending more time with her. He picked up the slim jim and wiped it on his pant leg, leaving a trail of mud on the already-muddied fabric, then shoved it into his back pocket. "But you know, today was the easy part. Spending the next couple of days with my family, and my brothers, is no easy task."

"They can't be that bad."

"You'll see." And he'd see if she'd last one day or if she'd head for the hills after a few hours with his crazy family. "We're having a barbecue out at the ranch tomorrow afternoon. Do you want to come out for that? It would give you a chance to get to know a few other people who will be at the wedding. And you can see if you can handle being around my brothers."

"Sure. I like a challenge."

"I'll remind you that you said that after the barbecue tomorrow." He narrowed his eyes at her. "You serious about this? Really?"

"Sure. I was going to spend a few days in Creedence anyway, and who knows, this could be fun."

"Well, I'm not promising fun, but I don't think you'll get bored. We've got three more full days until the wedding, and besides the barbecue, Rock has this alumni hockey game scheduled that we're all either playing in or helping out with, so you'd probably get stuck serving hot dogs at the snack bar with my mom and Quinn. And there's the rehearsal dinner, of course. Then the wedding itself. That seems like an awful lot to do just to pay a guy back for loaning you his shirt. You sure you're up for all that?"

His family would probably scare her off by the second day.

She shrugged. "I'm always up for an adventure. And it sounds like fun."

"Okay, then it sounds like we've got a deal." He held his hand out to shake.

She hesitated just a moment, as if contemplating what kind of crazy scheme she'd gotten herself into, then put her hand in his and squeezed. "Deal."

The handshake didn't seem like enough, and he was tempted to suggest sealing the deal with a kiss. But the woman had just agreed to spend the next several days with him as his date. He probably shouldn't push his luck. "I'll pick you up for the barbecue tomorrow around noon," he said. "You staying at the Lamplighter Hotel?"

"Um, yeah, I think that's the name of it. But don't bother picking me up. I'll come to you. Just give me the address of the ranch."

He pulled out his phone. "What's your number? I'll text it to you."

She gave him her number, and he texted her the address. "And now you have my number too, in case you want to call or text me to say you've changed your mind about being my date."

She tapped the screen of her phone, then his phone chimed.

He looked down at the text message she'd just sent him. I haven't changed my mind about being your date. Or the whisper.

Mason couldn't help the grin that crossed his face.

He texted back, I guess I'll see you tomorrow. He hesitated over the emojis, trying to pick the most appropriate one. Should he do the smiley face that was blowing a kiss? No. Too obvious. And too girlie.

What about just a heart? No. Still too feminine *and* too high school. He was a man. *Grunt. Grunt.* He scrolled through several screens.

Tess tilted her head to see his screen. "That's a lot of thought going into a simple emoji."

He shrugged. "I've learned women can read a lot into a *simple* emoji. I want to get it right."

"I'm learning something about you right now."

He raised his eyes.

"You're kind of a perfectionist." She grinned and nudged his shoulder. "Don't think about it. Just pick something you like."

He looked down at the screen he was on, tapped two pictures, and hit Send.

Her phone chimed, and she opened the message and burst out laughing. "You picked the emojis of a taco and a mug of beer?"

He grinned. "You said to pick something I liked. I like tacos and beer."

"Noted." She laughed again and pressed the phone to her chest. "I think this might be the most romantic text I've ever gotten."

"I aim to please." He aimed to figure out a way to kiss her good night. He shifted from one foot to the other. Where was the emoji for nervous idiot?

He had an idea and tapped out a message, then hit Send.

Her phone chimed, and a grin cut across her face as she saw his message. It had only had two symbols: a pair of red lips symbolizing a kiss and a question mark.

She tilted her head and offered him a shy smile.

He debated going for the brief peck on the cheek or really going all in with the full lip-crushing kiss.

Ah hell—just do something.

He leaned down and pressed a quick kiss to her lips.

It was a good kiss—although he would have been happy to have it linger a little longer—and it was definitely better than the chaste cheek peck he'd been considering.

"I'll see you tomorrow," she said, opening her car door.

"See you tomorrow." He offered her his most charming smile, still tasting the sweet flavor of spearmint lip gloss she'd left on his lips.

Tess bunched up the spare sweatshirt she'd had in the car and tried to pretend it was a feather pillow. Closing her eyes, she also tried to pretend she was in a cozy bed, instead of curled up in the back seat of her car in the alley behind the library.

She hadn't planned on sleeping in her car, hadn't planned any of this, but when Mason asked her to be his plus-one at the wedding, it was too good to pass up. The chance to be around his family was just what she needed. She tried to stuff down the part about also getting to spend the next three days with the handsome cowboy and what a dork she must have sounded like when he asked her.

She'd tried to come off all cool—as if it was totally

normal for her to hang out with celebrities and professional athletes, like she was so flirty and fun that she could easily pull off a weekend spent with a hunky guy trying to start small-town speculation about their "whisper" of a relationship. Where had that even come from?

And seriously? I'm always up for an adventure?

What kind of bull-pucky was that? She wasn't *ever* up for an adventure. She was the least adventurous person she knew. She didn't even like to try new kinds of toothpaste or shampoo. She'd used the same brand of both for years.

She didn't recognize half the stuff that was coming out of her mouth.

She did owe Mason a favor—or seven—for bailing her out so many times that day, and it wasn't a hardship to be his fill-in, but writing an exposé on his brother wasn't a great way to pay him back.

Guilt churned in her stomach, like acid bubbling against the inside of her gut. This wasn't the kind of person she was; this wasn't the kind of story she wanted to write. And she hated deceiving Mason. He was a good guy. As far as she knew.

But she'd thought the last one she'd dated was a good guy too. And look how that had turned out!

Tamping down the small inner voice that told her Mason was the real deal and she was being a real shit for doing this to him, she pulled the emergency blanket she always carried in her car—thank goodness for that—tighter under her chin.

Her acting as his date wasn't a totally terrible plan.

And he'd said she'd be helping him out too. He'd seemed genuinely annoyed by the well-meaning guests' comments on his marital, or *non*marital, status. So she was really doing him a favor. It was a win-win for everyone.

Mason would get to attend his brother's wedding in peace, and she'd get to spend time with Rock and Quinn. Plus, there was the added benefit of getting to cozy up to the cute cowboy. What could go wrong?

She looked around the inside of her car, her lodgings for the night, and let out a sigh. For starters, she had fibbed about staying at the Lamplighter Hotel. About staying at *any* hotel. She couldn't afford a hotel, couldn't even afford the gas to get up and down the mountain again for the next few days.

No, she was stuck. Stuck in Creedence, stuck sleeping in her car, because what she really couldn't afford was for her grandmother to lose her house.

She'd already called Mimi and told her she was staying up in the mountains for the next few days. She hadn't explained the exact situation, but she'd assured her grandmother she was working on a story that would help their situation.

Tess's mind raced with a thousand thoughts, and any hope of sleep she had was dissolving. Maybe she should work. Dragging her cavernous purse toward her, she pawed through the contents and pulled out a pen and a pink steno pad. She always carried one, or five, in case inspiration struck and she needed to scribble down a story idea.

She'd only been planning to be in Creedence for one day, so even though she'd brought three outfits, hair spray, and an emergency makeup kit with her, she hadn't brought her laptop or any electronics beyond her phone.

It seemed she was stuck with the old-school way of writing, which was fine with her. Sometimes, tackling an article with a pen and paper brought out a different side of her creativity. And she needed to come up with something creative if she was going to sell her boss on not only letting her stay with the magazine, but paying her big bucks for this article.

She held the notepad so the security light from the library illuminated the paper and jotted a headline at the top of the page: *Bad Boy Bachelor Becomes a Bridegroom.*

Hmm. Not bad. She wrote down a couple more.

Hockey-Playing Cowboy Gets Lassoed.

Does the Quickie Wedding of NHL Cowboy Mean He Scored a Goal, or Is He Going to the Marital Penalty Box?

Ugh. Funny. But no good.

Gordon didn't want funny. He didn't want light. He wanted dirt.

She drew a line, then wrote, *All the dirt I know on Rockford James,* followed by a short list of statements and questions to dig deeper into.

Rock's very handsome and known for his bad-boy ways. So why is he all of a sudden getting married?

This wedding was planned and executed in a very short time. Why?

Is Quinn using him for his money? Gold digger?

Quinn is already a single mom. Did she get knocked up by Rock to trick him into marrying her? Could her son actually be his?

High school sweethearts—but why are they suddenly back together now? Could Quinn be blackmailing him? Why?

What else could be involved? Drugs? Prostitutes? Gambling debts?

This list made her tired. And disheartened. She hadn't spent much time with Rock and Quinn, but they seemed genuinely happy. And like nice people.

Quinn had left her own party to find and loan a perfect stranger a pair of her shoes—which Tess had just realized she'd forgotten to return. She'd bring them with her to the barbecue tomorrow. But still, that didn't sound like the kind of person who'd blackmail her high school sweetheart.

But who knew what people did these days? As her scant dating history proved, she wasn't the best judge of character. She let out a sigh and shoved the notebook between the front seat and the center console. She'd work on the story again tomorrow.

Her head was starting to pound, and she couldn't afford to get a headache now. She suffered occasionally from migraines, especially on days with major weather changes, and always kept her prescribed pills with her. Although now that she thought about it, she hadn't seen the bottle in her bag when she'd been digging for a pen. Oh well, she could check tomorrow. Right now, she needed to sleep. She lay back down, pulled the meager blanket over her, and closed her eyes.

If only her brain would close the way her eyelids did. She couldn't seem to shut down all the thoughts that were flying around in her mind—worries about her grandmother, random lines of text that she might be able to use in the story, the feel of Mason's lips on hers as he'd given her the quick kiss. She tried counting to one hundred, tried imagining she was on a warm beach, but nothing worked.

Her eyes popped open as a low rumble of thunder sounded.

A flash of lightning lit up the sky, and fat drops of rain hit the roof of her car. She'd parked behind the town library, convincing herself it would be safe and no one would notice her car there. The library was on the north edge of town, across the street from the Lamplighter Hotel, so she'd gotten *close* to the truth on that one.

She'd driven up and down the streets of Creedence twice, looking for a good place to "camp." Thinking of it as camping made it feel a little less desperate and scary. There was an actual campground outside of town, but even a rustic tent site—one that might be out of the way enough for the other campers not to realize that she didn't have an actual tent—was thirty-five dollars. And she barely had thirty-five cents.

Besides, plenty of people had spent a night or two in their cars and been just fine. And it was safer, and warmer, than a tent. She'd settled on her current spot because her parents had often taken her to the library as a kid, and the building itself evoked feelings of warmth, security, and safety. And it was fairly secluded, with a good-sized alley running behind it that backed up to a forested hillside. The only thing behind the building was a steel Dumpster. And now her.

A shiver ran through her. As much as she told herself that it was a small town and no one would even know she was there and the library would be safe, if she were being truthful, she'd have to admit that she was scared to death—scared that someone would find her back there and drag her from her car to attack her. Or worse, break *into* her car and attack her.

She had no idea who all these random people were that were always looking to attack her, but she was sure they were out there. Another flash of lightning, followed by a loud roar of thunder, had her pulling the blanket over her head.

Then another sound, right outside her door, had her blood chilling and her heart thundering against her chest as she squeezed her eyes tightly shut. The tinny crackle of a can being rolled across the pavement as if a foot had kicked it. A foot belonging to a serial killer. Or a psychopathic rapist. Or worse—a clown.

What if a clown serial-killer psychopath was standing outside her car window peering in at her right now? She *had* to open her eyes, had to pull down the blanket and check. But she couldn't.

Fear paralyzed her. Just like with public speaking, fear of the unknown was feeling more dire than facing what was really out there in the darkness.

I can do this. I am strong. I can do this.

She repeated the mantra, steeling herself but keeping her eyes shut as she pulled the blanket down to her nose.

She couldn't breathe.

Seriously, if a clown was standing there, she'd scream, wet her pants, and most likely vomit—not necessarily in that order.

Do it.

She forced her eyes open, letting out a tiny squeal of fright as she did.

No clown staring menacingly into her car window.

No serial killer at all. Her breath came out in a stuttering shake. There was nothing there. Nothing to be scared of. It must have been her imagination.

Another sound, like someone—or something—scratching at the side of her door, had her yanking the covers back over her head.

Holy crap! Something *was* out there. Something was really out there.

She had to look. The sound came from somewhere low on her car. What if someone was *under* her car, waiting for her to step out so they could slit her Achilles tendon, leaving her crippled and crawling away from the car?

She'd seen way too many horror movies. This was ridiculous. She had to check it out. It wasn't as though she was going to be able to sleep anyway. Not with a knife-wielding serial-killer clown waiting under her car.

A high-pitched whine sounded, and Tessa's racing heart shattered. That was a whine of an animal. An animal in pain. The thought of an animal hurting was enough to break her out of her frozen stupor and get her to crawl across the back seat to peer through the window.

A gasp escaped her lips as she saw a small scruffy dog huddled under the Dumpster. It must have tried scratching at her door first, then headed for the shelter of the trash receptacle.

She squinted her eyes, trying to see through the rain. In the dark, it was hard to tell what color the dog was through the mud coating its fur. Poor thing. It looked like a drowned rat. She had to do something.

Pushing open the back door, she let out a whistle and called to the dog. "Come here, boy. Come on."

The dog crept forward a few inches but didn't leave the relative safety underneath the Dumpster. The rain pelted the side of the back seat and splashed against the door. Tess pulled the door shut, trying to think of what she could use to lure the dog to her.

Her purse still lay on the floor of the car, and she dug through its contents again, finding the napkin with the roll and cookie that she'd pilfered from the buffet table earlier that day.

Why she'd taken a roll and a cookie was beyond her. She hadn't really been thinking, just knew that it wouldn't hurt to stockpile a little grub, and the barbecued pork had been way too messy for her bag.

So, she'd settled for the carbs and figured a cookie sandwich was better than nothing. She'd been saving the food to have for breakfast, but this little guy looked like he could use it more than she could.

She opened the back door again, then broke off a piece of the bread and held it out toward the dog. "Here, boy."

The dog inched forward again, his nose lifting to sniff the air. The rain pelted the ground in front of the Dumpster. But the lure of food must have outweighed fear of the rain, or her, because suddenly the dog shot out from its hiding spot and sprinted for her car door.

Reeling back, she laughed as the little dog launched himself into the back seat and onto her lap. She fed him the chunk of bread, then reached around and pulled the back door shut and locked it as he happily chewed his reward. Now that he was in the car, she could see he was light brown and beige and had soulful brown eyes.

He finished off the roll, then licked his lips, and gazed expectantly up at her.

"Sorry, buster. I'm saving the cookie for me. That's my breakfast."

He let out a tiny whine, then crawled up her chest, sniffing and licking her face.

He wore a blue collar around his neck, but the ring around it had either been pried or broken open and the tags—if there had been any—were missing. Using the corner of the blanket, Tess wiped it down his face and back, cleaning off the mud and doing her best to dry his fur.

"What are you doing out here all by yourself, fella?" she asked. "Are you lost, boy?"

I know how you feel.

The fact that he was wearing a collar led her to believe the dog did belong to someone, but there was no way she was going out in that rainstorm to track down the owner. She'd bring him into the library in the morning and see if anyone recognized him or had heard about a missing dog. Librarians usually knew the lowdown on just about everything going on in town.

For now, he'd just have to be her guest for the evening. "Welcome to Chez Ford Taurus. We're delighted you'll be joining us tonight and hope you enjoy the posh accommodations."

The dog touched the end of his nose to her cheek, then laid his head against her shoulder. *Aww*. How cute was that?

"Fine. You can have the cookie. But we're splitting it." She pulled the wadded napkin from her purse, and the dog excitedly sniffed the air, his nose digging into the napkin and his tail wagging against her leg.

She freed the sugar cookie and split it in half, releasing

the heavenly scent of vanilla and sugar. Popping one half into her mouth, she rested the other half on her hand and held it out to the dog, who delicately licked it, then gobbled it off her fingers.

"That's all there is," she told him around a mouthful of cookie.

He stared at her for a moment, letting out another soft whine. Then, as if accepting her statement, he pawed at the blanket beside her and curled up in a furry circle in its folds. She let out a sigh. Guess the dog was sleeping with her tonight. Not that she minded. Lying back down, she pulled the blanket over her shoulder and curled her body around the small dog. He lifted his head, then rested it gently on her shoulder.

Dang. For the second time that day, she'd been done in by a cute male. But this time, she was pretty sure she really did fall in love. Closing her eyes, she rested her hand on the animal's furry back.

The scent of wet dog filled the car, and she could smell his cookie-scented dog breath as he settled into sleep, but she'd take a muddy, semi-smelly canine companion over a serial-killing clown any day.

Chapter 7

Tessa woke the next morning to the sun streaming in on her face and the sound of a soft whimper as the dog scratched against the inside of the door. She sat up, stretching her aching muscles as she reached for the handle of the back door and pushed it open just far enough for the dog to slip out. He raced for the grassy area behind the car, did his business, then ran back and jumped onto the seat next to her.

The alley was still empty, but she didn't know how long that would last. She had no idea what time the librarian would show up, but she knew she didn't want to be here when she did.

Climbing over the seat, Tess dropped into the driver's side and let out a yawn as she started the engine and pulled out of the parking lot. She might not be able to afford to stay in the KOA campground, but she figured she could probably sneak in and use their facilities. Plus, she really needed a shower. She smelled like a combination of musty closet and wet dog.

Thank goodness she'd packed the extra clothes and a few toiletries for the wedding-party events. She might not have an arsenal of makeup, but she could make do with shadow and liner as long as she had moisturizer, mascara, and a great lip gloss.

The KOA camp was fairly empty, and she parked her car next to a camper with Kansas plates. Mimi was originally from Kansas and had always told her you could trust a fellow Midwesterner.

Tess grabbed her bag and the spare toothbrush and paste she always kept in her glove compartment. She liked to be prepared in case she needed to interview someone and had coffee breath or had eaten too garlicky of a lunch. Thank goodness for her preparedness now.

The key to looking like you belonged someplace was to *act* like you belonged there. With the little dog trotting at her heels, she strode purposely up the road and into the camp's restroom facility. It was empty this early in the morning, and she was relieved to see a nice built-in area with shower stalls and wall dryers. She set her bag on the bench and popped into a bathroom stall. The dog followed her in and sat at her feet, which she guessed was only fair since she'd watched him take care of his business earlier.

Shedding her clothes, she stepped into the shower and was excited to see a container unit affixed to the wall that held shampoo, conditioner, and body wash. It might not have been the fanciest, but the shower had hot water and great water pressure, and Tess was just happy to have a place to soap up and wash her hair.

As she rinsed the conditioner from her hair, she was surprised to see the water at her feet turning a muddy brown. Glancing around, she let out a laugh as she saw the little dog standing behind her in the shower stall, soaking up the warm spray of water as if he was having a day at the spa.

She filled her hands with shampoo, then bent down and gave the dog a thorough scrubbing.

Not having an actual towel—she wasn't *that*

prepared—she made do with paper towels and quickly dried off herself and the dog as well as she could. She dressed in a pair of khaki shorts and a white tank top, then slipped her feet back into her sandals.

Using the hair dryer, she dried and fluffed both her hair and the dog's. Then he jumped up on the bench and patiently watched her put on her makeup and brush her teeth.

No one had come into the bathroom yet, so when she was done, she set the dog on the counter, turned on the tap, and let him lap at the water pouring into the sink.

"I'm afraid that's all I've got to offer you in the way of breakfast, boy," she told the dog, rubbing her hand over his now-clean-and-soft furry neck. "I know, I'm hungry too."

"A drink of water isn't much of a breakfast," a voice said behind her.

Tess let out a squeak, and her hand flew to her chest as she turned around to face an adorable little old lady standing in the doorway of the bathroom. She had to be at least eighty, but she wore a hot-pink tracksuit and a lime-green hat that read "Feisty" in sparkly rhinestones. A small poodle with matching curly white hair sat obediently at her feet.

"Oh my gosh, you scared me," Tess said, nonchalantly taking the dog from the counter and setting him back down on the floor.

He padded over to the elderly woman and sniffed at her ankles, then cautiously nosed the poodle.

"Didn't mean to startle ya, but I couldn't help but overhear your conversation with your pup. I'm Helen, and this is Benji." She gestured to the white dog, who was enthusiastically smelling the newcomer's ears. "My husband, Lee, is frying up a mess of bacon and eggs back at our RV. You and your friend here are welcome to join us."

"Wow. That's so nice. But we couldn't possibly impose." Tess's stomach let out a loud rumble, apparently voicing its displeasure over her turning down bacon and eggs.

"It's no imposition at all. We have more than enough, and we'd love the company." She leaned forward and lowered her voice as if she was sharing a secret. "To tell you the truth, honey, Lee and I have been on the road for two months now, and it would be nice to hear someone else's voice besides our own. Don't tell him, but after sixty years, I've already heard all his stories."

Tess let out a chuckle. "Okay. If you're sure."

Helen gave her a wink. "I'm sure. Just give me a few minutes to get washed up, and we'll walk over together."

She and Helen, and the two small dogs, were fast friends by the time they walked back to the camper. Her dog was a little shy of Lee, but his affection was easily swayed when the man offered him a dish of dog chow. He let Lee scratch his head as he greedily gobbled down the food.

Their RV happened to be the camper with the Kansas plates that Tess had parked next to. So apparently Mimi had been right. Because breakfast with Lee and Helen from the Midwest turned out to be a fun affair.

Lee was not just a great cook—he used actual bacon grease to scramble the eggs in—but also a masterful storyteller. He had Tess in stitches as he shared tales of their travels while she scooped scrambled eggs, toast, and some of the crispiest bacon she'd ever tasted into her mouth.

They had to have seen her pull up next to them, but they didn't ask her many questions. Such as why she was in a KOA campground with no camper. She told them she was in town for a wedding, and they didn't press beyond that—and she didn't offer anything more.

She liked this sweet couple and was blown away by their simple generosity. And sitting outside their camper soaking up the summer air and the mountain scenery made up for the awful night she'd just spent in the back seat of her car.

Holding her stomach, she heaved a contented sigh. "That was delicious. I can't thank you enough for feeding us. I wish I could do something to return the favor."

Helen raised an eyebrow at her husband.

He shrugged, apparently knowing exactly what his wife was thinking in that secret code of being married forever. "I don't care. You can ask her."

Uh-oh. Here it came—the real reason these folks had been so nice to her.

"Well," Helen said, "now that you mention it, I could use your help with something. My grandkids keep sending me pictures, and I'm sure Lee could figure it out, but I'm having a heck of time trying to save them on my iPad. If I brought it out here, could you show me how?"

Tess let out a laugh. "Of course. I help my grandma with this kind of stuff all the time."

"Oh, bless you. You'd be doing me a great favor." Helen disappeared into the RV.

"And you'd be doing me a favor too," Lee said with a conspiratorial wink. "Because then I won't have to hear about it anymore."

Tess chuckled and pushed her plate to the side as

Helen came back with the iPad. It only took her a few minutes to save the photos, and then she wrote down detailed instructions on how to do it for the couple to use the next time.

"This is wonderful. You have no idea how much this will help." The older woman patted Tess's hand.

"It's no big deal. And it was a cheap price to pay for such a great breakfast."

Helen snuck the scruffy dog a leftover crust from her toast. He was sitting between them, alternately resting his head on the lap of whoever was willing to pet him. "So, what are you going to do about this little guy?"

"I don't know. I was thinking I'd try to make up some flyers at the library this morning and post a couple of them at the grocery store and the police station." She'd told them that the dog was a stray, and how she'd only found him the night before.

Or rather, he'd found her.

"Good idea. In the meantime, what are you going to call him?"

Tess hadn't really thought about it. "I've been calling him 'dog' so far. I don't know if I should actually name him. He seems well-trained and is wearing a collar, so I assume he's someone else's dog, and I don't want to get too attached."

"Too late." Helen grinned as she peered down at the dog. "It wouldn't hurt to come up with something. Just for now."

Tess studied the dog's cute face. His brown eyes gazed up at her with admiration. She'd never had a pet and had no idea how one came up with a suitable name.

She had a friend who'd named her dog Montana

because that's where she'd found him. She thought about where she'd found this little guy, but she couldn't very well call him Dumpster or Dark Alley.

"I found him outside of the library, and I do love to read. Maybe I should name him after a character in one of my favorite books." She clapped a hand to her head. "Except there are way too many. I love so many stories, I could never choose. But I do remember spending a lot of time in the library, especially when I had a paper due and needed to do research. Remember back in the prehistoric days before we had the internet when we used to have to look everything up in the card catalog?"

The older woman nodded. "You're preaching to the choir, sister."

Tess chuckled. She tilted her head as an idea came to her. "That's actually kind of a cute idea for a name."

"What? You want to call him Card Catalog?"

"No. But I could call him Dewey for the Dewey decimal system."

Helen laughed. "That is cute."

She brought her face closer to the dog's. "Do you like that name, pup? Would you accept being called Dewey?" He tipped his snout up and licked her chin, which drew another laugh from her and Helen.

"I think we've got a winner," she proclaimed, wiping the dog slobber from her chin. "Dewey it is."

"That sounds just right." Helen nodded, her silvery curls bobbing with the movement of her head. "It's always a hard one when you find a stray. If he is lost, you want to return him to his owner, of course. But I've heard tales of folks dumping their dogs at rest stops or letting them loose because they can't take care of them.

And this little guy has obviously already fallen in love with you."

"The feeling is mutual," Tess said with a sigh as she scratched the scruffy mutt behind the ears. "I've never had a dog, or any pet, before."

"Looks like you have one now."

Tessa spent the next hour with the couple, helping to clear the dishes, then taking a walk around the campground with them and the two little dogs.

She felt like she'd known them forever by the time she said goodbye. Helen gave her a hug, and Lee offered her a grandfatherly pat on the shoulder accompanied by a reassuring wink.

"We'll be here all week if you want to come back anytime. Breakfast will be on about seven," he told her.

They assured her they had plenty of dog food and sent her off with one baggie crammed full of enough food to last Dewey for a week and another filled with treats.

She climbed into the car, and the dog jumped over her lap and into the passenger seat. He gave an excited yap, which she interpreted as the doggie equivalent of calling "shotgun." Raising her hand in a wave, she pulled out of the parking lot and headed back toward the library.

"Dang it." Mason scowled as the pliers slipped from his hands and fell into the dust of the corral. One of the horses whinnied at him, and he shook his head as he inhaled a deep breath.

"Sorry, girl." He scooped the tool from the dirt and crossed the corral to caress the chestnut mare's neck. Her name was Gypsy, and she'd been his horse for close to ten years now. She could usually be found somewhere around him whenever he was working anywhere near the barn. It probably had more to do with the sugar cubes in his pocket than their horse-and-rider bond, but he couldn't say for sure. He did know that he regarded the mare as one of his top-ten favorite females.

"I'm not mad at you." He ran his hand along her velvety neck, and she nuzzled his pocket with her nose. He wasn't really mad at anyone. He was just in a weird mood—one minute happy and smiling, and the next minute scowling and grouchy. And he hadn't been able to focus all morning.

Heck, he hadn't been able to focus since last night. Not since he'd met the dark-haired beauty who had haunted his dreams the night before.

Not even the extra-hard drills his brother had put them through that morning during hockey practice could take his mind off her. He'd narrowly missed getting beaned in the head when he'd lost his focus while trying to take a shot on goal. He'd been thinking about the feel of her legs wrapped around him when he gave her that piggyback ride down the trail.

Mason wasn't used to this much skating. He and Colt often accompanied Rock to the ice rink when he was in town, but they usually just messed around on the ice while Rock did laps around them. But with the alumni game coming up, his brother had been working them—and the whole team—pretty hard the last several weeks. Although they were all fairly competitive, they didn't care as much about winning this game as they did about not looking like idiots against the younger guys they'd be playing.

Mason had been skating hard and his muscles ached from the new drills they'd been working on, but the muscle he wasn't used to working was his heart. And that one had been put through the paces yesterday — pounding and racing and practically stopping when he chanced upon Tess in that closet.

What was going on? He couldn't remember the last time a woman had messed with his head the way Tessa Kane was doing. He liked her. He knew that; otherwise he wouldn't have asked her to be his date. But he didn't usually make impulsive decisions like that. He was the responsible brother, the one who looked out for everyone and made sure things got taken care of. He didn't usually worry about himself, as long as everyone else was okay.

Which made him wonder what the hell he'd been thinking by inviting this woman to spend the next three days with him and his family during the crazy wedding weekend.

And why the hell had she agreed?

Sure they'd had fun together, and he'd felt like they'd really hit it off. But most women liked to take things slowly, not jump right into the frying pan of a guy's whole family.

Maybe that's what had him scowling—wondering what her motivation was. Why had she agreed to be his date? Not just for one event, but for the whole weekend? It couldn't be just to repay the favor of him lending her a shirt. It wasn't that great a shirt.

A small, niggling thought crept into his mind that she was doing it to get close to Rock—just as other women in Mason's life had done. But that was ridiculous. Right?

That couldn't be it. She hadn't really spent any time

with his brother. She'd seemed only to have eyes for him. But he'd been fooled before.

I'll know soon enough. He glanced at his watch. She'd be here any time now. His pulse jumped at the thought of seeing her again.

"Mason Dean," his mom yelled from the front porch of the house. "Come on in and get washed up. Dinner's about ready."

"I'm comin'," he hollered back, then gave the horse's neck a final pat before heading toward the old farmhouse.

The house itself might be old, but his brother had insisted on adding some renovations to the inside, including giving their mother an updated kitchen. The wall had been knocked out between the living room and kitchen, and a huge center island had been installed, giving the house a great-room effect.

Vivi had put the larger kitchen to use today, cooking and baking up a storm, and the counters were covered with salads, breads, and assorted baked goods.

His great-aunt had arrived earlier that afternoon, and she sat at the table, her hands busy as she husked a giant stack of corn.

Mason leaned down and brushed a kiss on her cheek. "Hey, Aunt Sassy."

"Hey, yourself," she answered with a wry smile. "Hope you brought in your appetite. Your mom's cooked enough for eighty."

"Good. I'm starving."

"You're always starving."

He chuckled and grabbed a chocolate chip cookie— his favorite—from a plate and stuffed it in his mouth.

"Your 'new friend' should be here any minute," Vivi said, glancing up at the kitchen clock as he washed his hands at the sink.

"Yep," he mumbled around the mouthful of cookie, avoiding his mother's curious eyes as she handed him a towel.

"Whose new friend should be here?" Colt asked, dropping his hat on the table as he sauntered through the front door.

"Your brother's, apparently." Vivi nodded at Mason, her face wearing the slightest smirk as she leaned her hip against the counter. "As of yesterday, he's invited a girl to attend the wedding with him *and* all the prewedding activities, including the barbecue today."

"What? No way. Mace doesn't do spontaneous." Colt pulled a bottle of water from the fridge and twisted off the cap. Tipping the bottle up, he took a swig, then eyed Mason suspiciously. "Do you, Bro?"

"Yes, I do," Mason muttered. "Or I've been known to. Sometimes."

"So, who's the girl?" Colt scoffed.

"She's not a girl. She's a woman. And her name is Tess. You met her last night."

"So did you." Colt cocked an eyebrow. "She must have been one hell of a first date if you're already bringing her out to the ranch to meet Ma and hang with us."

That was the thing, the thing that had been gnawing at Mason. She *had* been one hell of a first date.

Not that spending time together at the party had been a date, but he'd had a great time with her. They'd laughed and talked, and he'd felt like himself around her. And he didn't feel like that very often.

Maybe it was because she didn't already know him, didn't know the history of their family, didn't know that he was Rockford James's little brother. He felt like he was just Mason to her. Without all the baggage.

He felt good. And that thought excited and terrified him.

Not that he could say any of that to his brother. Colt and Rock would rib him for a month of Sundays if they heard him spouting any of that mushy stuff. "Everybody needs to stop making such a big deal out of this," he said. Including himself. "She's nice, and she's fun, and I invited her to the wedding and to the barbecue today. End of story."

There. That ought to do it. Act like it's no big deal, and it won't be.

Although he had a feeling his mom wasn't fooled one bit. Vivienne James knew her sons, often better than they knew themselves. She offered him an easy smile. "I'm sure she is nice. Otherwise you wouldn't have invited her. I'm looking forward to her visit."

Colt studied him for another moment then shrugged and peered over the array of dishes on the counter. He snagged an oatmeal scotchie. "Whatever. She seemed cool to me. And we all noticed that she was wearing your shirt, so you must have already spent some 'nice' and 'fun' time together." He laughed as Mason threw the towel he was holding at his head.

The sound of a car's engine coming down the long driveway of the ranch drew their attention to the front window of the kitchen.

"Looks like your 'new friend' has arrived," Vivi said, a note of amusement in her tone.

Mason ignored her, too busy trying to quell the flurry of sensations that had just taken off in his gut. He pushed out the front door, pausing on the porch to steady himself as she parked her car next to his pickup. His border collie, Theo, raced up to greet her as she stepped from the car.

She had on a simple tank top and shorts, but her hair was loose and curled around her shoulders, and when she pulled off her sunglasses and smiled up at him, she took his danged breath away.

He sauntered down the porch steps, trying to act casual since he knew full well that his mother and brother would have their faces plastered to the kitchen window.

A grin broke out on his face as he approached her. Forget the food at the barbecue. Tessa Kane looked good enough to eat.

She took a step forward, and without thinking, he grabbed her hand and pulled her toward the barn. "Come on, I want to show you something," he mumbled.

"What is it?" she asked as they stepped into the cool shadow of the barn.

He turned to face her, suddenly feeling awkward and shy. "Nothing. My family was just watching us, and it felt weird saying hello to you while they stared at us through the window."

She smiled. "Understandable."

He rubbed his hand along the back of his neck. "And also, I've had something that's been bugging me all night, and I thought if I could take care of it right off the bat, we'd just get it out of the way and it wouldn't be between us all afternoon."

"Oh...kay. This sounds serious. What is it?"

"It's about that kiss I gave you…"

Her eyes widened, then she shook her head as she stared at the ground next to his boots. "Oh yeah, that. Of course. You were probably worried that I would get the wrong idea. Or that I would think this was more than just a casual date. I know you just asked me to help with the busybodies, and that I'm just a stand-in. I get it."

What the hell was she talking about?

"No. It's not anything like that." He lifted her chin, tipping her face up to his. "I just feel like maybe it wasn't my best work."

A grin tugged at the corners of her lips. "Oh."

"I think if I had another chance, I could do better. You know, make it a little more *memorable*."

She shrugged, looking up at him through her lashes. Her voice was soft, barely above a whisper. "I thought it was nice."

"Darlin', I never want a woman to think a kiss I gave her was 'nice.'"

A sly grin crossed her face, and she pushed her shoulders back and took a step closer. "In that case, I think you're right." She lifted her hands and rested them on his chest. "You'd better try again."

He swallowed, the heat of her hands warming his chest.

She scrunched the folds of his shirt into her fists. "I'm ready when you are." Her voice lowered, taking on a breathy tone. "But if you're going for memorable, you'd better make it a good one."

Chapter 8

HOLY SHIT. FLASHES OF HEAT DARTED DOWN MASON'S spine. And through his groin.

He loved the way she looked shy one moment, then her eyes flashed with the spark of a dare the next. He couldn't figure this woman out, but he liked her.

There was more to Tessa Kane than he'd imagined, and it would seem that she'd just thrown down a challenge. And he *was* up for it. If the tightening in his jeans were any indication, apparently in more ways than one.

He pulled back slightly, just enough to gaze down into her face. A light glaze of shimmery gloss coated her lips, and her cheeks were pink with color. She stared up at him, her expression holding a mixture of fear and anticipation.

He knew the feeling.

Then she pulled her bottom lip just slightly under her front teeth, and he didn't know anything—except that he wanted that pretty, pink mouth.

Keeping one arm around her waist, he reached up with the other and slid his hand along her slender neck, feeling her pulse race under his thumb. He held her gaze, his eyes not leaving hers as he cupped her cheek in his palm.

Her lips parted, anticipating his kiss, and his own pulse galloped through his veins.

"Comin' in hot," he warned as he tilted her face the

slimmest degree, then leaned in and lightly grazed her lips with his.

She tasted like spearmint and vanilla and something else—something that made him feel the same way he did on a warm summer night when the air was perfect, the stars were out, and the sweetest peace would settle in his soul.

A quiet sound escaped her lips, a cross between a moan and a sigh, as he pressed another soft kiss against her lips.

And it was about the sexiest sound he'd ever heard.

Her hands tightened the grip she had on his shirt, and he couldn't hold back a grin.

"You said to make it good," he murmured against her lips.

"Is that all you got?" she whispered back, her voice husky and breathless.

Aw hell. Now all bets were off.

Fire surged through his veins as he pulled her to him, dragging her body tightly against his, then slanting his mouth across hers, taking her lips in a passionate kiss.

She melted into him, matching the intensity of the kiss.

Everything else fell away—nothing else mattered. Nothing except the feel of this woman pressed against him and the taste of her lips on his. He wanted to pick her up and carry her into the bunkhouse, to drag that tank top over her head and rip those shorts down her legs.

Screw the barbecue and the family time. All he wanted was time with Tess. Time to explore and discover what she liked, what she loved, and what made her squirm with desire.

He wanted this woman under him.

And over him.

Sliding his hand from her cheek, he dove it into her hair, filling his fingers with the thick, silky strands as he imagined the way that tangled dark hair would look fanned out across his white pillowcase.

"Geez, get a room!"

The sound of his older brother's catcall broke through Mason's concentration. He took a step back, immediately missing the warmth of Tess's voluptuous body, and tried to catch his breath.

Rock and Quinn crossed the driveway toward the barn, his older brother's face holding an impish smirk. They must have walked over from Rivers Gulch.

Tess seemed a little off-balance herself. Mason could hear her quick gasps of breath, and her eyes were as round as shotgun shells. He reached out his hand and took hold of hers as they walked out of the barn and back toward her car. He told himself it was to steady her, but in truth, the feel of her fingers gripping his hand worked to calm him.

"It's about time you showed up," Mason shot back, ignoring the jab aimed at him and Tess.

"Oh yeah? It looked to me like you weren't exactly ready for company." His brother gave him a good-natured slug in the arm before turning to Tess. "Hi, Tess. I was going to say welcome to the Triple J Ranch, but it seems like you already got the red-carpet reception."

"All right, leave the girl alone," Quinn said, stepping up to Tessa's defense and smiling warmly at her. "It's nice to see you again, Tess. And I could use another woman around here, so don't let these two yokels run you off."

"Oh, I'm not going anywhere," Tess said, giving Mason's hand a squeeze.

The sentiment gave his heart a squeeze as well.

What was that about? Hadn't he just been telling his brother he didn't do spontaneous? Hadn't he just been reminding himself that he was the responsible one, the one who made smart decisions?

So what in the Sam Hill was he doing letting his heart get involved with a woman he'd just met, who had shown up out of nowhere, and who hadn't yet made it through even ten minutes of dealing with his family.

I need to take a giant step back, he thought and let go of her hand.

That had been one hell of a kiss though.

"I hope you don't mind that I brought another friend along," Tess said as she reached for her car door.

Here it came. Who was her friend? Could they coincidentally happen to be a big fan of Rockford James? He searched the interior of the car but didn't see anyone sitting there. Was this woman crazy?

Tess opened the door, and a small, scruffy dog leapt from the car and ran around her legs.

Mason let out a chuckle, laughing at the nutty dog and at himself for being such an idiot and jumping to conclusions. "Who's this?"

"This is Dewey."

"I didn't realize you had a dog. I didn't see him yesterday."

"I *didn't* have him yesterday. And I don't *have* a dog... I mean, he isn't mine. I found him last night. In a parking lot. He was scared to death and shivering in the rain."

"Poor little guy." Mason bent down and gave the dog a scratch on the ears. The dog leaned in and closed his eyes, clearly enjoying the attention and the scratch. "Do you think he's a stray?"

"I don't know what to think. He's a great dog, really well-behaved, which makes me think he belonged to someone. But his tags, if he had any, are missing from his collar. I stopped in at the sheriff's office to let them know I'd found him, and I left my number. And the librarian in town helped me to make a few flyers with his picture on it. I put them up in the grocery store and the pizza place and on that bulletin board by the courthouse. I figured I'd hold on to him for a few days…just until someone comes forward to claim him."

"He does seem like a sweetheart," Quinn said, smiling down at the dog, who had ventured away from Tess and was sniffing at her shoes. "That's nice of you to take care of him."

That's what Mason had been thinking.

The screen door slammed, and Colt and Vivi came down the stairs.

"Tess, you remember my brother, Colt, and my mom, Vivi."

Vivi smiled and gestured around the farmyard. "Welcome to the Triple J. We're glad to have you."

"She's already been welcomed, with Mace's tongue down her throat," Rock murmured under his breath to Colt.

Mason glared at his brothers, but they didn't care. They both shrugged, good-natured grins covering their faces as they tried not to laugh.

"Your house is beautiful. And the view is amazing," Tess said, nodding at the range of mountains that served as a backdrop to their ranch. "Thanks so much for including me."

"It's our pleasure. I hope you brought your appetite." Vivi turned to Colt and Rock. "Why don't you two stop behavin' like fools and make yourselves useful by firing up the grill."

"I hope it's okay that I brought the dog with me," Tess said as Mason's brothers headed toward the yard.

"Of course," Vivi told her. "There's always plenty of animals running around this place. We've got a handful of barn cats, and Colt's golden retriever, Watson, is around here somewhere. And that one's Theo... He's Mason's dog." She gestured to the border collie that had just raced out of the barn to run circles around her legs.

Tess knelt down to run her hand along the furry neck of the dog as he wiggled next to her. "Hi, Theo." She laughed as he lathered her cheek with a sloppy dog kiss.

Mason grinned. He'd introduced his dog to his last date, and she'd shrunk back from the excited mutt and spent the next thirty minutes discreetly trying to pick the dog hair off her pants.

Not Tess.

A blue pickup pulled down the drive and parked next to them. Hamilton and Quinn's son, Max, climbed out, followed by a huge brown dog.

"See what I mean?" Vivi said, planting her feet so she didn't get bowled over by the big dog who loped up to her in greeting. She ruffled his neck. "Hello, Truman. You're a good boy, aren't you?"

"He's not that good," Hamilton said, a scowl evident under his thick mustache. "He's the reason we're late.

He decided to sample the cake that was sitting on the counter."

"Oh no," Quinn wailed. "He didn't. He ate the whole cake?"

"Not the *whole* cake," Max explained. "We saved the one side. Grandpa and I are gonna eat that later."

"We still brought the baked beans," Hamilton said, hoisting a stainless-steel Crock-Pot from the bed of the pickup.

Vivi chuckled and rubbed Quinn's shoulder. "Don't worry, honey. We've got plenty of dessert."

Quinn sighed. "I spent all morning making that dumb cake."

"If it makes you feel any better, Mom," Max said, as usual sounding much older than an eight-year-old kid, "Truman obviously thought it was real good. He liked it so much, he would have eaten the whole thing if we wouldn't have caught him."

"Surprisingly, that does *not* make me feel any better," Quinn said in a wry tone. "Last week, that dog tried to eat a bottle of Elmer's Glue, so I'm not that impressed with his discerning palate."

Tess let out a snort of laughter. The group turned to her as if they'd forgotten she was there, and then they all broke into laughter.

"What did I miss?" Aunt Sassy asked as she pushed through the screen door. She held a basket of rolls in her hands. Mason loped up the stairs and took the basket from her, then offered his arm to steady her as she walked down the front steps.

"You didn't miss much…just some of Quinn's cake that Truman ate." He led her to Tess, who was kneeling and petting the cake-eating dog. "Tess, this is my great-aunt, Sassy. Well, Cassie, I guess."

His aunt smiled at Tess. "It's okay. You can call me Sassy. All the rest of these yahoos do."

"It's so nice to meet you." Tess stood and started to hold out her hand, then must have realized she'd been petting the dog and wiped her hand on the side of her shorts. "Sorry, my hand's a little slobbery."

Sassy took her hand anyway. "That's all right. A little dog slobber never hurt anyone. I was raised in the Depression, ya know?"

"Oh goodness. That must have been hard."

"It was." Sassy still had hold of Tess's hand and was studying her face. "Where do you live, Tess?"

"In Denver."

"What do you do?"

"I'm a writer."

"What's your zodiac sign?"

"Sagittarius."

"Favorite color?"

"Purple."

"Morning person or night owl?"

"Night owl."

"Milk chocolate or dark?"

"Milk."

"Favorite season?"

"Summer."

"If your house caught on fire, what's the one thing you'd save?"

"My grandma," Tess answered without hesitation. She'd answered all his aunt's rapid-fire questions with barely a blink.

A grin curved across Sassy's lips, and she patted Tess's hand, then finally released it. She gave Mason a small nod. "She'll do."

He let out his breath, not realizing he'd been holding it, as his aunt took the basket of rolls from his hands and crossed the yard toward the table.

"What the heck was that all about?" Tessa whispered.

"I told you she was sassy." He slid an arm around her waist and leaned toward her ear, not because anything he had to say was a big secret, but just because he liked being close to her. "She's a character. She does that to everyone. It's like a litmus test when she first meets someone."

"Did I pass?"

"She really only cares about the last question, and without missing a beat, you told her you'd save your grandmother instead of a family heirloom or the television. So yeah, I'd say you passed."

"My grandma *is* my family heirloom. And who's going to save their television? It's insured."

"You'd be surprised."

Thirty minutes later, the whole family, including Quinn's brother, Logan, an assortment of farmhands from both ranches, and Tess were seated around the long picnic table they'd set up in the side yard of the house.

Yesterday's party had been for the locals and Rock's team. Today's meal was just about family and celebrating Rock and Quinn. They'd selected choice steaks from their own stock to cook, and the scent of grilled meat filled the air.

Ham stood at the end of the table and took off his hat, signaling to the family that he was about to say grace. Mason reached for Tess's hand, glad to have another excuse to touch her. It was crazy the number of times he'd already found in the half hour that she'd been here.

A touch of her hand, a brush against her hip, a nudge on her shoulder. He didn't consider himself a touchy kind of guy, but something about this woman and the smooth, tan skin of her bare legs and arms had his palms itching and his body aching to run his fingers along her—hell, along her *anything*.

He just wanted to touch her.

What he really wanted was to whisk her away where they could be alone, and he could get not only his hands but also his lips and his tongue on her. Except that he wasn't sure what would happen if they were alone.

This way, when they were around others, he had an excuse to touch her, to hold her hand, to stroke his fingers down her arm and revel in the rash of gooseflesh that cropped up there.

He got a kick out of watching the skin on her neck blush a soft pink when he leaned down to whisper something in her ear. Which made him want to whisper *everything*, even if it was just to ask her to pass the salt.

She had an easy laugh, and he liked the way she seemed to blend effortlessly into his family, chatting with Quinn and giving his brothers a hard time. Heck, if she could handle Rock and Colt, the girl just might be a keeper.

Except that Mason wasn't looking for a keeper. He wasn't looking for anything. Except a quiet life on the ranch where he could farm, tend to the cattle, and ride his horse. He felt his scowl return as he sighed and dug into the food on his plate.

As it often did in their family, especially when they

had fresh blood for an audience, the conversation soon turned to telling stories and sharing memories of stupid things he and his brothers had done growing up. Most of their antics involved Quinn and Logan, so it seemed everyone at the table had a memory or a story to tell.

Tess held her sides, unable to stop laughing, as each one tried to top the craziness of the story before. They regaled her with tales of sneaking out at midnight, the time they'd tried to hook sleds to their horses, the time they'd hosted their own pie-eating contest, and numerous stories of teeth being knocked out—usually during another of the endless hockey drills Rock insisted on putting them through.

Max's small face beamed with pride as he watched Rock speak. He stood up on the bench seat and wrapped a skinny arm around Rock's neck. "Rock is the greatest," he told Tess, who was sitting across from them. "He's like a superhero. And I love superheroes. They all have superpowers. Rock's is that he can skate really fast, and he's superstrong. What's your superpower?"

"Excuse me?" Tess's eyes widened as all eyes turned to her. "I don't have *any* superpowers."

Quinn leaned forward and offered her an encouraging smile. "Don't worry. He does this with everyone. He thinks we all have superpowers. Mine are more like super *mom* powers, like finding lost items and being able to read minds."

The pink color rising on Tess's cheeks darkened. "I can assure you I don't have anything like that. I'm really pretty ordinary."

Mason didn't believe that for a minute.

"Your superpower is just something you are super

at doing," Max explained. "What do you think you're really good at?"

"Making poor life decisions," she mumbled.

A round of laughter rippled through the table, but Mason had an odd feeling she hadn't been trying to be funny. He remembered her earlier terror at speaking in front of people and slid his hand across her leg to twine his fingers through hers. Her hand was trembling.

"Actually, I think Tess's superpowers are telling good stories," he said.

Her hand gripped his tighter.

Maybe that hadn't been the way to go. Her face had just lost all color. She probably thought they were going to ask her to tell them a story. *Dang*. He'd been trying to help and had just put her more into the spotlight.

"But she doesn't tell them out loud," Mason said before anyone asked her a question. "She writes them down. She's a writer."

She shook her head and lowered her eyes to her lap as a ripple of interest flowed around the table.

He pointed at Max. "But you should tell us what your superpowers are. It seems like they change every week."

Max giggled and raised his arms above his head. "My superpower this week is talking to animals. And making cookies disappear."

Vivi, who had been watching him and Tess with her discerning mom eye—one of *her* superpowers—laughed and gave Max a round of applause. She must have realized all the attention was making Tess uncomfortable as well.

Mason leaned down and whispered into Tess's hair. "Sorry about that. I know you don't like to be the center of attention."

She offered him a thankful smile and whispered back, "Thanks for trying to help. I think your superpower is taking care of others. I know you keep saving me."

Hmm. That might not be too far from the truth.

Not the part about saving her. He hadn't really done all that much except loan her a shirt and get her mixed up in an entire weekend spent with his family and the small-town folk that believed every detail of anyone's life was everyone's business. That didn't sound like a superpower to him. More like an anti-superpower.

"I think I would like my new superpower to be skating," Max announced, grinning up at Rock with adoration. "I've decided I want to play hockey like you."

Mason's brother's eyes widened. "Are you sure, buddy?" The first time Rock had taken Max skating, the boy had fallen and broken his arm. He'd only recently got the cast off. Rock had been too freaked out to take him again, so he'd asked Colt to teach him.

Max bobbed his head enthusiastically. "Colt's been teaching me lots of stuff, and I've been working on my stickhandling."

Rock looked at his brother. "Stickhandling?"

Colt shrugged. "You asked me to teach the kid to skate. So I bought him a stick, and we've been tossing a puck around. That's how Dad worked with us. You know it helps to keep the focus on something other than your feet."

"Do they even have a Mites team here?" Rock asked, referring to the eight-and-under league.

"Some of the moms have been asking me about starting one," Quinn told him. "Apparently, now that I'm going to be the wife of a famous player, I have been elevated to expert status on all things hockey."

"What do you think about it?"

She raised a shoulder. "I'm okay with it. It's exercise, and I've always thought it was good for kids to be involved in a team sport. Although I have to admit I was picturing him playing soccer first. But if he wants to try hockey, I'm fine. And you can understand why he wants to, considering the majority of the male role models in his life either have played or are currently playing it."

"Not this role model," Ham said. "You couldn't get me on a pair of skates for a million bucks. I'll keep my feet in my boots, thank you."

Quinn leaned closer to Rock and lowered her voice. "You can't blame him for wanting to play hockey when everything about the sport gives you a zam-boner."

Rock grinned, then glanced over at Mason and Colt. "I guess Max is going to play hockey. But I'd only want him on a team where I knew and trusted the coach. And a young team like that would need a coach who was good with kids and had a lot of patience. And who knew the game inside and out."

Mason nudged his younger brother. "Sounds like he's talking about you, Brother."

"Me?" Colt asked, looking up from where he was spinning a quarter across the table to Max. "Why me?"

"Come on, Colt. You'd be the perfect choice," Quinn said. "You're great with kids, and you have the patience of a saint. You're already teaching Max how to skate and apparently to stickhandle. What's the big deal of adding one or two more kids to the lesson?"

"Or twelve," Mason said, thankful they were asking Colt and not him. With all the responsibilities of the ranch, there were days he didn't have time to eat lunch, let alone try to coach a kids' hockey team. But it was a great idea for Colt. He loved the sport, and this would give him a chance to be part of the game again.

"You would be an awesome coach, Colt," Max agreed. "Will you do it?"

Colt's brow pulled in, and he tugged at the side of his ear. He looked like he was thinking, but Mason already knew he was going to do it. That guy couldn't turn down a request for help if he tried. Half the town owed him a favor because he was the first guy they called when they needed something, whether that was someone to help them move a refrigerator or paint a barn. Colt was always willing to pitch in.

"Yeah, okay, I'll do it," Colt relented. "On one condition."

"What's that?" Rock asked.

"That you agree to sponsor the team so all of them get good equipment and new skates. I don't want anyone to feel like they don't get a chance to play just because they can't afford equipment."

Rock nodded and stuck out his hand. "Deal."

Max stood up in his chair and cheered as Colt and Rock shook on it. "This is so cool. I think I want to be the goalie."

Colt shook his head. "I don't know if I'd recommend that. You don't have to be crazy to play goalie"—he paused, and both of his brothers chimed in to help him finish the sentence—"but it helps."

Max shrugged his shoulders as he sat back down. "Okay, but what's a zam-boner? Do I need one of those?"

The table erupted in laughter.

That kid was too much. Mason leaned toward Tess. "Are you sure you're ready for a whole weekend of this?"

She chuckled and nodded her head. "Oh yeah, this is hysterical. And I'm getting great material for a future book. I've got to use that 'zam-boner' line somewhere."

The laughter around the table died at the sound of an engine. All heads turned toward the road as a white news van pulled down the driveway, its call letters boldly displayed on the side.

"So much for our nice family meal." Rock pushed up from his seat, an angry scowl already forming on his face. He slammed his fist onto the table, making his plate and silverware jump. "Why can't the damn reporters just leave me alone and let me enjoy a day with my family?"

Chapter 9

TESS GRIMACED, SHRINKING SMALLER ONTO THE BENCH seat. She *was* one of those damn reporters. But she was worse. Because she had finagled her way not just into the family meal, but practically into the family itself.

"I think I may have told you that Rock detests reporters," Mason said, his voice low next to her ear. His breath tickled her neck and sent a delicious shiver running down her spine.

"Yeah, I seem to recall you mentioning it."

Numerous times.

Mason stood up. "I got this one, Rock. I'll tell them to shove off."

Rock shook his head. "Not this one. I recognize those call letters, and they're particularly obnoxious. They don't take no easily."

Colt pushed to his feet, an excited grin tugging at the corners of his lips. "Sounds like this calls for Operation Gunslinger."

What the heck was *Operation Gunslinger*?

Whatever it was, it caused a ripple of enthusiasm to course around the table, and several of the men's expressions mimicked Colt's excitement.

A chorus of "Yeah" and "Let's do it" flowed over the table as the men all rose to their feet, their faces turned to Rock, waiting for confirmation.

Rock's scowl slowly turned to an impish grin. "Yeah, okay. Let's do it."

Vivienne added another spoonful of potato salad to her plate as she rolled her eyes. "Have fun, boys."

"What's going on?" Tess asked as she watched the men scatter, fanning out and disappearing into the barn, the bunkhouse, and the house.

"Just a display of cowboy machismo and a bunch of men who've watched way too many westerns," Vivi answered, snagging a chunk of pickle from her plate and popping it into her mouth.

Quinn laughed and came around to their side of the table, snatching another biscuit from the basket and squeezing in next to Tess. "I think it's hilarious. And they love it."

"Love what? What is happening?" Tess asked, wondering if she should be grabbing more food as well. Did she need more sustenance for this "operation" or were Vivi and Quinn just both still hungry?

"Just watch." Sassy, who sat on Vivienne's other side, nodded to the news van as it pulled up in front of the house.

The doors of the van opened, and a perky blond reporter stepped out, followed by a heavy-set guy with a bushy beard who hoisted a camera to his shoulder.

"Hi there." The blond waved, the sun glinting off her sparkling white teeth. "We're lost, and we were just wondering if you might be able to give us directions."

Tess started to open her mouth, but Vivi put a warning hand on her arm and lifted her chin toward the front porch of the house. She jumped as the screen door banged open, and the James brothers stepped out on the porch, all three of them armed to the teeth.

Rock stood in the middle, a shotgun resting easily on his shoulder. His eyes were fixed on the blond, giving her a steely stare. "Do you need a news camera to ask for directions?"

The man turned the camera toward Rock.

Mason took a step forward to stand even with his brother. He also had a shotgun in the crook of his arm. "I'm going to remind you that you're on private property and suggest you don't turn that camera on." His voice was lower than usual, tinged with the menace of a threat as he raised the gun and cocked the barrel.

The cameraman glanced from the reporter to the three cowboys but didn't lower the camera.

This time Colt stepped forward, his eyes narrowed into hard slits. He carried an older-model revolver that looked like it was possibly an antique. But he held it out in front of him and pulled back the trigger with a resounding click. "My brother might have offered a suggestion, but I'm giving you an order. Get back in your van, and get off our property."

The blond held up her hands and offered them an apologetic smile. "We don't want any trouble. Like I said, we were just looking for directions."

"You don't want to hear the directions I have for you," Rock answered.

"We're going to stick with 'no comment' and repeat our instructions to get off our property"—Mason used the end of the gun to direct their attention toward the barn—"before we do something you're going to regret."

The reporter and cameraman turned their heads, and

the color drained from their faces as one by one, armed cowboys stepped menacingly out from behind barn doors and the sides of the bunkhouses.

The air was still, quiet except for the audible clicks as each man cocked his gun in turn.

"You guys are crazy," the cameraman yelled as he scrambled to get back into the van.

The blond reporter pushed past him and climbed into the front seat signaling the driver to go. Dust filled the air as the tires spun out in the gravel and the van shot down the driveway.

Holy high noon.

Tess was witnessing "hot cowboy" multiplied to the nth degree. She blinked, surprised to feel the flame of heat in her blood at the rugged display of manliness. "Were they really going to start shooting at them?" she whispered.

Vivi let out a bark of laughter. "Lord no. Most of those guns aren't even loaded. And did you see the one Colt had? That was the antique revolver that sits on our mantel above our fireplace."

Laughter bubbled up her chest, and Tess let out a nervous giggle. "Are you serious?"

"Of course I'm serious." Vivi's eyes sparkled with mischief. "It's not even a real gun. It's a lighter."

Tess looked from Vivi to Quinn to Sassy; then the four women broke into laughter. Holding her sides, Tess tried to catch her breath as the men headed toward the table, laughing themselves and clapping one another on the back.

Colt dropped into the seat across from her, holding up the antique revolver and pulling the trigger. A small flame lit from the end of the gun's barrel, and he offered her an exaggerated wink. "And that, Hoss, is what we call Operation Gunslinger."

"That's what I call watching too many episodes of *Bonanza*," Vivi said, still laughing.

Ham jerked a thumb toward the house as he sat down on the other side of Vivi. "I left Max and Truman inside watching a movie."

"Thanks, Dad. I'll go check on him," Quinn said, sliding off the picnic bench and planting a kiss on Rock's lips as she passed him on the way up the porch steps.

Mason dropped into her vacated seat next to Tess. A shit-eatin' grin covered his face. "Bet you thought you were just coming out for a barbecue. Didn't know you'd get dinner *and* a show."

And what a show.

"Two for the price of one, I guess." Following Quinn's example, Tess pressed a quick kiss to Mason's cheek. "Very hot. But next time, do you think you all could find some chaps? I think that would really add the authentic Wild West touch."

Rock raised an eyebrow. "Mace, is your girl really requesting you wear chaps? At the dinner table? And around Ma?"

Heat flamed Tess's cheeks, but Rock let out a chuckle. "I like you already."

The group broke into laughter, but *with* Tess, not at her, and she joined in on the good-natured fun. Leaning in toward Mason, she whispered. "It's never a dull moment around here, is it?"

"Oh, it's usually extremely dull. You just caught us on a good day." He wrapped an arm around her waist and pulled her hip tighter against his, as if it were the most natural movement in the world. Her body softened against his, and she let herself sink into the curve of his arm.

She filed away the thought of how Operation Gunslinger was going to read in her article. She was really getting the inside flavor of Rock and his family.

Vivi flattened her hands on the table. "After all that excitement, who's ready for pie? You all carry your plates in and get this table cleared while Quinn and I put together the desserts," she said with the commanding authority of a drill sergeant.

Her crew must've been good at following orders because they all stood up and had their dishes in hand and the table cleared within minutes.

"I can help," Tess offered, grabbing her plate and the empty potato salad bowl and following Mason's mom into the kitchen.

"Thanks, honey, but you don't have to." Vivi grabbed the dirty plates and scraped them into a bowl before stacking them in the sink.

"I want to. Besides, my grandma would have my skin if I didn't help with the dishes after such a great meal."

"She sounds like my kind of woman. Mason told me your grandmother raised you and that you still live with her."

What else had Mason told his mom about her? "I do. And she's an amazing woman. Except we're more like roommates now."

"I can't imagine being roommates with my grandmother," Quinn said with a chuckle.

Tess laughed with her. "We do pretty well. There are definitely positives and negatives. I mean, she's my best friend and a wonderful cook, and she likes to eat dinner together and always listens when I talk about my day, so that's all great, but she's also super nosy and constantly gives me advice, whether I ask for it or not. Sometimes it's like rooming with a really bossy friend who still tells me to go to my room if I disagree with her."

Vivi grabbed a stack of plastic containers and set to putting the leftovers away. "There's plenty of times I wish I could still send my boys to their rooms."

A flush of heat worked up Tess's neck as she thought about Mason's bedroom—well, more about his bed and, actually, more about his bed with him in it. Turning away so his mom wouldn't see her blush, she crossed the room to where she'd left her purse on the sofa and dropped her sunglasses inside. It was at least something to do so she didn't look like a dork staring at the wall.

A gnawing ball of guilt settled in her stomach like a rock. She liked these women, liked this whole family, liked how they had already taken her in and accepted her. She hated the fact that she was deceiving them and hated to imagine what they would think of her when the article came out.

Being around Mason was easier than Tess had thought it would be—especially since he was hotter than the Colorado sun. And he seemed like a good guy. A guy she could really be interested in.

But he wasn't going to be interested in her once he found out she was really a reporter. And he *would* find out. Once the story came out, everyone would find out.

Maybe she could get her boss to run the story under a pen name.

Or maybe she could forget about the story altogether. But she couldn't do that to Mimi.

Her grandmother wouldn't approve of all this deception, but it didn't matter. Saving her grandmother's house and keeping them both from getting tossed out into the street is what mattered. She'd already spent one uncomfortable night sleeping in her car. She didn't want that back seat to turn into her permanent bedroom.

No, it didn't matter what these people thought of her. What mattered was getting the story and saving her grandmother from financial devastation. Getting duped by a devious reporter and one revealing story in a magazine wouldn't really hurt this family; they were strong.

She pushed down the thought of what it would do to her and how it might break the heart that was already connecting to the tall cowboy, because her feelings didn't matter either.

Her heart would mend. It always did. But not doing the story would ruin her grandmother.

Unless she could think of another idea to raise the money and forget the article altogether. But how could she raise a quick couple thousand dollars? Selling either drugs or her body could net some quick cash. But the only drugs she had at her disposal were Advil, prescription migraine medicine, and an expired bottle of pills that helped with an occasional acne flare-up.

So becoming a dope dealer was out of the question. And she wasn't sure how much she could get for her tall, curvy, big-footed, squishy-bellied body. She'd have to put the idea of selling her body on hold for now.

Taking a deep breath, she pasted on a smile and headed toward the sink. She lifted the faucet and directed the spray of water over the stack of dishes. "Do you have a system for loading your dishwasher?"

"She doesn't use it enough to have a system, so I just load it how I think it should go," Quinn told her, pulling the dishes from the sink and stacking them in the rack. "Rock bought it for her when he had the kitchen and living room remodeled, but she still likes to wash things by hand."

Rock had their home remodeled? It seemed like there was more to the guy than just the arrogant playboy the press made him out to be. "Your home is lovely," Tessa remarked, then glanced at Quinn as she put the last bowl in the dishwasher. "Do you know where you're going to live after the wedding?"

It was an innocent enough question—something anyone might ask. That rock of guilt pitched in the pit of her stomach, reminding her she wasn't asking it innocently. She was asking it to get information about Quinn and her fiancé. Before Quinn could answer, Rock and Mason sauntered into the kitchen.

"Ah dang," Mason said. "It looks like you're just finishing up. Rock and I were just coming in to do the dishes."

"Yeah, right." Vivi smirked, obviously used to this game. "It's too bad we've already finished. But you two can help carry all these desserts out."

She loaded Rock and Quinn's arms with two pies, a coconut cake, and a platter of cookies. Picking up a fresh pitcher of iced tea, she gestured to the remaining apple pie and pan of brownies. "I've got the tea if you all can grab those last things."

"Sure, Mom," Mason said, holding the door for them all to walk through. "But I'm not sure we're going to have enough dessert."

"I swear I don't know where you got that smart-aleck mouth," Vivi mumbled, giving him a grin and a swat on the arm as she passed through the door.

Tess's heartbeat tripled in her chest as Mason turned his grin toward her and ambled across the kitchen. "Are you a fan of pie, Tess?"

He somehow made the simple question sound flirty and sinful, and all she could do was nod as her mouth went dry.

"My mom makes the best apple pie in three counties. And she's got the blue ribbons to prove it." He broke off a piece of the crust and held it up to Tess's lips. "It's a little bit like how I imagine heaven would taste."

She opened her mouth and let him feed her the offered piece of crust, biting into the flaky shell. A line of filling rimmed the crust, and she tasted the cinnamon tinged with the sweet tartness of apple and brown sugar. It was amazing, and she let out a soft moan as she licked the excess sugar from her lips.

"It's good, right?" He dipped his finger into the pie and lifted a chunk of apple into his mouth, holding her stare as he took a step closer. A dab of pie filling glistened on his lip, and she watched, transfixed, as his tongue darted out and licked the dab clean.

"It's delicious," she whispered.

He narrowed his eyes, dropping his gaze to her mouth as he circled her waist with one of his large hands. He brought his other hand up and cupped her cheek, then ran the edge of his thumb over her bottom lip. "Your lips look delicious."

He tilted his head, leaning his face toward hers. "I can't tell for sure until I taste them though."

Tess swallowed, every nerve ending in her body

surging with electricity. He'd kissed her before, but that had been standing in a barn, and his brother had seen them. There was no one to see them now; they were all alone. Just the two of them. And the pie.

Her back was against the counter as he closed the rest of the space between them and dipped his mouth to hers.

The kiss was gentle, tender, his lips barely skimming hers. Her lips parted, and she inhaled a trembling breath, sure he could feel the thumping of her heart against her chest.

"I was wrong," he said, his voice husky and low. "It's not the pie. It's you." He pulled back, just the slightest, and gave a gentle nip to her bottom lip. "*You're* a little bit like how I imagine heaven would taste."

He brushed her lips again, then his mouth slanted across hers as he deepened the kiss.

A low growl rumbled in the back of his throat, and he tightened his grip on her back, dragging her against his chest as his mouth explored hers.

Tess's hands had somehow moved to his shoulders—his very broad and muscular shoulders—and she gripped the folds of his shirt in her fingers, clutching the fabric between her fingers as her knees threatened to buckle. All she could do was hold on as she felt the strength of his embrace and the desire in his lips as the kiss deepened further.

He tasted sweet and warm—like cinnamon and brown sugar and a cozy blanket on a cold day—and she melted into the kiss, into his strong arms, letting the moment sweep her away.

All she could focus on was this man and the way his

lips felt on hers and the feel of his hands as they caressed and touched her cheek, her hip, the small of her back.

He drew back as if trying to catch his breath and his eyes searched hers, as if he were looking for clues to see if this was really real or to decipher how she felt about him.

She wanted to tell him. Tell him that she really liked him, that she was falling for him. Falling for his easy charm and his gorgeous eyes. Tell him that this was more than just a fill-in date to her, more than some silly favor to pay him back for loaning her his shirt.

Opening her mouth to speak, she willed the words to come, but instead she asked, "What was that for? You realize we're alone in here. We can't start a whisper of a rumor if no one's around to witness the whisper."

He blinked, and she swore she saw a hurt look cross his face, just for a moment, just a slight crinkle around his eyes.

Why was she so stupid? Why didn't she just tell him how she felt? That she didn't care about starting a rumor or keeping the locals off his back, that she just wanted him to kiss her again. And again.

He recovered quickly—maybe she hadn't seen anything at all—and offered her an impish grin. "You never know who might be watching."

A smile pulled at the corner of her lips. "Then you'd better kiss me again, just to be safe."

His grin broadened, flashing her the pearly whites of his teeth before he leaned back down and took her mouth again.

Her body came alive under his touch, flashes of heat and electricity swelling through her veins and across her skin. His hand gripped her waist and, as he pressed his hips against hers, she could swear she felt a pulse of vibration flare between them.

Oh wait...that *was* an actual vibration.

He pulled away, grumbling as he tugged his phone from his pocket and checked the screen. "I should probably take this."

She nodded, sucking in a ragged breath and already missing the warmth of his body against hers. Shaking her head, she tried to clear it, tried to focus, but her thoughts were jumbled, and all she could think about was how well and thoroughly she had just been kissed.

Mason grinned down at her, twisting a lock of her hair around his finger as he put the phone to his ear. "Hello?"

He dropped his hand as his grin fell away and his mouth tightened into a thin line. "Ah shit," he said, followed by a couple of "yeahs" and "uh-huhs" before he hung up. His forehead creased as his expression darkened. "That was the sheriff. We've got a problem."

Chapter 10

TESS'S ALREADY-POUNDING HEART LEAPT TO HER THROAT. *A problem? What kind of problem?* Like an "I just found out you're a fraud" kind of problem?

Stop it. That's ridiculous. There was no way the sheriff would have any idea who Tess was or who she worked for. She hadn't even met the man. But what if he'd found out she'd spent the last night camped out in the parking lot behind the public library? That could be a problem.

"What's wrong?" she asked, her voice shaky.

But Mason was already heading for the front door, the pie—and the kiss—apparently forgotten. She followed on his heels, both anxious and terrified to hear what he was going to say.

He hurried down the front porch steps, calling out to the men sitting at the picnic table. "Sheriff just called. He's getting reports of a herd of cattle spread out across County Road 9. Whoever called it in claimed they were Black Angus and carried our brand. We must have a fence down."

The group rose as one, leaving their plates as they climbed over the picnic benches and headed toward their vehicles.

"Where do you want us, Mace?" Rock asked, nodding to Quinn and Logan as he crammed the rest of a cookie in his mouth.

Mason called directions as he headed toward his pickup. "You three take the four-wheelers through the pasture and meet us there. See if you can get an idea of how many cattle we're missing as you go. Ham and I will meet you over there. Buck, you want to start checking the fence line to make sure we're not down anywhere else?"

"Sassy and I will stay here with Max," Vivi said, already clearing the plates from the table. "Check in with us when you've got 'em all rounded up."

All the dogs scrambled out from under the table where they must have been waiting for scraps, and Theo and Dewey raced along at Mason's heels. Not knowing what else to do, so did Tess. Mason climbed into one side of the truck, and she climbed into the other.

He raised an eyebrow at her as he started the engine. "What are you doing?"

"I'm coming with you."

"You don't have to. You can stay behind with my mom."

"I might be able to help." Although she had no idea how. But she still felt like she should be in on the action.

He shrugged. "Suit yourself. We can always use an extra hand."

Before she could pull the door shut, Colt squeezed in, tossing a roll of duct tape and a couple of pairs of gloves on the dash. "Scoot over."

Dewey bounded into Tess's lap as Colt's golden retriever jumped into the cab as well.

The smell of dogs and horses filled the cab, but all Tess could think about was the way Mason's thigh pressed against hers and the way her shoulder bumped his as they bounced over the dirt road.

Oh—and the way he'd just kissed her. She couldn't stop thinking about that either.

Mason surveyed the large tree that had fallen across the section of broken fence. A split down its trunk suggested that it had been hit by lightning in the storm the day before.

The others were rounding up the cattle and moving them back onto Triple J property while he and Tess went in search of how the cattle had gotten out in the first place.

This was obviously the place. When the tree fell, it had knocked down two fence posts, and one had broken free of the barbed wire strung around it. A large section of the fence lay open, and this had to be where the cows had been getting out.

They'd received another call from a neighboring rancher who'd seen a couple of their cattle in one of his pastures. Colt had gone back with Ham, figuring it would be easier to transport the last few strays to the ranch with a trailer.

"Do you think we can move it?" Tess asked, her brow furrowed as she studied the tree.

She was trying to help—Mason knew that and appreciated it—but the sight of her long legs and the memory of kissing her in the kitchen kept distracting him from what he needed to be focused on. Which, for the moment, was trying to figure out how to get this stupid tree moved and the fence repaired so no more cattle could get out.

"Let's try," he answered, bending his knees and putting his back against the gnarled trunk.

She grabbed the other side, and their muscles strained

as they tried to move the dead tree. "Dang. It won't budge," Tess said, stepping back to catch her breath.

"We're going to have to use some chains and the truck." Mason dropped the tailgate and hoisted himself into the bed of the pickup. A large truck toolbox filled the front half of the bed, and he lifted one side of the lid and pulled out some rope and a set of chains.

He spied the chain saw they'd been using earlier in the week to collect firewood and grabbed it as well. "I'll try to cut some of it back first," he said, hoisting the chain saw above his head.

Dropping the chains on the ground, he jumped up onto the trunk and fired up the chain saw. They'd had fallen trees on the ranch before, but he'd always had one of his brothers or a ranch hand to help him take the limbs apart.

I'm going to be on my own with this one, Mason thought as he sawed through several of the bigger limbs and let them fall to the ground. Satisfied that he'd made a good start, he cut the chain saw's engine and turned to survey his work.

He couldn't have been more surprised to see Tessa hauling the dead limbs away from the fence. Her hair was pulled back in a ponytail, and a fine sheen of sweat had broken out on her forehead. She wore the other pair of leather work gloves that Colt had thrown in the truck to protect her hands as she wrangled huge branches off the fence and pulled them clear.

"What are you doing?"

She glanced up, giving him a look that might have implied he was an imbecile. "I'm helping. What does it look like?"

"That's exactly what it looks like."

She gestured to the sky where a series of dark clouds were traveling quickly across the blue background. "It looks to me like we need to work quicker."

"You don't have to do this. I can get it. And I don't want you to get hurt."

She tossed a smaller branch out of the way. "You're going to be the one that gets hurt if you're suggesting I can't pull my weight and help you with this tree."

Mason held his hands up in surrender as he let out a chuckle. "Okay, sorry. You're doing amazing."

"I'm not doing amazing, but I'm doing my best." She blocked the sun with her hand as she looked up at him. "I just wish I had grabbed my sunglasses before we left."

"There's usually an extra pair in the truck's glove box. I can check for you."

"Don't bother. It's too late now, and I don't think we're going to have to worry about the sun much longer."

Almost as if responding to her request, the dark clouds thickened and shifted, blocking the sun from view. A low rumble of thunder rolled across the sky. Tess's shoulders shrank against another flash of lightning.

"Yeah, we'd better get it in gear." Mason climbed back up on the tree trunk. "And Tess, you really are helping. And I totally appreciate it."

A grin tugged at the corners of her mouth. "Appreciate me later, cowboy. For now, let's get this tree out of here."

Mason yanked the cord of the chain saw, commanding the machine to life. Small fragments of wood shot through the air as the teeth of the saw bit into the dry timber.

He sawed through the last stray limb as another crack

of lightning ripped through the air. Jumping down from the trunk, he barely got the chain saw back into the toolbox before the sky opened and let loose a torrent of rain.

"Seriously?" Tess shouted over the din of the rain as she planted her hands on her hips. "What is it with you and thunderstorms? Was your dad Zeus?"

He crossed to her, grabbing the last two felled branches and pulling them out of the way. "As much as I love the idea of you thinking of me as a demigod, I'm fairly certain my father was not Zeus." He flashed her a flirty grin. "But we can check with my mom when we get back, just to make sure."

She offered him a wry smile. Her bangs were plastered to her forehead, and water dripped from her ponytail.

At least he had his hat to protect his head. He pulled it off and dropped it on her head. "We should go back. We're drenched. We know where the break in the fence is, and I can get my brothers to come out and help me move this tree later."

"Don't be ridiculous. If we leave, there's a chance that more of your cattle will get out this way again. If we can do it, let's just get it done." She raised her hands to the sky. "It's not like we can get any wetter."

Her clothes were soaked through, and he swallowed at the way her white tank top clung to her skin, outlining every curve and leaving nothing to the imagination.

Well, nothing and *everything*.

His imagination was running wild with thoughts of what he could do with those curves and how it would feel to get his hands—and his mouth—on the taut, pebbled nipples that were perfectly outlined through the wet fabric.

Which only served to make her body look ten times sexier than it already did.

Forget the stupid tree. He could care less if all the cows got out. He just wanted to get his hands on this woman.

"Hello? Mason, did you hear me?" Tess was yelling as she waved her hands in front of his face.

"Wha—? Yeah. No. I didn't hear you," he said, shaking his head to clear it.

"I was asking you about what ideas you had in mind for this tree."

He blinked. He had plenty of ideas in mind for the tree, and several of them involved her naked and pressed against it. But somehow he didn't think that's what she'd meant.

"We need to get the chain around it, then we can use the truck to pull it off the fence," he said.

"Okay, let's do it."

Another flash of lightning spurred him into action. They needed to get this done and get inside. Lightning had already struck this tree once. They worked together and quickly got the chain around the old trunk, then hooked it to the hitch on the back of the pickup.

Theo ran around the tree, acting as though he was trying to herd it off the fence and barking his support, but Dewey sat under the truck and out of the rain. Both dogs jumped into the cab when Mason opened the door. Tess climbed in from the other side, shivering in her wet clothes as she yanked the door shut behind her. Dewey hopped into her lap, and she wrapped her arms around him.

"Hold on," Mason told her, starting the engine and putting the truck into gear.

She let go of the dog and braced her arms against the dashboard as he lightly pressed the gas, letting the power of the truck do the pulling for them.

As they inched slowly forward, the cab jerked while the chain pulled taut and dug into the trunk of the tree. The wheels of the pickup spun in the mud, but the tree moved forward, drawn by the circle of chain.

"You're getting it," Tess cried. "It's working."

Another foot or two, and the tree dropped free of the fence. The barbed wire still sagged and strands of it were still embedded in the soft wood, but the trunk no longer impeded the fence line.

"Whoo-hoo." Tess offered Mason a high five, grinning at him as though he'd just hung the moon or become a national hero.

He wasn't totally against the idea of her seeing him as a hero. Or as a demigod.

Except I'm not a hero, he thought as his temporarily inflated ego came crashing down.

Rock was the hero.

Mason was just an ordinary guy. He wasn't even doing that extraordinary of a feat. It's not like he lifted the tree over his head or anything. He couldn't lift it at all. And he'd used the power of the truck to even move the dang thing.

Shoving the truck door open, he grabbed a pair of pliers from the glove box, then stepped back out into the rain. "I'm going to get the fence line back up, and then we can get out of here. You might as well wait in the truck."

Apparently, Tessa Kane was not good at heeding directions, because no sooner had he lifted the downed fence post than he could feel her at his elbow, adding her weight as she helped to pull it back in place.

The rain continued to fall as they sloshed through the mud, Tess's white tennis shoes now a muddy-brown mess. Fat flecks of mud were crusted to her legs, and her clothes were stained and smudged with dirt and rust from the fence.

Despite the guilt he felt for her ruining her clothes and getting her filthy, Mason was glad to have her by his side. She was a big help, lifting and holding sections of barbed wire so he could twist and pull it into place. It didn't take them long to get the fence back up and into a sufficient state of repair. He waved for her to head for the truck.

"I'm sorry. I'm getting your truck all m-m-muddy," she said, her teeth chattering as she climbed back into the cab. The dogs jumped in after her and curled next to each other on the floor.

"That's what trucks are for." He held out his arm. "You must be freezing. Slide over here and let me warm you up."

She took his hat off and set it on the dash, then scooted across the seat and into the crook of his shoulder. "I'll bet you say that to all the girls."

"Nah. Just the ones I sweet-talk into coming to a family barbecue, then end up taking into a field in the rain and getting them soaking wet."

"Oh, well, if that's all." She laughed and pushed her dripping bangs off her forehead, then let out a gasp as she looked down at her practically see-through shirt. "Oh my gosh," she cried, crossing her arms across her chest.

He couldn't help his chuckle as he pulled her tighter against him, rubbing her arm to warm her up. Dipping his head, he spoke into her ear. "I don't mind telling you that the sight of you in that wet shirt has warmed me right up."

She raised an eyebrow, then let out another shiver. "As much as I'd love to come up with a witty and flirty comeback to that semi-dirty comment, I'm too cold to be witty or flirty."

He let out another laugh and turned up the heat as he put the truck in gear. "Let's get you back to the ranch and out of those clothes."

"You are incorrigible," she said, but she laughed with him.

Putting his arm back around her, he pulled her close and headed toward the ranch. "I meant out of those wet clothes and into some dry ones."

"Of course you did."

He tried to focus on driving, to keep his mind off the beautiful woman that was huddled against him, but it was hard. And if he didn't quit thinking about her, that statement was going to get very literal, very fast.

Thankfully, it only took a few minutes to get back to the ranch. He pulled up in front of the bunkhouse. "Come on in. I can't promise the latest fashions, but I can at least find you some clothes that are warm and dry."

Tess's brow creased as she looked from the bunkhouse to the main farmhouse. "Is this your place?"

"What? Did you think I still lived with my mom?" he teased.

"Well, yes, I guess. I mean, not like that." She clamped her lips together, then eyed the bunkhouse suspiciously. "But I didn't think you lived in the barn."

A hearty laugh escaped him as he climbed from the

truck and held out his hand to help her. "It's not the barn. It's one of the old bunkhouses. And don't worry, it's been renovated."

Her look of skepticism changed to amazement as he opened the door of the bunkhouse and let her and the two dogs in.

It had taken close to two years to renovate the old building, tearing down walls and gutting the interior. He'd designed the layout himself and ended up with one large great room combining the kitchen and living room, a small guest bathroom, an office, and a large master bedroom with an impressive master bath.

The rough planks of the torn-out sections and old floors had been saved, then stained and used to create a shiplap effect on the walls. A huge stone fireplace took over one wall, and thick beige rugs covered the hardwood floors.

A heavy, overstuffed couch with matching chairs sat in front of the fireplace, and Mason had found an old trunk that he used as a coffee table. He was a tall guy, and he liked big, comfortable furniture.

He'd also tried to make the space suitable and useful for a guy who worked on a ranch, so the entryway had pegs for jackets and a rack for cowboy hats. A substantial wooden bench sat inside the door, offering a place to sit to take off his boots.

The dogs ran into the house ahead of them and curled up together on Theo's bed. Mason stopped and used the bootjack to pull off his boots, then peeled his wet socks off and dropped them on the rug.

Tess held a hand on the wall to steady herself as she toed off her sneakers and low-cut socks. "Oh my gosh.

It's gorgeous in here." She wrapped her arms around herself as she padded barefoot across the room to stand before the large windows that looked out over the back pasture and the mountain range in the distance. "This view is incredible."

"That's one of my favorite parts. I knew when I was designing the renovation that I wanted to make sure I could see that great view."

"You did all of this yourself?"

He shrugged. "I don't know. I guess. I mean, I designed it all myself, and I did a lot of the renovation myself, but I had help too. I hired out the electrical and the plumbing, and my mom helped with the decorating. I picked a lot of things out myself, but the throw pillows and some of the decorative stuff is all Mom."

"You did an amazing j-j-job," she said, her body shivering as her teeth chattered together.

"Thanks." He wrapped an arm around her shoulder and led her toward the master bathroom. "Come on, let's get you warmed up. One of my other favorite things in this place is the shower."

He took a small measure of pride when he saw her eyes widen as they stepped into the bathroom and she took in the rustic tiled floors, the gleaming copper bathtub, and the huge shower with multiple showerheads.

Stepping into the glass-enclosed shower, he turned on the hot water with one hand and pulled Tess into the space with him with the other. The smooth river-rock tiles were cold on his bare feet, but the water quickly warmed. He switched the nozzle so the hot water sprayed out from two of the showerheads on the wall, then positioned Tess in front of the warm spray.

A shiver ran through her, but she stretched her neck to let the water run down her throat. She was only doing it to warm her skin, but the gesture itself was so sexy that he wanted to dip his head and press his mouth to the soft bend where her slender neck met her shoulder.

She still had her arms crossed in front of her chest, but the wet fabric of her thin tank top clung to her skin, outlining the lace edges of her bra and the tops of her breasts.

He swallowed at the dryness in his mouth as his gaze traveled over her body. He wanted more than his gaze to journey across her curves. He wanted to get his hands, his lips, his tongue on her.

He wanted to peel her wet clothes slowly from her body as if unwrapping a present—a present that he hadn't realized how badly he'd wanted until she'd walked into his life the day before.

Tipping his head back, he closed his eyes. How could this be happening? How could he be standing in the shower with this gorgeous woman, both of them fully dressed in soaking-wet clothes? Stuff like this didn't happen to him. He was just an ordinary guy. This whole thing was supposed to be a simple gesture of asking her to accompany him to the wedding. No big deal, just a normal guy asking a pretty girl to be his date. Just because his feelings were crossing over the "simple gesture" line didn't mean that hers were.

Just because his skin was heating with desire and want—and it was taking all his willpower not to press her against the shower wall and kiss her senseless—didn't mean that she was feeling the same way or that she was interested in being kissed at all.

But she *had* kissed him back when they were in the

kitchen earlier. Kissed him back with a passion that had taken his breath away.

So he might have a chance.

But he didn't want to push. The woman had just helped him fix a fence and was standing in his shower shivering.

He could feel her shaking but didn't know what to do. Should he wrap her in his arms? Should he quit taking up space in the shower with her and let her get warm? Should he get her naked and find another way to warm her skin?

Her body was so close to his, but they weren't actually touching. Still, it was if an electric charge flowed between them, and he swore he could almost feel her against him.

He knew the right thing to do, the chivalrous thing. Finding his voice, he leaned toward her ear. "I'll give you some privacy and see if I can find you some dry clothes."

She whispered one word, but he heard it as clearly as if she'd shouted.

"Stay."

Chapter 11

It was one word, but it was the only word Mason needed to hear.

He didn't answer, didn't have to, but something in him—some tightly wound coil in his chest—loosened a little, and he let out a shaky breath.

Okay. Yes. He would stay.

Something told him that he still needed to take it slowly, that this woman was more fragile than she let on. He took the smallest step forward, closing the distance between them and sliding his arms around her waist.

She leaned back against him, letting out a sigh as she melted in to his chest. Steam rose in the shower as the space and their bodies warmed.

He didn't know what to do, what to say. So he did nothing. He just stood with her, holding her, letting her get comfortable with him, letting her get to know his body and to feel the weight of his arms around her.

Tessa Kane was a mystery to him, sometimes acting fun and flirty and full of confidence—he loved that—but other times acting timid and shy and unsure of herself. He had to admit, he kind of liked that Tessa as well. That Tessa was the one he wanted to shelter, to take care of, to prove to that he was a guy worthy of her attention.

The only problem being that he wasn't sure if he was that guy.

But he wanted to be.

So, he'd wait. He'd be patient. He could do that. He could let her take the lead, let her direct the next step. She'd already asked him to stay, so he knew she wanted something. But he'd let her be the one to decide what that something was.

She could decide to keep things light and in the zone of first or second base, which was fine. He would enjoy kissing her and touching whatever she let him get his hands on.

Or…she could take it to the next level, the one where their clothes disappeared and he had her naked and gasping against the shower wall.

He held his breath, his patience already failing him, as he hoped like hell she'd pick the latter.

She turned around and took a deep breath, almost as if she were gathering her courage. Then she glanced down at his waist. "Those wet jeans look heavy. And uncomfortable."

He cocked an eyebrow at her. "Yeah. They are."

She raised her eyes, staring straight into his with a boldness that sent licks of heat curling down his spine. Her voice was low, but direct. "You should take them off."

Yes, ma'am.

His lips curved into a grin as he fumbled with the button of his jeans. His hands shook, but it wasn't from the cold.

Hadn't he just been hoping that she'd make a move? So why was his heart slamming against his chest and his pulse racing as if he'd just run a hundred-meter dash?

He couldn't believe how nervous this one woman was making him. And how much he wanted to please her.

Hell, how much he *wanted* her, period.

They were still fully clothed, but the outline of their bodies through the wet fabric was almost more enticing than if they had been naked.

Almost. But not quite. Naked was always better.

The denim was stiff and unwieldy as he pushed his jeans down his legs, stepped out of them, and kicked them to the back of the shower.

He was wearing boxer briefs, but of course they were white. And would leave little to her imagination. It would only take one glance to know that the denim of his jeans was not the only thing around here that was stiff.

She boldly gazed down, and another smile crept across his face, this one of pride as he watched her eyes widen and the corners of her lips curve.

He pointed to her waist. "So those shorts you're wearing look pretty heavy and uncomfortable too."

She smiled coyly, jutting one hip out just the slightest. "You're right. What do you think I should do about it?"

He swallowed. Damn, but he did like this woman. Finding his voice, he huskily ordered, "You should take them off."

She narrowed her eyes. "Only if you take your shirt off first."

He whipped his shirt over his head, cussing as the wet fabric caught for a second on his ear, then tossed the shirt to the floor. He lifted his chin, silently challenging her to make the next move.

He couldn't take his eyes off her. He didn't want to miss one moment of this show.

And she did put on a show.

She slowly—Lord help him, so slowly—unbuttoned her shorts, slid down the zipper, then inched them over her hips. Wiggling a little, she worked the shorts down, then kicked them over next to his jeans.

A tiny scrap of pink silk held up by a lacy band was all she had on for underwear, and Mason silently thanked whoever had invented thong panties and convinced women to wear them.

She stood in front of him, her fist planted on her hip, as if daring him to look at her.

That was a dare he would take.

His gaze traveled over her. All she still wore were the tiny panties, her bra, and the white tank top. And all of it was clinging to her skin, the fabric sheer and clearly showing every part of her. With her arms at her sides, every detail of her full breasts was on display, and the pink nubs of her nipples poked through the thin cotton.

His hands itched to touch her, to be filled with her lush curves. And his mouth craved to taste her, to lick, to nibble, to suck.

But as bold as she was acting, he was pretty sure this was an act. Somehow he didn't think she was actually as confident as she was leading him to believe. So he held back, giving her the reins and letting her make the moves. Letting her direct this scene.

She picked up the soap, slowly rolling it in her hands, working up a lather before she set it back down.

He caught his breath, anticipating the feel of her fingers against his skin as she moved her hands toward his chest.

Sliding her soapy hands along his shoulders, his chest, and his stomach, she left a trail of frothy bubbles.

Her fingers were slick as she circled his chest, then traced his nipple. His heart was tripping so hard she had to feel it under her palm.

His blood, hot, pounded through his veins. He was surprised the water wasn't steaming as it hit his heated skin and washed the soap away.

She leaned toward him, her beautiful mouth coming close to his neck. Slowly, seductively, she pressed her lips to his throat and ran her tongue against the hollow. She was tormenting him.

And he loved it. Loved the way she touched him, the way she moved, the way her wet skin glistened. He couldn't take his eyes off her.

As hard as it was, he kept his hands to himself and instead lifted his gaze from her body and looked into her eyes. "Can I touch you?" he whispered.

Her voice was low, raspy, as if she couldn't quite find her breath. "I think I'll die if you don't."

Hearing the sexy confidence in her voice was utterly intoxicating.

And that was all he'd needed to hear.

He wanted to touch her, to taste her, to adore her.

She was his fantasy. Actually, she was beyond anything he'd ever fantasized about.

The heated tension in the air between them seemed to hum as he lifted his hand to her waist, then let it travel up her side in a slow, deliberate slide.

She was watching him, her eyes half-closed and her lips slightly parted. She watched as he slowly ran the backs of his fingers across her stomach and up between the center of her cleavage, then across the perfect round tops of her breasts. And she watched as he circled her hard, taut nipple, then leisurely slid his thumb over the pebbled tip.

Her eyelids fluttered, but she kept them open, letting out a soft moan as he drew the wet fabric of her shirt and bra down, dragging the lace edge across the delicate nub before fully exposing one lush breast.

Even though he could see every detail through the wet fabric, the contrast of having one breast free and bare was beyond arousing.

And he couldn't get over how exciting it was to have her watching every move he made. Every rub and caress of her breast, every stroke and squeeze that tightened her nipples even more.

He forced himself not to take one between his lips. Not yet. Instead he drew out the delicious torture of touching her. She was so beautiful, everything about her perfect.

Finally, slowly, he leaned down and pressed his lips into the soft curve of her shoulder. She dropped her head back, and a soft sigh escaped her lips.

And he wanted to take her then.

But instead, he took his time drawing it out. It was his turn to torture her with a slow seduction. He kissed his way down her throat to the swell of her cleavage, then across the breast that was still covered by her shirt. He'd been dying to touch it, touch her, since they'd first been caught in the rain and her shirt had gotten wet.

Sliding his tongue over her shirt, he circled her nipple, then drew it into his mouth, sucking her through the fabric.

She wriggled and let out another moan, and he

couldn't take it. He yanked the fabric down, freeing both of her breasts and finally taking them in his hands, filling his palms with their fullness as he licked and kissed and tasted her, sipping and sucking at each tip.

Her hands splayed against the shower wall as she arched her back, offering more of herself.

And he took it. He pulled her against him, her round breasts slipping and sliding against the soap still clinging to his chest. He kissed her mouth, darting his tongue between her lips as he ravaged her.

Her lips were warm and pliant, and she urged him on with moans and whimpers, her hands tangling in his wet hair.

Bracing his hands on either side of her, he pressed her against the shower wall, every inch, every curve of her body enveloped by his.

He loved the way she moved, the way she writhed against him, loved those freaking sexy-as-hell sounds she made and gritted his teeth to stay in control.

He couldn't get enough of her, of the way her flesh quivered under his touch. He wanted more, wanted to touch every part of her. His hands roamed over her skin, learning her body, discovering what she liked and what seemed to make her crazy.

Those were his favorite parts.

She was so damn sexy, tempting him with every inch of her creamy skin and her luscious curves.

His hand slid down her side and over her hip, then she parted her legs just slightly, just enough to serve as an invitation, and he slipped his hand between them, skimming around the tiny scrap of silk as he claimed her.

He held her in the palm of his hand. Literally.

Her fingers dug into his shoulders, and she pressed against his palm, urging him on. And he obliged her with slow, steady strokes, giving her all his attention until her gasps became shuddering cries and her knees gave way as she sagged against him.

He lovingly kissed her shoulder, then pulled her tank top over her head and dropped it to the shower floor. She let him undress her, her body languid as he peeled the rest of her clothes off, then turned off the spray of water.

Opening the shower door, he grabbed a towel and wrapped it around her, then twisted another one around his waist before leading her into the bathroom.

With slow, deliberate movements, he dried her off, pressing the dark lengths of her hair between the folds of the towels. It took only seconds for him to swipe the towel across his body and call it good.

He didn't care if he was still a little wet; he needed her in his bed—and needed her now.

Dropping both towels on the floor, he bent down and slid his arm behind her legs, lifting her up and cradling her against his body as he carried her into the bedroom.

The late-afternoon light filled the dim room. The rain had let up to a steady drizzle, but the storm was still raging inside Tess as Mason stepped into his bedroom.

She couldn't breathe. Couldn't believe that this ridiculously hot cowboy had just taken her to O-Town *in the shower* and was now carrying her to his bed.

Carrying her.

All five feet, nine inches of her.

This was the kind of night every woman dreamed about. Was she really doing this? She felt like a different person. Like someone she didn't even recognize. Like a woman playing a part in a movie. A seriously sexy, hot-as-hell movie.

And she was the star.

It was almost as if having Mason ask her to be his date had given her license to actually make herself over into that role, to imagine herself to be the kind of woman who would casually be invited to accompany a seriously sexy cowboy on a weekend of fun.

The kind of woman maybe she really wanted to be.

Because the funny thing was, as different as it felt to let that part of herself loose, she loved the woman she'd been portraying, the woman who was sexy and confident, who lived in the moment, and who took what she wanted.

And she wanted this man. She wanted Mason, not just with her body, but with her entire soul.

He pulled back the comforter and laid her gently on the bed. The sheets were soft against her skin, and she fell back, her head nestling in the pillows.

She didn't care that she was naked, didn't care that he was staring at her body with a look of ravenous desire. *Let him look*. Because the *way* he was looking at her made her feel different, like a new Tess. A Tess who could seduce a cowboy right out of his jeans.

Her pulse raced as he climbed onto the bed and braced his arms around her head, holding himself above her.

He looked down at her, their stares locked.

Her mouth went dry. She licked her lips, and a growl sounded in the back of his throat. His excitement fueled her own, and she looked into his face, losing herself in his brown eyes.

He moved slowly, with utter restraint. The opposite of her. She felt anything but restraint. All she wanted was full abandon and more of the frenzied, heated passion they'd had in the shower.

Her gaze traveled over him—over his strong jaw and down to the muscles in his neck—and she couldn't get enough. He was so damn handsome.

He lowered himself down onto one elbow. As his chest pressed against hers, she swore she felt his heartbeat, its rhythm seeming perfectly matched to her own.

He lifted a hand to her face and cupped her chin. "Are you good?"

Lord, could this man be any hotter?

"I'm more than good," she said, offering him her most wicked, come-hither smile. "I'm excellent."

"Yes, I would agree. You are." He grinned, then pressed a kiss to her lips.

His kiss was a soft promise, not a demand.

She kissed him back, loving the feel of her bare breasts against his muscled chest and the way his large hand gripped her waist and pulled her snug against him.

Then his hands seemed to be touching her everywhere at once.

And she was touching him, running her hands over his muscled back, kissing the hard planes of his shoulder, the soft indents of his neck. His body was like a treasure that she'd just discovered, and she let herself explore every measure of him. *Every* measure.

And he certainly measured up.

The new Tess—the confident, brazen Tess—came unbound, guiding her hands and her mouth and urging her to be bold and ask for what she wanted. "I want you," she whispered against Mason's ear. "Now. Now would be good."

A quiet chuckle escaped him as he leaned over and pulled out the drawer of his nightstand. She heard the whisper of a foil packet and watched as he moved back to his knees, tearing the packet open and covering himself.

He gazed down at her, the passion in his eyes so intense that it made it hard for her to breathe. But she couldn't look away. She wanted to see him, to see them, to experience every delicious moment of this night.

He brushed his fingers across her stomach, and she arched her back, her body crying out for more.

She needed to feel him, all of him.

Skimming his hand down her thighs, he gently pressed her legs wider and settled between them. She could feel her legs trembling as his muscular thighs met hers.

Her chest rose and fell with each jagged breath she took. She wrapped her legs around him, pulling him closer. She was ready for him, so ready.

And so *not* ready.

Not ready for the depths of desire, the heights of passion, or the intensity of the emotions that were flowing through her.

Their bodies seemed to have been made for each other, and she savored the weight of his body on top of hers, delighted in the fullness of him. She buried her face in his shoulder and loved hearing the soft, rumbling moans that came from deep in his throat. His breath came in rough gasps, almost animalistic in his response to her, and she loved that too.

This was real. This had to be real.

Her mind spun with conflicting thoughts about how amazing this all seemed, and yet tiny doubts crept in of why he would pick her and if this really meant anything to him.

Stop thinking! Stop analyzing!

Forget rational thought. She wanted to feel, not think. She let everything else go and simply gave in to the desires racing through her.

She let the sweet sensations build in her, swirling and spinning, until they were soaring through her entire body, until shudders ran through her and she cried out and fell apart in his arms.

Hours and several more sweet sensations later, they lay naked and tangled together in the sheets.

Tess snuggled against Mason's body, still amazed at the way their bodies seemed to fit so perfectly together. Still amazed at his body, period. All that raw muscle and those hard abs. This afternoon had been like a fantasy, like something out of a movie, and she didn't want it to end.

But she knew it would. Knew it had to. Knew the real world would come crashing back in, and the pretend world they'd created this afternoon would fall apart.

Mason brushed a loose lock of hair from her cheek and tucked it behind her ear. "You want to stay?"

"Yes. No. Yes." She chewed her bottom lip. "I do want to, but I'd better not. I think it would be awkward to have my car sitting in front of your mom's house all night."

"I'm not a child. I've had overnight guests of the female persuasion."

She didn't want to think about any of the other women that had been persuading Mason to do anything. She liked the idea that her body was the only one that his hands had roamed over.

That was ridiculous, of course. She knew he'd been with other women, but she wanted to believe there was something special about the way he was with her.

Because she definitely felt something different with him. She couldn't put her finger on what it was exactly. It might have been the way she felt so comfortable with him, so at ease, whether they were eating a meal together or lying in his bed. Or maybe it was the way he made her laugh. Or perhaps it was the push and pull of their conversation—the way that she teased him, and he grinned and teased her back.

Mason was smart. She liked his wit and his dry sense of humor. But somehow she didn't think he saw himself that way. Maybe it was the curse of living in the shadow of a famous older brother, especially one who was larger than life like Rockford, but Mason had plenty of charm and charisma of his own.

He had more than enough attributes that he didn't need to compete with or compare himself to Rock.

Mason was a great guy all on his own. And he was a guy who deserved a woman who saw that and appreciated it.

Guilt roiled in her stomach like a prickly ball, poking and tearing at her insides. She liked this guy, liked him a lot. It was more than just his hard abs and his seriously muscled body—and even more than that incredible thing he'd done with his tongue.

She liked *him*.

And hated herself for deceiving him.

For one moment, she considered coming clean with him. Telling him the truth—but what would she say? That she started out using him to get a story on his brother, but she really liked him now. *Yeah, that would go over really well*.

And she still didn't have enough on Rock—didn't have enough dirt to write an article that would earn her the kind of money that she needed to save her grandmother's house.

And she needed to save her grandmother's house above all.

But just thinking about what was going to happen when they all found out caused a dull ache to pound in her skull. This whole family was going to hate her.

She'd already blown it, already gotten too close. Even though she'd told herself, promised herself, that she wouldn't get involved again. That she wouldn't risk her heart with another guy.

Apparently she was a slow learner.

But she didn't have to be. She could stop this now. Before she did any more damage. Before she made the situation any worse.

She scrubbed her palm against her forehead, trying to think of another solution, anything to get her out of writing this article. Maybe she could become a stripper, except that she had no rhythm and the only dance moves she knew were the ones to the music video of "Thriller," which she didn't think would make much of a striptease routine. Not to mention the fact that she had no upper-body strength, so she'd probably slide off the pole.

She'd heard people could make quick money with virtual currency. Maybe she could mine for Bitcoin. Oh wait, she forgot about a few minor problems, like first of all, she didn't know exactly what Bitcoin was or how it worked, and second, she had no earthly or virtual clue how to mine for it.

"I'd better go. I've got a bit of a headache coming on, and I'm sure you still have work to do tonight."

He narrowed his eyes and studied her face. "You know, that headache excuse is supposed to be used *beforehand* to get you *out* of doing the deed."

"I wasn't trying to get out of doing *the deed*. In fact, the deed itself was really quite amazing."

A cocky grin tugged at his mouth. "Yeah, it was."

"But I really should go." She crawled out of bed, bringing the sheets with her and wrapping them around her body. "But my clothes are still lying in a soaking-wet pile in the bottom of your shower. Do you think I could borrow this sheet? I've heard togas are coming back in style."

He chuckled as he turned on the bedside lamp, then pushed off the bed and crossed to his dresser.

She admired the view as he dug through the drawers. Mason James had one hell of a body.

He turned around, a T-shirt and a pair of sweats in his arms. "Were you checking out my butt?"

"I was." She grinned and lowered her eyes. "But now I'm checking out some of your other finer assets."

"Oh yeah?" He took a step closer and tugged on the

corner of the sheet. "Then it's only fair that I get to check out your assets too."

"You've been checking them out for the last several hours."

"It wasn't enough. I want more." He gestured to the sheet. "I want to see you. All of you. With the lights *on*. Lose the sheet."

With the lights on? Come on.

She hardly ever let a man see her like that. Naked in bed was one thing—that was different. That was on her back so her stomach looked flat, and it was usually in a haze of passion, and sometimes alcohol, so she wasn't thinking about it.

This was another thing entirely. This took guts and confidence—attributes that she was sorely lacking. This took the new Tess.

The new Tess was brave and gutsy, and she tried to channel her alter ego.

She reminded herself that he had already seen her… well, her everything, and he made her feel confident. Made her feel brazen and bold. She didn't need an alter ego. She just needed to be herself. She took a deep breath and let the sheet drop to the floor.

She stood naked in front of him, her bravado dropping with the sheet.

Even though he'd already seen and touched every part of her, this was different.

This was her, the real Tess, standing naked before him, letting him fill his gaze with her, letting him study her imperfections and flaws.

And he was filling his gaze. His eyes were hungry, feasting on her every curve.

"You're looking at me like you're the Big, Bad Wolf, and you want to devour me."

"I do. Especially since you just lost your 'riding hood.'" He licked his lips and flashed her a roguish smile.

His playfulness emboldened her, and she planted her fist on her hip, pushed up her chest, and batted her eyes. "Why, Mason, what big teeth you have…"

"The better to eat you with, my dear."

He let out a low growl, then tossed the spare clothes he'd been holding and lunged at her, grabbing her around the middle and playfully nibbling at her neck.

She shrieked with laughter as they fell onto the bed, her headache forgotten as he nibbled at more than just her neck.

Chapter 12

As the screen door of the bunkhouse slammed behind her, Tess was already rethinking her decision to leave the comfort of Mason's bed.

The rain had stopped, and dusk was settling on the farm. Sounds of the animals filled the air, and light spilled from the big, open barn door. She looked around the ranch and tried to envision a life there, tried to imagine waking in the morning with chores to do or sitting on the porch in the evening with Mason watching the sun dip below the horizon.

It could be a good life. The kind of life she could only dream about. Because that's all it was—a dream. A beautiful fantasy that could never, would never, be hers. She did not get a dream life like this. It simply was not in the cards for her.

At one time, when she'd been a young girl—back before her parents' accident, back when life was wonderful and simple—she did believe. Believed that she would grow up and marry a handsome prince, a good man like her father.

But then everything changed. One tiny moment, a scant shift in circumstances, circumstances that she'd caused, had changed her entire life.

And now she didn't get to have wonderful and simple; she didn't get to dream of a beautiful life on a ranch with a cute cowboy who made her heart flutter. Not after what she'd done.

Even though she'd spent her life trying to make up for that one catastrophic mistake, it was always there under the surface, waiting to remind her that she didn't deserve happiness, wasn't worthy of love, and didn't get to have the happy life that she'd robbed her parents of.

She could have glimpses of it, moments like tonight spent in the arms of a man who made her feel special, made her feel worthy, but those moments didn't last. She knew it, could feel it coming like the change of pressure in the air before a storm. A storm of her own making.

Mason was a good man, a decent man, a man she could imagine herself with. Maybe. If she'd met him under different circumstances. If there weren't other people involved—like her boss, Mason's brother, and her grandmother.

If it had been just the two of them, they might have had a chance. But not now. Not with what she had to do.

She let out a sigh as she opened the door to her car and gestured for Dewey to get in. But the little dog must have heard something in the barn. His ears pricked up, and he lifted his snout to sniff the air. He let out a small yip and took off running, barreling full speed across the driveway and through the barn door.

Tess tossed her things in her car and took off after him. "Dewey, get back here." She rushed through the barn door, imagining the dog getting trampled by the animals inside the barn.

But instead of running toward the animals, Dewey had run to the man standing at the workbench.

"He's okay," Rock said, bending down to scoop up

the dog. He scratched him behind the ears. "You're a funny little thing, aren't you?"

"Sorry, he got away from me." She couldn't believe her luck. This was her chance to talk to Rock alone. To ask him some questions and see if she could dig out anything useful to use in the story.

"No biggie."

She glanced down at the lumber and tools on the workbench. "What are you working on?"

"I'm making a frame for Quinn."

Her brow creased. "Why? I thought the NHL paid you pretty well." Maybe there was a story here—maybe Rock was having financial difficulties. "Can't you just buy her one?"

He chuckled. "Yes, I could. But not like this one." He pointed to the large branch that lay on one side of the bench. "I cut that from 'our' tree, and I'm making a frame out of the wood."

Ah. Finding a flaw in this guy was going to be harder than she'd thought. "Wow."

"I know. I can be kind of a sentimental sap sometimes," he said with a shrug.

"I think it's nice. How do you even know how to do that?"

"My dad taught me. From the time we could hold a hammer or read a level, he was always teaching all of us boys how to use tools to build or fix stuff." He took a sip of beer from a bottle on the bench, then held it up to her. "Want one?"

"Uh…sure." She didn't really want one but thought maybe if they were having a beer together, he might open up to her, share a few stories.

He crossed to an ancient refrigerator against the side wall, the dog still clutched to his chest. The fridge was full of pop, beer, and bottled water. He pulled a bottle free and twisted the lid off before handing it to her.

She took a swallow, then leaned against the side of the workbench. "I think it's pretty cool that all of you boys got a chance to know your dad before he… Well, you know…"

"Died?" Rock finished for her.

Grr. She was such an idiot. Why would she bring up his dad? Talking about someone's deceased parent usually immediately shut the conversation down—at least it did when anyone brought up the subject of her parents. "Sorry."

He shrugged. "It is what it is. He was a good man, and we're lucky we got the time with him that we did. I think he, and my mom, shaped us into the men we are today."

"And now you get a chance to be a dad to Max. He seems like a great kid." There, that ought to do it, swing the conversation back to him and Quinn and their new family.

Rock chuckled. "He is. And I love him like he was my own. I'm planning to adopt him." He held Dewey up, the little dog looking even smaller in his large hands. "What about this guy? Mason said you found him in a parking lot. Are you going to adopt him?"

She grinned. "I think so. I've never been a dog mom before."

"He's going to need you. Because this little mutt has the kind of face that only a mother could love." He chuckled and passed the dog to her.

She burst out laughing, both at Rock's joke and the

way Dewey's legs frantically bicycled in the air as he tried to get to her.

"Well, isn't this cozy?" a voice asked from behind her. A voice that did not sound happy.

She turned to see Mason standing in the doorway of the barn, a scowl on his lips.

"Hey, Mace," Rock said, finally succeeding in dumping the squirming dog into her arms. "I was just telling your girl here…"

"She's not…" Mason stopped himself, clamping his lips together in a tight line, then glared toward her. "I thought you were leaving."

"I was. I mean, I am. The dog got away from me and ran in here."

"Yeah, I see that. Did he also run to the fridge and crack you a beer?"

"What? No, of course not." Why was he so angry? "What's wrong?"

"Nothing. Nothing's wrong. I'll leave you to your beer." He let out a sigh, his shoulders sinking as he turned and walked out of the barn.

She ran after him, catching up to him as he neared her car. "Mason, wait."

He whirled around, his mouth set in a hard line. "Wait for what?"

"For me to talk to you. To explain."

"To explain what? That you barely left my bed and somehow conveniently ended up in the barn drinking and giggling with my older brother?"

Her back bristled. "I wasn't giggling."

He stared at her, his eyes dark and angry.

She tried to imagine how it would have looked from

Mason's perspective, coming into the barn and seeing her drinking and laughing with his brother. Okay, it might have looked bad, but nothing had been happening. "I didn't go looking for him. The dog ran into the barn, and he was just there."

"So you decided to hang out and have a beer? I thought you had a headache."

"I did. I do." It had only been a dull throb before, but it was pounding against her forehead now.

"It didn't look like it to me."

His tone was starting to annoy her. A spark of temper lit, and she lashed back, "Surely you don't think I was trying to come on to your brother!"

"It wouldn't be the first time," he muttered.

"Well, it would be for me," she spat back, her anger really rising now. "What kind of woman do you think I am?"

He shrugged. "I wouldn't know. I only just met you yesterday."

"Well, that fact didn't seem to affect your earlier decision to take me to bed."

"Hey, don't get mad at me. I didn't do anything wrong here."

Except jump to some pretty terrible conclusions.

"Neither did I." Guilt slammed into her like a Mack truck. Because she knew she had been doing something wrong. Nothing like he was suggesting. She wasn't interested in Rock romantically, but she was interested in his story, in finding out the facts behind his hasty wedding to the girl back home.

Mason scrubbed a hand across his eyes and forehead. "I think you should go."

She clutched the dog tighter to her chest, holding on to him as if he were a life vest in a raging storm. "Yeah, I think I probably should."

He shoved his hands in his front pockets and stared at the ground next to her feet. "We can talk tomorrow." He turned his back and headed toward the bunkhouse.

Home sweet home.

Tess glanced around the parking lot before pulling her car into the spot behind the library.

It was already past eight, and the sky had gone dark, with just a sliver of a moon shining through the clouds. The rain had returned, and a light mist and fog blanketed the trees behind the alley. She hoped the darkness and the gloomy weather would help conceal her car.

When they'd finally crawled out of bed again, she'd tugged her hair into a ponytail and put on the sweats and T-shirt that Mason had dropped on the floor. Her bra and underwear were still soaked, so she'd gone commando, and when she'd left the bunkhouse, she'd felt sexy and a little racy.

Now she just felt cold, and hurt, and ashamed. And anxious about spending another night in her car.

Dewey whined in the seat next to her, almost as if he could sense her apprehension.

"I know, boy. It's not the Ritz, but it's all we've got for tonight." She stroked his head and tried not to think about her wonderfully comfy bed at home.

Or her anxious grandmother.

Thankfully, she'd left her phone in her purse so it hadn't gotten soaked along with her clothes in the afternoon rainstorm. But when she'd finally gotten back to it, she saw several missed calls and worried texts from Mimi.

She'd called her grandmother as she'd pulled away from the farm to let her know she hadn't fallen victim to a horrible accident or a serial killer—Mimi had the same kind of imagination she did—and that she just hadn't had her phone on her.

Her chest ached from wanting to tell her grandmother everything that was happening—the cute guy, the dilemma of the story, the predicament of having to hurt and deceive people she was really starting to care about. There wasn't much she kept from her grandmother, but this was a hard one.

She knew Mimi wouldn't approve of the way she was treating Mason just to get a story. Especially since she was doing it to save Mimi herself. Her grandmother would throw herself in front of a bus rather than let Tess get hurt in any way.

Tess couldn't tell her everything, but she couldn't help sharing a little bit about Mason, telling her that he was a guy she'd met at the wedding and that she'd been spending time with his family out at the James's ranch.

Mimi knew that Tess was going to Rockford's wedding and had guessed Mason was his brother. Tess told her she was attracted to Mason but didn't share their disagreement about his brother. The taste of the beer had gone sour in her mouth as she thought about the hurt look on Mason's face. She was embarrassed and ashamed, and Mason had every right to be hurt. And Tess knew if Mimi asked her too many questions, she'd easily figure out she really did like Mason and there was something more going on.

Her grandparents' relationship had been a passionate, whirlwind affair, and Mimi was a big believer in love at first sight and that love conquers all.

Tess knew Mimi would tell her to forget the dumb argument—and the stupid story—and go for it with the cute guy who was making her heart pound and her palms sweat.

And maybe she should.

The headache had already been building behind Tess's eyes so she didn't talk long, just enough to assure her grandmother she was safe and would be spending another few nights up on the mountain.

Tess had told her grandmother the magazine was paying for her lodging, just to keep Mimi from going to an early grave. Knowing her granddaughter was sleeping in her car in an alley would surely bring on a coronary.

Just add it to the big, old pile of BS she'd been shoveling up the past few days.

The pressure behind her eyes had Tess begging off the phone, and she'd promised she'd call her grandmother again the next day.

That pressure was now ten times worse. She pressed her hand to her forehead, fighting the familiar signals of the migraine headache. She knew she was going to pay for not having her sunglasses on this afternoon.

But she needed to get down all the great material she'd heard today before she forgot it. She pulled out her notebook and spent the next fifteen minutes jotting notes as fast as she could while willing the migraine to hold off until she'd at least captured some of the stories about the James brothers playing hockey as kids and

Rock making a picture frame with his own hands and planning to adopt Quinn's son. She crammed the notebook back between the seats as soon as she'd reached the end of her notes, then leaned her head back against the seat rest and closed her eyes.

The phone call with her grandmother was already getting fuzzy in her head. They'd skimmed over the impending house payment, but she was sure now that Mimi had said something about having things under control. That she'd talked to "some people" and was working on a plan.

What people? What kind of plan?

Any time her grandma mentioned anything about having a "plan," Tess knew some kind of trouble was about to follow. Mimi's plans never quite worked as expected. Maybe she should call Mimi back.

Pain seared through her head, and a wave of nausea rolled within her stomach. Maybe she'd call her later.

She crawled into the back seat and reached for the thin blanket, her hands already shaking as the chills started.

She'd suffered from migraines for years but could often fend them off with medication, especially when she felt the onslaught of a bad one starting. This one had taken her by surprise, sneaking up on her as she drove away from the farm. What had started as a nagging annoyance had built further toward full-blown agony with every mile she drove.

It made perfect sense though. The day had consisted of the perfect storm of migraine triggers—the bright sunlight coupled with clouds and drastic weather changes, the fact that she'd had too little sleep and not enough caffeine that day, and that she was most likely dehydrated after working with the tree and sweating throughout the afternoon.

Fumbling for her bag, she pawed through the contents, remembering that she had meant to check it and praying she'd thrown the bottle of migraine medication into her purse.

Her search proved fruitless, and she let out a cry of frustration as she threw her bag onto the floor of the car. She'd been in such a rush when she'd left Denver and preoccupied with her grandmother's situation that she hadn't even thought about it. Besides the fact that she hadn't been planning to spend even one night in Creedence, let alone two.

She needed water and some ibuprofen, but the water bottles she had in the car were empty, and she couldn't find the strength to crawl back into the front seat and drive to a convenience store. Not like she had any money to buy aspirin anyway.

Curling into a fetal position, she pulled the blanket over her shoulder and tried to breathe through the pain. The migraine was coming fast and hard, slamming into her body in a storm of pain and distress.

Dewey curled up next to her on the seat, giving her comfort in that amazing sixth-sense way dogs have of knowing exactly what a person needs.

The realization that she had no medication at all only served to increase her stress and intensify the severity of the migraine.

Only the barest sliver of moonlight shone into the back window of the car, but even the slightest amount of light had pain searing through her head. Another wave of nausea rolled through her, this one worse than the first. She grabbed for the empty fast-food bag she'd spied on the floor earlier, leaning over the seat as her body heaved.

She let out a sob as she wiped her mouth with the back of her hand, then squeezed her eyes shut against the pain in her head.

Foul sweat covered her skin, soaking through her shirt, but her body still felt cold, and she shivered under the blanket. She heard Dewey whine and tried to lift her head to find and comfort the little dog. But she couldn't see straight, and dizziness swept through her.

Smudges of black blurred her vision. Her head fell back against the seat.

Tears of pain and frustration leaked from the corners of her eyes. She hated this feeling of helplessness, of not being able to control her own body. Her eyes stung from the tears. Her mouth was dry, her throat burning from the bile of the vomit. She needed water, could already feel the dehydration settling in.

But her limbs were too heavy and the pain in her head too severe. She couldn't move, couldn't even sit up.

Her throat was parched, dry as cotton, the discomfort made worse by the sound of the steady rain now hitting the roof of the car. If only she could open the window, she could stick her head out and let the rainwater fill her mouth. She'd already cracked the window a few inches for the dog. If she could only sit up.

But the effort was too much.

Pain seared through her head, and stars sparkled in the air just before her vision blurred to a muddy brown, then an inky black as she lost consciousness and collapsed back against the seat.

This is probably stupid, Mason thought as he glanced down at the picnic basket on the seat next to him. But he'd acted pretty stupid, and this was the only way he could think to apologize. He'd let his temper and his imagination get the best of him. And he'd been a jerk to Tess.

She hadn't really done anything wrong, not as far as he knew. And what had he really seen? Her laughing as his brother passed her a dog. That same scenario wouldn't have fazed him if he had been in the barn with them. If they hadn't been alone and swigging beer.

But sharing a laugh, or even a drink, didn't mean that Tess was interested in his brother. He'd automatically jumped to the conclusion that she'd been after Rock all along. His worst fear was that he was going to care about another woman, and she was going to end up using him again to get to his brother.

But he'd thought Tess was different, had believed that she was something special. So when he'd spied her in the barn with Rock, he'd automatically seen red. And he hadn't given her a chance to explain, even to listen to her side of the story. He'd just stormed back into the house and let himself have a good sulk. Until his stomach started growling, and he'd settled down and realized that neither he nor Tess had eaten any supper. *And* that he probably owed her an apology at the very least and a chance to talk this through. It seemed like his apology would go better if he was bearing food.

He knew she was staying at the Lamplighter Hotel, so he'd decided to drop off a sandwich to her. How the hell a sandwich had turned into a full-on picnic complete with a bottle of wine and a couple pieces of leftover pie was beyond him. And if that wasn't bad enough, as he'd walked to the truck, he'd pulled a handful of wildflowers to give her. He'd seen the patch of yellow daisies and couldn't resist. He figured she'd love them, and maybe they'd soften her up a little and give him a better chance to explain.

What in the Sam Hill was wrong with him?

He didn't do picnics, and he sure as hell didn't pick wildflowers for anyone other than his mom. And he hadn't done that since he was nine years old.

But he also didn't spend hours languishing in bed, exploring the curves and valleys of a woman he'd only met the day before.

This was probably coming on too strong. He'd just give her the sandwich. And maybe the pie. She didn't have to know he'd packed an entire picnic supper. Or that he'd picked her a handful of posies.

Cut it out, man. He was overthinking it. It was just a simple gesture. Just a sandwich, for crying out loud.

But he wasn't fooling himself. Nothing about this was simple.

Not the sandwich, not the handful of stupid flowers, not the fact that he was in his truck driving into town at nine o'clock at night to follow after a woman. A woman he'd just met. A woman he barely knew.

A woman he was falling for. And falling hard—as in face-first, no-hands, full-speed, crash-and-burn falling, with no safety net in sight.

And he had no idea if she felt the same.

He knew she felt something—she had to. With the kind of day they'd just had, she had to at least like him a little. That couldn't all be pretend. But one bout of great sex didn't mean she cared about him or was interested in anything more.

And since when had he even considered "anything more" with a woman? Especially a woman who didn't even live in his town. Or his county. It had been so long that he couldn't even remember. Couldn't remember the last time he'd let his guard down enough to even consider the possibility.

But he'd let his guard down today. Hell, his guard had come crashing down the minute he opened that closet door and saw Tessa Kane standing inside. Her shirt busting open was just the icing on the cake.

He was in trouble here. This was all happening too fast. He needed to pump the brakes and slow this ride down.

He should turn around now. Forget the sandwich, forget the stupid picnic.

This afternoon had been great—hell, it had been knock-his-socks-off amazing—but he wasn't looking for a relationship, especially with someone he'd just met. The relationships he did have were built on trust and honesty. And how could he trust a woman he'd bumped into in a closet at a party and knew nothing about?

But his truck seemed to have a mind of its own as it pulled into the parking lot of the Lamplighter Hotel. Regardless of what his truck wanted, he knew he wanted it too.

Even if this whole idea was a little bit crazy. Maybe he could use a little crazy, a little impulsive. It was certainly impulsive to drive into town and try to track her down. He didn't even know what room she was in, he suddenly realized. He didn't suppose it would be too hard to figure it out though. It wasn't a really big hotel, and her car would most likely be parked in front of her room. If he had to knock on a couple of doors, it wouldn't be that big a deal.

Except that her car *wasn't* parked in front of her room.

It wasn't parked in front of *any* room. In fact, it wasn't anywhere in the lot at all.

Hmm. That was weird. Maybe she'd stopped to get something to eat. Except that the diner and the grocery store were both already closed for the night. The only other place to buy anything to eat was the convenience store, and the parking lot had been empty when he'd driven by just now.

His eyes narrowed as he stared at the four cars that sat in the hotel parking lot: an old Honda, a red pickup, an SUV, and a new sporty compact. None of them were a crappy Ford Taurus.

He pulled up in front of the office and cut the engine to his truck. So much for trying to surprise her. He pulled out his phone and tried her number, but it went to voicemail after four rings.

He didn't bother leaving a message. What would he say anyway? "Hi there. I'm kind of an idiot and brought you some food, but you're not here. Call me if you're still interested in either me or a sandwich."

Yeah, that sounded real great. He blew out a sigh as he tapped his fingers on the steering wheel. He wasn't sure what to do. He could always leave her the sandwich and the pie. That would mean he wouldn't get to see her again, but at least she'd get fed.

An awful thought struck him—maybe she'd gone

home for the night, back to Denver. Maybe this whole thing *had* been too much for her, and she'd said *screw it* to the whole weekend and driven back down the pass.

The hotel office was lit up, and he could see one of the Johnson girls sitting behind the counter. He couldn't tell which one—there were three girls, all teenagers—but this one's red hair was pulled up in a messy knot and falling across her face as she studied her phone. They'd gone to church with the Johnsons for years and had known all the girls since they'd been born. The joys of a small town. Only in this instance, the small-town connection might come in handy.

The desk clerk knew him and knew he wasn't a weird stalker. Maybe she could tell him about Tess. If she'd seen her tonight. Or knew where she was. Or when she'd be back. Or *if* she'd be back.

It couldn't hurt to ask.

He pushed through the door of the hotel office, cringing as the bell rang, signaling his entrance. "Hey there." Easiest to go with the generic greeting until he figured out which girl he was dealing with.

She looked up, startled, then a grin split her face. "Hey, Mason."

"Hi, Sarah." He recognized her now. She was the oldest of the girls. "Sorry to bug you, but a friend of mine is staying here. You know, she's in town for Rock's wedding. I wanted to drop something off for her, but I can't remember her room number. Her name's Tessa Kane, and she drives a beat-up little Taurus."

Sarah's brow furrowed, and she frowned. "Are you sure she's staying here?"

"I'm pretty sure. Why?"

"I haven't seen a car like that here, and I don't have anyone registered by that name."

That was weird. This was the only hotel in town, and Mason was sure she'd said she was staying there.

"Really? Because I thought she said she was staying here. She would have checked in yesterday. Can you look again?" That was a dumb question. She hadn't looked at anything the first time. "Maybe you missed her registration."

The exaggerated roll of her eyes told him she didn't think so. "I don't need to look. We only have three rooms rented out for tonight. One is to a fly fisherman who comes up here once a month, and the other two are to families that are traveling through and just checked in tonight. We were full last night because of your brother's party, but none of the rooms were rented to a single woman."

A sinking feeling settled in his gut. "You're sure?"

She let out the kind of sigh only teenage girls can seem to perfect. "Yes, I'm sure."

"All right. I must have heard her wrong." He trudged out to his pickup.

What the hell? Where was she? He was sure she'd told him she was staying there.

Why would she lie?

And if she'd lied about this, what else was she lying about?

He raked his arm across the seat, sending the picnic basket crashing to the floor, then threw the truck in gear and peeled out of the parking lot.

And then he slammed on his brakes as a Volkswagen Jetta laid on the horn and swerved around him.

Shit. He hadn't even seen the guy.

He needed to get off the road. Give himself a minute to calm down. To take a breath. He pulled into the next closest parking lot across the street from the hotel. The library was closed, and the lot was empty.

The wild daisies had slid off the seat when he'd slammed on the brake. They lay on the floor, mocking him with their cheery yellow color. He rolled down the window, then grabbed them and flung them out onto the pavement.

What the hell was going on?

This didn't make any sense.

He leaned his head back against the seat and closed his eyes, trying to relax, to think about this rationally. But how could he think when all he could hear was the sound of a dog barking? And not just barking, but barking interspersed with yapping and whining. Somebody needed to let their damn dog inside.

He shook his head. Now he was cussing at a dog. It wasn't the dog's fault.

This was stupid. If he wanted to know what was going on, he needed to go to the source. He needed to ask Tess. He'd already tried her cell once, but he needed to try again. And again after that. As many times as it took to figure out what was going on.

He pulled his phone from his pocket, then jabbed at her contact information. Holding his breath, he listened to the phone ring. Once. Twice.

Realizing he was clenching his teeth, he intentionally relaxed his jaw. The phone rang a third time, and he let out his breath as he heard a click. This time she picked up. Or at least it sounded like she did.

Except that she didn't say hello. She didn't say anything at all.

"Hello? Tess?" He pressed the phone to his ear, concentrating as he listened for her response. Damn it—he couldn't hear anything over the sound of that damn dog barking.

Wait a minute.

He pressed the phone closer to his ear. *What the hell?* It sounded as if the barking was coming *through* the speaker of the phone.

"Tess," he practically yelled into the phone, fingers of alarm creeping into his chest. "Can you hear me?" He held the phone away from his ear, then put it back again.

Yep. Same barking.

What in the world was going on? It sounded as if the barking was coming from the trees behind the building. Mason put the truck in gear and pulled around behind the library.

He blinked.

What the hell? he thought again for the umpteenth time.

Tess's car was parked behind the library. But the car appeared to be empty. Except for the dog. He could see Dewey pawing and scratching at the window as he barked through the crack at the top. But there was no sign of Tess.

What was Tess's car doing back here?

She wouldn't leave it in a secluded spot like this. And there was no way she would leave the dog alone in the car.

Had something happened to her? Had she been kidnapped?

Cut it out. This was Creedence. Shit like that didn't happen here. But something was happening here. Something that felt very wrong.

A shiver of apprehension skittered down Mason's spine as he killed the engine and climbed from the truck. He grabbed a tire iron from behind the seat and guardedly approached the car.

The dog was in the back seat, his eyes wild as his barking and yapping became more intense the closer Mason drew to the car.

"Whoa there. Take it easy, buddy." He spoke calmly to the dog, trying to soothe both of their nerves. "It's okay, Dewey. It's just me."

The dog's head disappeared from view, then popped back up. A bead of sweat broke out across Mason's back as he cautiously peered into the back seat.

He caught his breath.

Oh shit. The body of a woman lay curled in the back seat.

And not just any woman.

Tess.

Chapter 13

"Tess! Are you okay?" Mason pounded on the window, sending the dog into even more of a frenzy, but the woman in the seat didn't move.

He considered breaking the window with the tire iron, but he remembered he still had the slim jim he'd borrowed from the sheriff the day before.

Racing to the truck, he threw down the tire iron and grabbed the thin tool, then ran back to Tess's car. It only took a few seconds, but it felt like hours as he maneuvered the tool into the seal of the window and released the lock. Yanking open the door next to her head, he reeled back at the stench of sweat and vomit.

But he was a rancher—he'd smelled a lot worse—and he leaned into the back seat and cradled her head. "Tess? Darlin'? Can you hear me?"

She let out a groan and raised her hand. Her eyes stayed closed as she pressed her fist to her forehead. "Mason?" she whispered.

"Yeah, it's me. I'm here. I've got you." He stroked his hand across her damp forehead. Her skin was clammy but cool, so no fever. "Can you tell me what's wrong?"

His eyes searched the back seat for a clue to what was going on. A pink tote bag and her purse were on the floor behind the driver's seat, the contents of the purse scattered on the carpet. Next to it were two paper cups fashioned into what appeared to be dog dishes.

The other floor well had the evidence of her feeling sick, and it looked like she'd thrown up at least twice.

A thin emergency blanket and the sweatshirt he'd loaned her the day before were covering her, and he could see her cell phone clutched in her other hand.

Was she living in her car? Was she homeless?

He couldn't wrap his head around the situation or come up with any scenario that made sense.

None of that mattered right now. He needed to figure out what was wrong with her. Did she have food poisoning? A sudden bout of the flu? Had she taken drugs?

The car didn't smell like booze, so he ruled out that she was drunk. Plus, it hadn't been that long since they'd been together. Certainly not long enough for her to go on the kind of bender that would cause her to black out.

She curled tighter into a ball, her voice barely audible as she mumbled. "Migraine."

He let out a sigh of relief. He could deal with a migraine. His mom got them occasionally, so he was familiar with the symptoms.

The dog had thankfully stopped barking. It stood on the seat next to Tess, careful not to stand on her as it leaned forward and licked Mason's hand.

"Good dog." He stroked the dog's head. "You did good, boy." He needed to get her out of here, get them both some water, then get her somewhere other than the back seat of her car. "I'll be right back," he told her.

She reached for his hand, clutching it in a death grip. "Don't leave me."

"I'm not leaving. I'm just getting you some water." He left the back door of the car open, thankful it had finally stopped raining, and raced back to his truck.

Clearing off the seat, he made a place for her, then grabbed one of the half-empty water bottles that were always rolling around his pickup.

"I'm here," he said, minutes later as he slid into the back seat with her and lifted her head onto his lap. "I brought you some water. I need you to try to sit up."

She nodded, grasping his hand as she tried to lean forward.

He held the water bottle to her lips and persuaded her to take a few sips. Her lips looked dry, and he was pretty sure she was dehydrated. Which, he knew from his mom's experiences, only made the migraine worse.

He poured a little water in the cup on the floor, and for the first time, Dewey left Tess's side to jump to the floor and lap at the cup.

Mason may not be good at a lot of things, but he excelled at taking care of sick animals. He had the patience and the heart to tend to their wounds and coax them back to health. He'd even at one time considered being a veterinarian. Not that Tess was a sick animal, but he knew she was in trouble and she needed him.

"I'm gonna get you out of here," he told her, brushing her hair back from her forehead and laying a tender kiss on her forehead.

He backed out of the car, gently sliding her body along the seat until he could get his arms under her. Then he cradled her body against his as he carried her to his truck. Thankful that he'd brought the older truck, he laid her out on the bench seat. Dewey followed at his heels, jumping into the seat and curling against Tess's body.

After getting her settled on the seat, he ran back to her car, grabbed her purse and tote and the keys from the floor, locked the car, and slammed the door shut. He'd come back and get the car later. For now, he needed to focus on Tess.

He tossed her things into the truck and slid in next to her, gently lifting her head and resting it on his lap. Lifting the water bottle to her lips, he tried to get her to take another drink before he pulled out of the lot and headed back to the ranch.

Tessa rolled over in bed, smooth cotton sheets caressing her skin, as the pounding in her head thankfully subsided.

Wait. There were no smooth cotton sheets in the back of her Ford Taurus. And there definitely wasn't enough room to stretch out her legs the way she was doing now. Where the heck was she?

Her eyes popped open, and she squinted back against the soft sunlight that streamed through the window of the bedroom. She glanced around, recognizing the dresser, the window coverings, the bed. Mason's bed.

She was in Mason's bedroom. But how the heck had she gotten here?

She distinctly remembered getting in her car and driving away from the ranch the night before. She remembered pulling into the alley behind the library and climbing into the back seat of the car as the shooting pain of the migraine pounded against her skull.

And that was the last clear thing she remembered.

The rest of her night had been in-and-out fuzzy moments and dreams filled with riding in Mason's truck, her head cradled in his lap, and memories of her mother taking care of her when she was sick. If she closed her eyes, she could almost feel her mother's soothing touch as she stroked her head or brushed back her hair.

Snippets of voices and murmurs blended together with sensations of soft, warm fabric and a dimly lit room.

Mason must have found her somehow and brought her back here. But how had he found her?

Oh my gosh. He had to have seen me sleeping in my car.

What could he be thinking of her now? And had he spent the whole night taking care of her?

She pushed up against the pillow, leaning her back against the headboard.

Dewey was curled on the bed by her feet. He stood and carefully walked toward her as if he knew she'd been hurting. He tipped his nose to her face, sniffing her once, then gently licked her cheek.

"You're such a sweet dog," she whispered, running her hand down his back as he lay down on the pillow next to her and rested his head on her arm.

The scent of bacon and coffee filled the air, and her stomach let out a loud rumble.

It was a good sign that she was hungry. It wasn't a good sign that she was wearing a faded blue T-shirt that read Creedence High School Football on the front.

That was not the shirt she'd been wearing when she'd left.

She heard hushed voices in the next room and recognized one as Vivi's.

Oh no.

When she'd left here the night before, she'd been wearing a similar T-shirt, a pair of sweats, and nothing else. She did not want to face Mason's mom from under the covers of his bed wearing only a thin T-shirt and no undies.

She peeked under the covers and let out a sigh of relief when she saw her bottom half ensconced in a pair of black gym shorts.

"Good morning. How's the head, honey?" Vivi sailed into the room, a cup of steaming coffee in her hand. She held out the mug. "You take cream and sugar?"

Tess shook her head. "I'll take it however you got it. I'd take an intravenous drip if you think you could manage it."

Vivi chuckled as she handed her the cup, then gestured to the end of the bed. "Okay if I sit?"

"Sure."

"You gave my boy quite a fright last night. He called me on his way home, and I met him over here. I haven't heard him that upset in a long time."

"I'm sorry. I didn't mean to scare anyone. I usually have a better handle on my migraines. This one just got away from me."

"I hear you. I get them every once in a while as well. I know how they can throw you for a loop. This one seemed pretty bad. How are you feeling now?"

Tess stretched her neck from side to side. "My body aches, but my head is clear."

"That's good. We pulled out all the stops last night. Warm compresses, lavender oil, peppermint oil, sips of ginger root tea, and ibuprofen. Mason said you had an empty bottle of Advil in your bag, so we assumed you could take it okay."

Gah. Mason had been in her bag. Her mind raced with thoughts of what he could have found in there as she nodded. "Yeah, I'm fine taking it. I just didn't have any. And didn't have the strength to go to the store and buy any." *Or the money*. There was that too.

"We're just glad you're okay." Mason's mom patted her leg, and Tess's throat tightened with emotion as she realized her dreams of her mother's hands might have been Vivi's instead.

"How's the patient?" Mason's low voice asked as he sauntered into the room and leaned a hip against the dresser. His dark eyes were narrowed as he studied her and didn't contain any of the teasing glints they usually held.

The fabric of the air seemed to change when he walked in, as if all the oxygen had been sucked from the room.

He was so dang hot.

He wore jeans and the same square-toed leather boots he'd had on the day before. A faded red T-shirt stretched across his broad chest, and a faint hat ring circled his head.

It seemed as if his eyes saw right through her—saw every fib and half-truth that she had told him. Yesterday she'd seen affection, tenderness, and lust in his eyes. Now she only saw distrust and suspicion.

She could understand his wariness. She probably wouldn't feel too trusting of a guy she'd found sleeping in his car either.

If he'd only let her explain…

And say what? More lies? Maybe she should just tell him the truth. She could start by simply answering his question. "I'm fine. Better. Thanks to you. And your mom." She smiled shyly at Vivi.

Mason's features softened as he glanced at his mother. "Yeah, she was great. She knew a bunch of tricks I never would have tried. Thanks, Mom."

Vivi shrugged and patted Tess's leg again. "It's nice to be needed sometimes. And I'm just glad you're feeling better."

"I can take it from here," Mason said.

His mom stood up and laid a hand on his arm. "I'm here if you need me. And I'll see you later at the exhibition game."

"Thanks. I'll be there."

Tess noticed he didn't say "*We'll* be there." Vivi had asked her the day before if she'd be willing to help her and Quinn with the snack bar during the game, and Tess had been excited to be part of the day. But was her time with Mason James now up? Was he waiting for his mom to leave so he could chew Tess out, then send her packing?

Neither of them said anything as they listened to Vivi collecting her things and leaving the bunkhouse.

Mason let out a sigh as they heard the screen door slam.

Tess hoped he would sit in the spot Vivi had just vacated, but he stayed where he was, leaning against the dresser. His stance was seemingly casual, but she could see the stiffness in his shoulders, the solemn line of his lips.

"You really feeling okay?"

She nodded, unable to speak around the lump forming in her throat. She didn't want to lie to him anymore. She wanted to come clean, to tell him everything. But that was the fastest way to ruin everything between them. And she liked what they'd started.

"I'm glad you're feeling better. But I gotta tell you, I have a lot of questions."

"I know," she whispered. And prayed she would have the answers.

"I came into town last night to apologize for getting so worked up about you and Rock. And I figured you might be hungry, so I made you a sandwich and brought you some supper."

"You made me a sandwich?" A flicker of happiness rose in her chest. She didn't think anyone other than her family had ever made her a sandwich before.

"Yeah, I did. I thought I was being nice, but I ended up feeling like a fool when I went to the hotel to give it to you and found out you weren't checked in there."

His eyes focused in on hers, piercing her heart with the hurt she saw there. She looked down at her hands, clasped tightly in her lap.

"No," he continued. "In fact, you hadn't been staying there at all. Apparently, you've been sleeping in your car in the alley behind the library." He paused, as if waiting for her to explain.

She didn't know what to say. Where to even start. How to even find her voice. "How did you find me?" she finally managed to ask.

A faint smile tugged at his lips, and he pointed to Dewey. "It was your miniature Lassie over there. He was barking up a storm. I called your cell, and you must have had enough wits about you to pick up. I could hear him barking through the phone."

She peered down at the little dog, his brown eyes looking up at her with what could only be described as devotion. "You are a good dog." His tail beat a quick tap against the pillow.

If only she could appease Mason as easily. "I'm sorry."

"Sorry's fine, but that doesn't explain what the hell you were doing sleeping in your car. Are you homeless?"

She let out a humorless laugh. *Not yet, anyway.* "No,

I'm not homeless. Just broke. I really do live with my grandmother in Denver, but I couldn't afford the gas to come up and down the mountain, and I couldn't afford to stay several nights in a hotel."

"Then why did you agree to be my date for the wedding? To stay up here all weekend? Was it just to get a chance to meet Rock?"

Pain tore through her heart—his question was hitting way too close to home. She shook her head. "Of course not." She choked out the words. His assumptions may not be true now, but they certainly were at the time. "I'd never even heard of your brother. That's the truth." She could say that honestly; she hadn't known who Rock even was before a few days ago.

She could also be honest with Mason about something else. Her feelings. She glanced up at him, her voice barely above a whisper as she answered, "I agreed to be your date because I liked you."

He sighed and scraped a hand across his face. "I liked you too."

Liked?

Mason finally moved. Pushing away from the dresser, he crossed to the bed. She scooted over, making room for him to sit next to her.

He settled on the bed, his hip barely brushing hers as he leaned forward, his elbows on his knees. Turning his head, he stared at her, studying her face as if looking for the truth.

A fist squeezed around her heart.

She waited, barely able to breathe. Knowing that was the one thing that she couldn't give him.

He took a deep breath. "I *still* like you. My heart

damn near stopped when I saw you passed out in that car. But I was also pissed off. Pissed that you wouldn't come to me. Pissed that you made me think you were staying at the hotel. Pissed that you made me feel like an idiot you'd tricked into believing one thing when something else was really happening. I hate being lied to, Tess. And I hate being made to feel like a fool."

She nodded. "I'm sorry."

"So you said." He blew out his breath. "Just tell me the truth. All I want to know is what's really going on here."

This was it. The perfect segue to tell him everything. No more lies.

Chapter 14

"The truth is..." Tess paused, swallowing the bitter acid burning her throat.

Could she really tell him the truth?

That she had tricked him—and not just about the hotel, but about her whole reason for being here? Could she tell him she'd used him? That this whole weekend was one big calculated move to find out information about his brother?

It would crush him.

She might not know him all that well—although she felt like she did, felt like they'd made a real connection—but she did know Mason felt the heavy weight of living in his famous brother's shadow. She'd gotten a taste of that the night before. And she knew telling him the truth would destroy whatever trust they had been starting to build.

And it would destroy any relationship as well.

As much as she wanted to tell him the truth, to come clean about who she was and why she was really there, she wasn't ready to let him go. Wasn't ready to let this go.

Maybe if they had a little more time to build their relationship, to strengthen what they had between them, they'd be strong enough to handle her deceitfulness. Her head was telling her that was total bullshit. They couldn't build anything real on a foundation of lies. That was like trying to build a house on shifting sand.

But her heart was telling her it might work, that it was

worth the cost to try, that it was worth the risk to have more time with him. Even if he wasn't truly interested in building anything with her, she wanted more time to live in this imaginary world where a cute cowboy was falling for her. Wanted one more night spent in his arms, in his bed. One more night of feeling wanted, desired, loved—even if it was all in her imagination.

She would take it.

Because she wasn't ready to let go of Mason. Not yet.

So she wouldn't tell him the whole truth, but she could be honest about some of it. She could be honest about how she felt.

She rested her hand on top of his, brushing her thumb across his callused palm. "The truth is that I like you. I really like you. I know this started out because you needed a fill-in date for a big wedding weekend, and I was okay with that. I knew that you couldn't really be interested in me, that I was just standing in because there was no other choice, but I couldn't say no. You're this charming cowboy who's so handsome, you take my breath away. And then we spent more time together. I felt like I was getting to know you, and I wanted more."

A gentle smile played on his lips, but he shut it down, tightening his mouth back into a severe line as his forehead creased in concentration. "I get that. I really like you too. But that doesn't explain…"

"Why I was sleeping in my car?"

"Yeah."

"I told you. I'm broke, and I lost my job."

"I thought you said you were a writer."

"I am a writer, but I still need a day job to pay the bills." *Please don't ask what kind of job I had.*

She hurried on before he could ask. Kept talking, kept tying together the braid of lies and half-truths. "I apparently wasn't cut out for the job, and I got fired. Look, it's been a rough year. It started with a bad breakup, and I closed myself off from dating, from doing much of anything. But I was having dinner with a friend, and she told me her brother had been dumped and needed a plus-one for a wedding weekend. She knew I hadn't been on a date in a year and convinced me that her brother would be a safe, easy way to ease back into the dating world. It sounded kind of fun, so I figured what the heck. Why not?"

She stopped and peered at him, trying to convey the emotion she felt. The emotions were real, the only honest things she had to offer him. "Then Mick-the-Dick stood me up, and I met you. And you were funny and charming and so cute, and I wanted you to like me. And somehow leading with 'Hey, I'm an idiot and just got fired from my job' didn't seem the way to impress this hot guy I'd just met."

"Okay, I get that. But that was the first day. What about yesterday? Or last night? You could have told me you didn't have a place to stay. Hell, you could have stayed here. I *asked* you to stay here."

She lowered her eyes, unable to look at him. A thread had come loose on the bedspread, and she stared at the broken strand, feeling as though it somehow represented her—that she'd been going along fine, her life creating neat little stitches, then one thread broke and the whole thing was coming unraveled.

"I know. And I wanted to. I really did. But I just couldn't. Look, I lost my job. I don't have enough money to fill my gas tank or even buy a stupid hamburger, but I still have my pride." She let out a shaky breath. "Or at least I did."

"You still do."

"I feel awful…like a total schmuck for deceiving you." For *still* deceiving you. "It was a stupid thing to do, and I truly apologize. Can you forgive me?"

The tightness in his shoulders eased, and his expression softened—just a little. But enough to give her hope. She wanted to reach out, to touch his cheek, to run her fingers through his dark hair, but she kept her hands in her lap, twisting the folds of the sheets between her fingers.

He nodded, a small shake of his head. "Yes, of course I can forgive you. I feel like a schmuck too. For everything that happened last night with Rock…for jumping to conclusions. For not being the kind of guy you could just talk to. Or that you could turn to. You can tell me anything. Just talk to me. And no more lies, okay?"

Before she could answer, a fist pounded at the door, and they heard Quinn's voice through the screen. "Mason? Tess? Are you guys decent? We need to go. The alumni game starts at eleven, so we've got to get over there pretty soon and get set up."

He studied Tess's face. "Do you still want to do this?"

Her heart leapt. Was he offering her a second chance? "Which this? The game? Or…?"

"All of it. The game. The rehearsal dinner. The wedding."

"Yes."

"Yes to which?"

"Yes, to all of it." She slid her hand into his and entwined their fingers. "I want to be here. With you."

A smile spread across his face. "Good. Me too. With you. You know what I mean."

Hope bloomed in her chest as he leaned forward and pressed a tender kiss to her lips.

Quinn banged on the door again. "Hello? Can you guys hear me?"

Mason let out a chuckle, his breath tickling Tess's cheek as he tipped his forehead to touch hers for just a moment, then hollered back to Quinn. "We hear you. The whole ranch can hear you. You can come in."

The screen door opened, and in the next second, the bedroom was chock-full of craziness as Quinn burst in with Mason's dog hot on her heels. Theo jumped on the bed, sending Dewey into a frenzied circle as they barked and jumped on each other in greeting.

Tessa laughed, holding her hands up to fend off the chaotic licks and slobbery kisses. "Besides the obvious issue of getting mauled by these puppies, I do have a problem with the game though. I don't have any clothes to wear."

"I can help with that," Quinn said, tossing a blue-and-red Colorado Summit jersey on the bed as she shushed the dogs and scolded them to get down. "We're all wearing them. To support the guys on the team."

Tess lifted the jersey, smiling at the name "James" spelled out across the back.

Mason nodded to the chair in the corner that held a pile of her clothes. "I washed your other stuff from yesterday."

She glanced at him, a secret smile on her lips, silently sending him a message that said she was thinking about the way he'd peeled those wet clothes off her in the shower the day before.

His flirty smile in return told her he'd gotten the message and was thinking the same thing. "I also grabbed your bags from your car in case you'd need anything else."

Her smile fell, replaced with an expression of remorse. "Thank you. I really do appreciate you helping me."

Quinn snapped her fingers. "Hello? You do remember I'm standing here. You two can make moony eyes at each other later. Right now, I need you to get dressed."

"All right. Can I have twenty minutes to take a quick shower and brush my teeth?"

"You can have thirty," Quinn said, already heading for the front door. "We'll meet you at the ice arena."

Forty minutes later, Mason and Tess were driving down the highway toward the ice arena. Tess's hair was still damp, and the smell of her shampoo—his shampoo, actually—filled the cab of the truck, making Mason a little crazy as it evoked images of her naked and sliding against his skin the way she'd done the day before.

It had been hard enough trying to find things to occupy his thoughts while she'd been in the shower today and doubly hard not to strip down and join her. But his ego was still bruised, and he wasn't ready to jump back into the bed or the shower with her quite yet.

Or so he kept trying to tell himself.

Mason had driven the newer truck, the one with a center console instead of the long bench seat, and wasn't sure if he'd consciously made that decision so she would have to ride on the other side of the console instead of in the middle next to him as she'd done before. He didn't want to think too hard about it.

He didn't want to think too hard, period. This whole thing made his head hurt. Which made him think of Tess and her migraine and finding her in her car.

Dammit—everything seemed to make him think of her.

She'd only been in his life two and a half days, yet she seemed to already have touched every part of it. She'd met his family, been in his truck, his house, his bed. Heck, she'd even been in his shower.

Ah hell, now he was thinking about the shower again.

He needed to do something to get his mind occupied. Start up a conversation. Say something. Anything.

Anything to get his mind off the memories of her naked curves slick with soap.

He cleared his throat, readying to speak as he searched his brain for a safe subject to discuss. Anything would do—the weather, the traffic, the State of the Union.

They'd left both dogs at home, and the cab was quiet without the activity of the pets. The last two days, he and Tess had talked easily as they rode together, but now he couldn't think of a single thing to say.

"Have you heard anything from the flyers or the sheriff about Dewey?" he finally asked.

Tess shook her head. "Not a single call. It's like his real owners vanished. Or they really did abandon him."

"Who would do that to a dog? Especially a cute little guy like Dewey?"

"I can't imagine." She let out a sigh, then gazed out the window as if she was also searching for something to say. "Tell me more about the game today. All I know is that you and your brothers are playing, and it's some kind of fund-raiser."

"We've been doing it for five or six years now. It was

Mom's idea to begin with. Probably as a way to get Rock home for a few days in the summer. But it usually raises several thousand dollars that they use toward college scholarships for the local high school. And it's fun for the kids to get a chance to play against Rock and some of their dads. They break the teams into twenty-and-under and twenty-one-and-over. Anybody who's played club or for the high school can come out and be on a team."

"That sounds fun. But isn't it a little unfair to have kids playing against a professional NHL player?"

Mason laughed. "Some of those kids are pretty good. And some of the guys are pretty old and only skate a couple of times a year, so it evens out. Besides, we have a rule that Rock isn't allowed to score. He can only pass."

"Smart."

"It evens things out a little. And there's no checking allowed."

"That makes sense." She absently twisted a length of her dark hair around her finger. "How about you? Are you excited for the game?"

He shrugged. "It's no big deal. I mean, it's kind of fun to get on the ice with my brothers again, and we have a good time with the kids. It's usually a pretty fun deal. But the timing sure could have been better. I wish it weren't in the middle of Rock's wedding stuff, but it couldn't be helped. The date had already been set months ago."

"Do a lot of people come out for it?"

"Just about the whole town."

"That sounds exciting. Too bad I'll miss the game." She held up her hand. "Don't get me wrong. I'm happy to help out in the snack bar. Your mom helped me so much last night that I'll do whatever she needs me to."

He chuckled. "Don't worry. You won't miss the game. Mom never wants to miss out on it either, so the snack bar is only open before the game and in between periods. You'll be able to come out and watch all the action."

A smile curved her lips, and she offered him a shy glance. "Good. I wasn't much into sports in high school, but I've always kind of wanted to go to a game and cheer for my guy."

A twinge of pride bloomed in his chest at the idea that she wanted to watch him play. When they were younger, all the girls had come out to see Rock. It was a new feeling to have someone who would be there just to watch him.

Besides his mom, that is. Vivi didn't count.

And he didn't miss the fact that Tess had just said "my guy." Was he *her* guy? Did he want to be?

She reached over and tentatively rested her hand on his.

His head might still be asking that question, but his heart had already made up its mind. He turned his palm over and entwined her fingers with his.

He might be only holding her hand, but she was holding his heart.

What the heck am I doing here? Tess thought as she approached the snack bar. She could see Vivi and Quinn inside, laughing and talking easily as they set out paper plates and plastic cups.

Her heart yearned to be part of that easy sisterhood. She liked these women and enjoyed laughing and joking around with them. Who was she kidding? She loved being around this whole group. She wanted to be part of this family.

A pain in her chest, like a stab of heartburn, reminded her she wasn't part of the family and never would be. She might have had a chance if she'd met Mason in a different place, in a different time. But she hadn't.

She took a deep breath, pushed back her shoulders, and walked through the door of the snack-bar area. "Tessa Kane reporting for duty."

"There she is," Quinn said, crossing the room to give her a hug. "Thanks so much for helping us out."

"I'm happy to. What can I do to help?"

Vivi narrowed her eyes, studying her face. "You sure you're feeling up to this? Your head okay?"

Tess smiled, the heartburn pain flaring again. Except that it wasn't due to gastric issues; it was a real burn, a hard ache to her heart. An ache caused by the knowledge that she was deceiving this incredibly nice woman who needed her help but was more concerned about her health.

"I'm fine. Really. The migraine is gone, and I'm ready to go." She looked around the snack bar. "So put me to work."

"Me too." A petite, curly-haired brunette woman poked her head in the door.

"Hey, Chloe. I'm so glad you could make it. Here, put this on," Quinn said, grabbing the last hockey jersey from the counter and tossing it to her. "Team James is now complete."

The brunette woman flushed, her cheeks turning pink with color as she twisted the fabric of the jersey in her hands. "Oh gosh. It's fine. I'm glad to help," she mumbled. She wore a light blue T-shirt that read "Don't make me use my teacher voice," which seemed funny for the soft-spoken woman and made Tessa like her immediately.

Quinn chucked. "Then get your jersey on and get in here."

Chloe pulled the shirt over her head and rolled up the sleeves as she stepped into the room.

Tess guessed her to be in her late twenties, early thirties, but with her cropped jeans, Converse sneakers, and the too-big jersey, she could have passed for much younger. Her face had a youthful appearance, with big blue eyes and a small pert nose, and her hair was a mop of gorgeous unruly curls that other women paid top dollar to try to emulate. She pulled an elastic from her pocket and tried to confine the mass to a messy bun, offering an apologetic smile as if she were asking forgiveness for her chaotic hair.

"Tessa, this is Chloe Bishop. She was Max's teacher last year. And will be again this year, I guess," Quinn said, nodding her head between the two as she made the introductions. "And this is Tessa Kane, Rock's brother's new girl."

The other woman's face paled. "Colt has a new girl?"

Chloe couldn't see it, but Tess couldn't help but notice the intrigued smiles that flashed between Quinn and Vivienne.

"No. Rock's *other* brother," Quinn explained. "Tess is Mason's girl, or his date for the weekend or whatever."

Tess offered the other woman a little wave. "Nice to meet you, Chloe."

"Oh yes, of course. And I didn't mean anything by that." Her cheeks were crimson again as her hands fluttered in front of her, smoothing down the folds of the jersey. "Colt could absolutely have a new girl. It wouldn't mean anything to me. I don't even really know him."

Tess offered the woman a kind smile. She had a feeling it did mean something to Chloe, and if she didn't really know Colt, it was only a matter of time before that situation would be remedied.

"All right, ladies. We have a lot of work to do here in a short amount of time, so we need to get to work," Vivi instructed, then showed the women around the snack bar.

She assigned each woman to a station—Chloe to drinks, herself to the food, and Tess and Quinn to the registers. "It's not too complicated. We only serve hot dogs, chips, and soda or bottled water to drink. We have popcorn and candy bars for snacks, and the board tells them what varieties we offer for drinks and candy."

Vivi pointed to the menu board on the wall behind her. "These are the choices we have, and if they don't like it, tell them they git what they git and to not throw a fit."

Chloe let out a chuckle. "Oh, that's good. Can I steal that for my classroom?"

"You're welcome to it. And it's nothing Max isn't used to hearing." Vivi looked at Quinn. "You're welcome to use that with my son as well. It's a phrase that comes in handy in lots of scenarios. Not what he expected for dinner? Too bad. Not the flavor cereal he normally buys? Not content with a quickie squeezed in between the third load of laundry and trying to get supper on the table? Tough shit. You git what you git, and you don't throw a fit."

Quinn's eyes went wide, then they all exploded into laughter.

Tess was having the best time. The snack bar was a hoot to run with the other women, and the game was a blast to watch.

Mason looked as much at home on the ice as he did on the ranch.

She was surprised at the ease with which he handled the puck, skillfully taking it down the ice and passing to the other players. He moved as if he'd spent his whole life on skates, easily maneuvering backward and forward.

His shoulders looked even broader with the help of the pads under his jersey, and he seemed impossibly tall as he skated off the ice and dropped onto the bench.

Tess caught her breath as he pulled off his helmet. His black hair was soaked with sweat and sticking up in spiky bunches, and his face was flushed with exertion. A happy smile covered his face as he joked with his teammates. He looked hot as hell, and she couldn't believe she'd been in that guy's bed the night before.

He glanced up in the bleachers and caught her eye, raising his chin and offering her a grin, and she melted into her chair. Feeling a sizzle of electricity surge up her spine and her face heat with warmth, all she could do was grin back and lift her hand in a little wave. She couldn't stop smiling, couldn't hold back that grin if she tried.

Then she couldn't help wondering how many people had just seen that little exchange and how many women had just died a little inside from jealousy.

It was the third period, and she sat in the bleachers

with Quinn. Vivi had told them they'd earned a snack, so they'd each grabbed a soda and a bag of popcorn before they'd shut down the snack bar for the period.

Vivi and Chloe sat a few rows up with Max and Ham. Between the three James boys and Quinn's brother, Logan, they had a family member on the ice to cheer for during most of the game.

The clock had sixteen minutes left, and the younger team had just tied the score, giving the teams two points each.

"Let's go, boys!" Quinn cupped her hand around her mouth and yelled down to the ice. "Come on, Rock." He must have heard her, because he turned his head and flashed a cocky grin, then spun around and skated backward a few feet.

"Show-off," Quinn said, but her smile lacked any malice as she tossed a piece of popcorn toward the glass.

"You guys seem really happy," Tess said, trying to tear her eyes away from Mason, who had put his helmet on and was skating back onto the ice.

"We are."

"I heard somebody say you were high school sweethearts, but then someone else said you'd only been together a few weeks." She hadn't actually heard anyone say that. That was just part of the information Gordon had given her.

"They were both right, in a way," Quinn told her. "We were actually junior high sweethearts and went together all through high school. Then Rock went off to college and started playing hockey with the big leagues. His head and his ego convinced him he was bigger than this small town—and apparently his small-town girlfriend—and he broke things off with me, breaking my heart in the process."

"Oh gosh." Tess knew making small, noncommittal remarks was the best way to keep someone talking.

"Don't worry. I got him back. I got drunk at a party and slept with a local guy I knew Rock would hate. But my plan backfired, because Rock didn't care, or I didn't think he cared at the time, and I ended up pregnant. I'm not complaining. Max is the best thing that ever happened to me, but I was pissed as hell at Rock for years."

"What changed?"

"He did, I guess. Or maybe we both did. He came home at the beginning of the summer to recuperate after getting hurt in a game, and we found our way back to each other. Neither of us are those dumb kids we were in high school. We've both changed. We've grown up, and we've apologized and forgiven each other."

"That's great you found each other again," Tess said around a mouthful of popcorn, trying not to seem too eager to hear the details but loving everything Quinn was telling her.

"It was great. It was kind of funny how it happened. The day he came home, he pulled up beside me on the road to the ranch, all hot and handsome, and I was wearing a pirate costume and riding a kid's bicycle."

Chapter 15

"You're kidding!" Tess couldn't believe it. This story just kept getting better and better.

Where was her notepad? The stuff Quinn was giving her was pure gold.

For the rest of the period, the other woman told her the story of how she and Rock had found each other again, how they'd overcome their differences, and how they'd never stopped loving each other.

Totally engrossed in the story, Tess felt her eyes fill with tears as she heard about the events that had played out over the last several weeks. She forgot she was digging for information and just enjoyed the details of Rock and Quinn's love story.

Quinn wound up her narrative, and Tess realized the game had less than a minute left. They stopped talking and turned their attention toward the players.

Rock was on the bench, but Mason and Colt were on the ice. Colt had just won the face-off and was skating forward.

He slipped between two defensemen, breaking away and charging the goalie. The rest of the team was skating forward, putting all their effort into getting to the net.

Colt skated up to the crease, pulled back his stick, and fired the puck, but didn't aim for the goalie. Instead he passed neatly to Mason, who had just skated to the net.

The puck hit Mason's stick with a smack, and he shot

it forward, sending it sailing over the right shoulder of the goalie and into the net.

The crowd went wild, jumping to their feet and cheering. No one really seemed to care which team won. They had cheered just as crazily when the younger guys had scored earlier. They seemed to love seeing them all play, and everyone appeared to be having a great time.

The teams lined up again in the middle, the clock allowing one more minute of play. Colt was playing center and facing off against a skinny kid who couldn't have been more than sixteen.

The crowd cheered as the ref dropped the puck and the kid snagged it, skating past Colt and breaking away down the ice.

Quinn had told Tess that the older team's goalie was a college kid, home for the summer. He'd played in this game every year, but this year was his first time playing on the men's team.

He crouched low, hitting the ice with his stick as if egging the younger guy on. His college team was the Tigers, and his goalie mask was painted to resemble a tiger's head, with yellow and black stripes slashing across the sides.

One of the older guys tried to catch the kid with the puck, but he weaved around him with the ease of a pro and sped toward the goalie, keeping the puck tight against his stick. The crowd was still on their feet, yelling and cheering as the kid skated toward the left side of the goalie.

At the last second, he dinked to the right side, pulling back his stick and firing a shot at the net.

The goalie's glove shot out and the puck sailed neatly

into its center, landing with a thud as the goalie snatched the puck from the air just as the buzzer sounded, ending the game.

"They won!" Quinn shouted, her popcorn flying as she jumped up and down.

Tess jumped up and down too. Quinn's excitement and the crowd's enthusiasm were contagious. She hadn't been to a lot of hockey games, and never one where she'd cared much about who won. But tonight, cheering for Mason, and being with his family, made her feel as if she'd actually had some skin in the game, and she was thrilled they had won. And that Mason had made the winning goal.

He was going to get the glory for the win tonight, not Rock. She somehow knew Mason would never admit that he cared about that, but the simple fact of it made her heart sing for him.

Whether he talked about it or not, he would know. And the town would know.

She and Quinn raced up the bleachers to hug Vivi and cheer with her and Hamilton. Max was beside himself, shouting and flinging popcorn into the air. Tess couldn't be happier.

For a minute, she let herself believe this was all real. That she was actually part of this family, that Quinn and Chloe were her friends, that Mason was really her boyfriend, and that she wasn't about to pull the rug out from under all of them with an exposé on Rock.

Guilt settled in her stomach like sand at the bottom of a pool. Like when the water looked clean and refreshing, but when someone jumped in, a hard layer of dirt and grit scraped at the bottom of their feet. She knew that feeling. Knew the gritty, sandpaper-against-your-soul feeling of having someone treat you as if they really cared about you, but in reality, they were just using you to get what they wanted.

But this was different from the way she'd been treated. *Wasn't it?*

It had to be.

It was. It *was* different. Because she really did care about Mason.

But I'm still using him.

She pushed the thought aside. *Just enjoy the moment. Enjoy the feeling of belonging to something—to a family. A whole family.*

Vivi clapped her hands together. "All right, girls. Let's head back to the snack bar and get everything cleaned up while the guys shower and dress. Then we can go celebrate."

Ham nodded. "We'll help. I know the fellas are going to be hungry, and I could go for a burger myself."

Really? She'd just seen him and Max scarf down several hot dogs, a bag of popcorn, and some M&M's. Not that it mattered. Hamilton James didn't have an ounce of fat on his wiry frame.

She'd never spent so much time surrounded by gorgeous men whose bodies were muscled and tanned and ridiculously hot. Even Ham, who was old enough to be her dad, still had a rugged handsomeness to him. It was as if they were all versions of the Brawny man, but in western shirts and cowboy boots.

Ham and Max followed the women back to the snack bar to help clean and pack up the extra supplies. With all of them working, it didn't take long. Chloe and Vivi filled the coolers with the extra food while Tess wiped down the counters. Quinn cleaned out the register, compiling the receipts and putting the cash into a plastic money bag.

They'd had a tip jar sitting between their two registers, and Quinn dumped the contents of it into a paper sack and handed it to Tess. "This is yours."

She held her hands up, not taking the bag. "What? No. We should split this between all of us."

Quinn shook her head. "We're good. We want you to take it. Besides, it was your smile that got the majority of these tips."

Yeah right. Quinn was a cowgirl bombshell. With her blond hair and tall, curvy figure, she could have been a model.

"Oh, come on. You got just as many of these, especially because you knew almost every person that we helped."

That was true. Between Quinn, Chloe, and Vivi, they really did know almost everyone who had approached the counter.

"Tess, it's okay. I'm not worried about it. Really. I'm getting married to an NHL hockey player in two days." Quinn nodded her assurance again as she pressed the bag into Tess's hands. "Take it. You worked hard today. You *earned* this money."

Tess blinked at the prick of tears behind her eyes. Quinn got it. She understood. "Fine. I'll take it."

"Good." Quinn turned to finish packing a box with the extra supplies, cutting off any further discussion about the matter.

Tess stuffed the bag into her purse. She *had* earned

this money. She'd worked hard today. And at this point anything would help.

She'd seen several people drop singles into the cup and imagined there were enough to at least put some gas in her tank to get her home and back. She could use a trip home to get fresh clothes and use her own shower. Although no shower would ever be as good as the one in Mason's master bathroom.

Images of her and Mason in the shower filled her mind. Quick flashes of wet hair, slick skin, and being pressed naked against the tiled wall while the steam rose around them had her skin heating, and she hoped no one noticed the blush she was sure was coloring her neck and cheeks.

"Any hot dogs left for the winning team?" Rock's voice boomed as he, Mason, and Colt stepped into the room.

The air filled with the scent of freshly showered men—a heady combination of shampoo, masculine-scented soap, and expensive, musky aftershave.

Quinn let out a cheer, then squealed as Rock crossed the room and lifted her off her feet with a giant bear hug. He grabbed Max with one hand, lifting him into the mix of the family hug as the boy laughed and joined in the happiness.

Tess swallowed at the sudden emotion clogging her throat. She wasn't sure if the feeling was coming from remembering her parents and what it was like to have the bond of a family unit, or if it was from the guilt that filled her, knowing she was an intruder here, an imposter who had wormed her way in.

She didn't have time to think too deeply about it

because her concentration and her breath were taken by the hot cowboy who sauntered her way, a roguish grin covering his face.

"Any chance you've got a hug like that for me?" He opened his arms, and she stepped into them, wrapping herself around his body and pressing her face into his delicious-smelling neck.

"You want a kiss to go with it?" she whispered against his ear.

A low rumble sounded in his throat before he whispered back, "It's all I've been thinking about for the last few hours."

She chuckled. "You were supposed to be thinking about the game."

His lips curved into a grin as they brushed hers. "I'm a good multitasker. I can do two things at once."

"You *are* good with your hands. *And* your lips," she whispered before he captured her mouth in a kiss. A kiss that robbed her of any other thoughts. A kiss that consumed her.

And that was over too soon.

He pulled back as Colt jabbed him in the side. "Dude, you do realize there are other people in this room."

She'd forgotten. For just a second. For just a wonderful, heady, passion-filled second.

Mason grinned down at her, and it was as if the sun had come out on a cloudy day. He really had forgiven her from earlier.

Tess smiled back at him, knowing the kiss was over, but her world had still been rocked. She held on to him, a fold of his shirt clutched in her hand as she tried to regain her bearings. She only hoped Mason was too busy punching his brother in the arm to notice the way her hand shook against his back.

"Great game, guys." Ham congratulated them with a hearty cheer. "And nice work, Mace, with the winning goal. You're the hero of the game."

Mason shook his head. "Thank you, sir. But it was a team effort. And really, Colt was the one who got the puck down the ice, then deked the goalie to make the pass to me. I just fired it in."

"Don't be modest, Brother," Colt said, shoving him in the shoulder. "You owned that goal."

Tess loved watching the slow, almost shy grin of pride spread across Mason's face. It only lasted a second before he shrugged it off, but she'd seen it.

"Whatever," he said. "Where are we going to eat? I'm starving."

"I thought we'd head over to The Creed. That way, you guys can get burgers for a late lunch, and those of us who've been gorging on hot dogs and popcorn can get an appetizer or dessert," Vivi said.

"What's The Creed?" Tess asked Mason.

"It's really The Creedence Tavern. We've just always called it The Creed. It's like a restaurant and pub. It's got pool tables and darts and has the best burgers in town."

"Sounds good," she answered, thankful for the tip money she'd stowed in her purse. She could now actually afford a hamburger.

Mason nudged her and gave a slight raise of his chin toward his brother, who was awkwardly approaching the third-grade teacher who had been quietly blending into the wall at the back of the snack bar.

"Hey, Chloe," Colt said, ducking his head at the petite woman. "I don't know if you remember me. We met earlier this summer at the drive-in. I was with my brother."

Her cheeks went crimson, evidence that she did indeed remember. "Of course. I mean, yes, I do remember you. Hi."

The exchange was almost painful to watch, but also sweet. The bubbly wit Chloe had shown earlier with the women was gone, replaced by a shy demeanor that had the woman's eyes downcast and her body practically shrinking into itself.

"It sounds like we're all going over to The Creed. You're coming along, right?" Colt asked, his voice soft and easy, almost as if he were approaching a skittish horse.

"Oh gosh. I wasn't planning... I'm not sure," she mumbled. "I don't want to intrude."

"What? You wouldn't be intruding. Besides, it looks like you worked hard selling hot dogs today. You earned it. Plus, I want you to come along. I mean, *we* want you to come. With us. All. All of us."

"Oh geez," Mason said under his breath. "Somebody's gotta save this guy." He took a step forward, breaking the connection with Tess as he swept an arm toward the door. "It sounds like there's no arguing, Miss Chloe. You're coming with us. Colt, why don't you grab that cooler, and we'll head out?"

The monster cheeseburgers at The Creed lived up to their names—thick, juicy patties of meat with slabs of cheddar cheese and strips of crispy bacon that melted in the mouth.

They had wrangled a big table in the corner, and Mason and Tess sat across from Colt and Chloe.

Mason was glad to see Tess enjoying her burger and making a dent in the huge pile of fries that covered one side of her plate. Having her appetite back was a good sign she was feeling better, and she wasn't showing any symptoms that the migraine had come back.

Which was good news. She'd scared the hell out of him the night before.

He still wasn't happy that she'd hadn't been completely truthful with him, but the memory of their earlier quarrel faded with every brush of her arm against his, every smile that she flashed his way.

The truth was that he wanted to forgive her, wanted to let this transgression go. Because he really liked Tessa Kane. And he wanted to believe in her, wanted to believe she was the person he thought her to be.

Because the real truth—the secret truth hiding right below the surface—was that he more than *liked* Tess. He wasn't sure when it had happened... Heck, he'd only known her a few days, but he'd always heard that when it happens, the person just knows. And he knew. Knew he was falling for this woman. With her long legs and her infectious laugh, with the clever way she teased him and the tender way she touched him—not just his body, but his heart.

She was a good person, a person who would pitch in to help run a snack bar; who saved ugly, scruffy stray mutts; and who talked about her grandma as if she was her best friend.

Tess had a good heart.

Mason knew they were still getting to know each

other, but in the time they'd been together, whether they were fixing fence in the middle of a thunderstorm or exploring each other's bodies in the shadows of his shower, he felt that she'd shown him her real self.

And Lord help him, he'd shown her his. For the first time in a long time, he'd let down his guard, let himself feel and trust in the company of a woman.

Tess had no ties to his family, no connections to his famous brother. Despite what had happened the night before, he felt that this woman liked him just for him. That she actually thought of him first. And that was a great feeling. A feeling he didn't want to end.

She was just what he needed. Just the kind of woman he wanted. She'd come in as an outsider and, so far, hadn't fallen victim to the hero worship that seemed to overtake women when they were in the presence of Rockford James. And that's just how Mason wanted to keep it.

Tess nudged him, bringing him out his musing as she leaned sideways to whisper in his ear.

All those sappy hearts-and-flowers thoughts of love must have jinxed him, because the words she whispered into his ear had his heart dropping to his feet and his blood rushing to his head.

"Look at your brother," she'd whispered. "He is *so* cute. I think my heart's going to melt."

Chapter 16

Mason whipped his head toward her, expecting to see the familiar look of adoration in her eyes as she stared at his older brother.

But she wasn't looking at Rock.

Mason's shoulders relaxed as he realized she was looking at his *younger* brother. His lips curved into a grin as he watched his normally charismatic and outgoing baby brother stumble over his words and appear almost shy, and his heart felt like it might melt too.

Tess reached under the table and entwined her fingers with his, then laid her head on his shoulder as they watched the timid exchange of conversation between Colt and the third-grade teacher.

"That jersey looks good on you," Colt told her, eliciting a bashful smile.

Chloe reached for the hem of the shirt. "Oh yeah, I almost forgot about this. I should give it back to you. Or I can wash it first and then give it back."

Colt chuckled. "No, it's yours. I want you to keep it."

"Okay." Her hands were still in her lap, and she twisted the hem of the jersey nervously between her fingers.

Mason leaned down, the scent of Tess's hair filling his senses. He wanted to nuzzle his cheek into the silky brown strands, but instead he whispered, "You want to get out of here?"

His lips had touched her ear, and he liked the way

her shoulders had scrunched as if a shiver had run down her back.

She smiled up at him. "Sure."

"I need to get back and get a few chores done, but then…" He'd started to say *I'm all yours*, but couldn't quite get those words out. Even though he knew he was.

Somewhere in the last few days, he had become all hers. And no matter what happened next, whether she stayed in his life to see where this led, or if she went back home after the wedding, Tessa Kane had ruined him for any other woman.

"…we can hang out," he finished, then tapped the table to get his brother's attention. "Hey, Colt."

The other man's head popped up as if he'd been caught stealing a cookie from the cookie jar, and Mason held back a smile, clearing his throat instead. "We're gonna head back to the ranch. I'll get the cattle fed in the main corral, but can you run a couple of bales of hay out to the south pasture when you get home?"

"Yeah. Sure. No problem."

"Thanks." He pushed his chair back and directed his comments to the rest of the table. "We're taking off. See you all later."

Tess leaned into him, her voice low. "But we haven't got the check yet," she said, reaching for her purse. "I earned some tips at the snack bar this afternoon, and I can pay for my own meal."

He put his hand on top of hers. "Don't worry about it. This one's on me."

"But…"

"Seriously, save your money." He wrapped an arm around her neck and spoke into her ear, partly because he wanted to keep his voice low and partly because he just liked having his mouth that close to her neck. "I always pay when I take *my girl* out for a meal."

He was testing the words a little, seeing how it felt to have them roll off his tongue in a casual sentence. He liked it.

And from the smile he caught forming on her lips, Tess liked it too.

Tess followed Mason around as he ran through his afternoon chores.

She liked watching him—liked the way the muscles worked across his back as he tossed sections of hay over the fence, liked the way his biceps flexed as he shook grain into the troughs, and especially liked the way his butt looked as he swaggered into the corral.

Besides how great his butt looked—and he truly had an amazing butt—she also liked listening to him talk to the farm animals. He had an easy way of speaking to the cows and horses as he walked among them, and he chatted amicably with all the ranch dogs as if they could actually understand him and respond back.

It was fun to see how little Dewey had inserted himself into ranch life, running around with Theo and Watson, and Tess liked the way Mason had adopted him too and treated the little dog as if he were one of his own.

"That's the last of it," Mason said, as he stepped out of the barn. He brushed the dust from his pants and tilted his head at her. "You want to go for a ride?"

"Sure." She took a few steps toward the truck.

But he touched her arm. "Not in the truck. On the horse."

"Oh yeah. Okay," she stammered.

He narrowed his eyes. "You ever been on a horse before?"

"Once. When I was about ten, and I spent a long weekend at a summer church camp."

"Did you like it?"

"I'm not sure. I fell off before we made it out of the corral, and I never tried again."

"Well, you know what they say about falling off a horse?"

"Yeah. I do. And it sounds like I'm about to get back on one."

He reached up and skimmed the back of his fingers against her cheek. A spark of heat flickered down her spine. "Don't worry. I won't let you fall this time. I'll hold on to you."

The spark of heat turned into a full-blown flame, and she was tempted to fan herself.

"I just got an idea," he said.

She'd been getting plenty of ideas.

He held up his hand. "Wait right here."

Tess stood where she was, unable to do anything but obey his commands, her skin still warm from where his fingers had grazed her. She watched him hurry across the driveway and bound up the porch steps and into the main house.

He came out a few minutes later, a leather saddlebag slung over his shoulder and a shit-eatin' grin on his face.

What was he up to now? She didn't know. And she didn't care.

But she couldn't wait to find out.

He led her into the barn and over to a stall where a

gorgeous brown horse stood lazily munching some hay. She lifted her head and let out a soft whinny as Mason approached the stall.

"Hey, Gypsy," Mason said, setting the saddlebag on the ground and holding his hand out to stroke the horse's neck. She nuzzled her nose against his chest, drawing a soft chuckle from him. "She thinks I have a sugar cube for her."

A sugar cube? Tess hadn't seen a sugar cube since she was a kid.

Everything here was so different from what she was used to. The pace of life seemed slower, the sense of community seemed stronger, and everything just seemed simpler. She liked it.

"Do you?" she asked. "Have a sugar cube?"

He offered her a flirty grin, then drew a Ziploc bag full of small white cubes from his front shirt pocket. "Darlin', I've always got a little sugar for my favorite ladies."

She laughed out loud, a full hearty laugh. "Oh my gosh. That might just rank in the top-ten cheesiest lines I've ever heard. Does that ever work?"

He laughed along with her. "I don't know. It's the first time I ever tried it. Did it work for you?"

"I don't know." She lowered her voice, affecting a sultry tone. "You haven't given me the sugar yet."

He opened the bag and hooked a cube out with his finger, then slipped his arm around her waist and pulled her to him. "Open your mouth."

She did as he said, sucking in a slight gasp at the sudden nearness of him.

"Lick your lips."

How could such simple directions sound so indecently sexy?

She swallowed, trying to keep her lips from trembling as she ran her tongue across them.

He watched the motion of her tongue, his eyes going dark and greedy. Then he lifted his hand, and holding the sugar cube between his fingers, he ran it over her bottom lip, leaving a sweet trail of sugary granules. Dipping his head, he kissed her mouth, a light kiss, just enough to dust his lips with the sugar as well.

She let out another soft gasp as he ran his tongue along her bottom lip, licking at the sugar.

Pulling back, he again slid the cube along her mouth. This time, more sugar stuck to her moist lips. Then he slid the cube between her lips.

"Hold it on your tongue," he whispered, his voice husky. "Let it dissolve before you swallow."

She knew he was talking about the sugar—of course he was talking about the sugar—but the way he said it was just about the sexiest thing she'd ever heard.

Holding the square cube on her tongue, she let the sweet sugar dissolve, just as he told her to do, but before she could swallow, he captured her mouth in another kiss. This time, it wasn't a slow, soft brush of his lips. This time it was full and deep, mouths open, and the sugar, grainy and sweet, swirled and graded between their tongues.

He kissed her a long time, longer than the sugar lasted, and when he finally pulled back, her lips were swollen and she felt like she had been thoroughly kissed.

She let out a deep breath. "Wow. I'm going to go ahead and give you that one. We're going to call the 'I've always got a little sugar' line a definite win."

He chuckled as the horse nudged his arm. "I think my other girl is jealous."

My *other* girl? That was the second time tonight he'd made that reference. Did he consider *her* his girl? Did she *want* to be considered his girl?

If he kissed her like that again, she would consider being just about anything of his.

He fed the horse a sugar cube and gave her a quick nuzzle on the neck. He held out another cube, and Tess's pulse raced at what he had in mind for this one. "Why don't you give her one too?" he suggested, nodding at the horse.

"Oh, okay." Not exactly what she had in mind, but she was up for it.

"Hold your hand out flat, and let her take it off your palm."

She did as he told her, trying to hold her hand steady as the horse jutted her head forward. Tess let out a small nervous laugh as the horse's velvety muzzle nibbled the sugar almost daintily from her palm.

Mason patted the horse's neck. "She's a sweetheart. I've had her for close to ten years, and she's the best horse I've ever had." He pointed to the stall gate. "You can stand there while I get her saddled up."

Tess took a few steps back and leaned on the gate as she watched Mason saddle the horse. His movements were confident and steady, and she liked the way he talked easily to the horse the whole time, telling her about his day and the alumni game.

She had to bite her lip to keep from laughing when he told the horse he'd scored the winning goal. Her eyes widened as the horse stamped her foot and gave her head a nod, as if she understood and was offering him congratulations.

He was right. She was a great horse.

Finally, he slipped the saddlebag over the saddle horn, then led the horse from the stall. He folded an extra blanket and secured it behind the saddle and across the horse's rump.

"It would be better if you were wearing jeans, but this will at least be softer on your legs and give you a little more cushion," he said, climbing into the saddle. He reached a hand down for her. "You ready?"

"No." She wiped her suddenly sweaty hands on her shorts. "Are you sure we can both ride her?"

"Oh yeah. She's a workhorse. Don't worry. She's strong." He patted the horse's neck, then pulled his foot from the stirrup. "Lift up your foot and put it in the stirrup, then grab my hand, and I'll pull you up."

She stared at his hand. Why did this have to involve him *lifting* her up again?

Although Mason had proved his muscles weren't all for show. The last few days, he'd carried her on his back and cradled her against his chest. He could probably pull her up on this damn horse.

Lifting her leg, she awkwardly stuffed her sneakered foot into the stirrup then grabbed his hand and heaved. Pushing off with her other foot, she half climbed, half fumbled her way up as he pulled her by the arm, and she swung her leg over the horse's backside.

"See, that wasn't so hard."

Not for you.

She tried to slow her breathing and pretend she hadn't just worked muscles that hadn't been used in ages. Blowing her bangs from her sweaty forehead, she wiggled around, situating her legs as she settled in behind the saddle.

"You good?"

She pulled at her jersey and the hem of her shorts, trying to adjust her clothes back into place without falling off the back of the horse. Letting out a breath, she pushed back her shoulders and gathered her courage. "Yeah."

"Hold on."

She wrapped her arms around his middle, pressing her chest to his back as the horse trotted toward the mountain range behind the ranch.

They rode for close to an hour, the horse plodding up the side of the hill and along the dirt trails. The horse was obviously used to this ride, and Mason assured Tess that Gypsy knew what she was doing and didn't want to fall off the side of the mountain any more than they did.

Once Tess settled down, she relaxed and enjoyed the ride. She and Mason chatted easily, mostly with him telling her stories about the ranch, but they also rode in companionable silence at times and just enjoyed the view.

"Here it is," Mason said, as the horse trotted to the top of a ridge. "Isn't it gorgeous?"

Tess caught her breath as she took in the beautiful landscape.

In the small valley below them, a crystal-blue lake shimmered in the late-afternoon sun. One side of the valley was a rugged cliff, and a series of thin waterfalls fell down its face, splashing into the far edge of the lake.

It looked like a painting. Or like something out of a movie. Tess considered pinching herself to make sure this wasn't a dream.

But the ache in her legs from an hour on the back of a horse told her this was indeed real.

The horse descended into the valley, confidently plodding its way down the path.

They stopped in a clearing at the water's edge, and Mason helped her climb down. Her legs felt like jelly, and she reached for his arm as he dismounted next to her.

"It takes a minute to get your legs back," he told her. "It helps to walk around a little."

She took a few tentative steps toward the water's edge as Mason let the horse get a drink, then led it to a giant cottonwood and wrapped its reins around a low branch. Tess grinned as she saw him sneak it another sugar cube.

He untied the blanket and spread it on the ground in front of the tree. The large roots snaked in and out of the ground, forming a perfect hollow where they could sit and lean back against the tree. "You can rest here while I collect some wood to make a fire."

"I can help," she said, already searching the ground for loose branches.

He chuckled. "Somehow I knew you'd say that."

They worked together to collect enough branches and dry wood for Mason to build a small fire, then sank down on the blanket to watch it burn. He grabbed the saddlebag and pulled it toward them.

"I'm dying to see what you brought in that bag," Tess said, peering over his hand.

"It's almost worth dying for," he told her as he drew out a blue metal tin and a mason jar. The jar was filled with chunks of strawberry and slices of lemon floating in a pink liquid.

He lifted the lid on the tin, and the heady scent of chocolate wafted into the air. "These are my mom's chocolate chip cookies, fresh baked this morning." He took out a cookie and split it in half, feeding her one side and popping the other half into his mouth.

An explosion of vanilla cookie and thick, chocolaty chips hit her tongue, and she groaned at the delicious flavor. She tried to ignore the fact that there were probably a zillion calories in each and pretended that calories fed to you by a hot cowboy didn't count. "These *are* amazing," she said around the mouthful of cookie.

"I told you. Wait until you try this." He held up the mason jar. "This is my Mom's strawberry wine. It was my grandma's secret recipe, but my mom perfected it and makes a batch every summer. It's a little sweet, but I think you're gonna like it."

"I love anything that starts with, 'This was my grandma's secret recipe.'"

He twisted off the lid.

"Did you bring glasses too?"

"No, babe. Strawberry wine is best when you drink it straight out of the jar." He held the jar to her lips and tipped it slightly forward.

Had she ever drunk anything out of a mason jar before? She couldn't think of when, but there were a lot of new *Mason* experiences she was trying, and so far all of them had rocked her world and turned out to be amazing. She hesitantly took a sip. A piece of strawberry slipped in, and she bit into it as she swallowed.

The wine was sweet, but the mixture of strawberries and lemon gave it a bit of a tart bite. The fruity flavor combined with the tang of the alcohol gave it a kick, and the flavors mixed deliciously with the chocolate of the cookie she'd just eaten.

She was a fan. "It's good. Delicious." She took another drink.

"I told you." He took a swig, and they passed the jar back and forth between them, sharing the sweet wine.

It went down as smoothly as actual lemonade, and it didn't take long for them to polish off the cookies and most of the wine.

Tess's head felt a little spinny, but her body felt loose and light. She let out a sigh as she leaned back on her elbows. Everything about this day seemed perfect. The campfire, the sweet strawberry wine, the blanket laid out in front of the most beautiful lake. And the gorgeous man who sat beside her, absently running his fingers along the edge of her bare leg.

He had his back against the tree, leaning casually against it as if he didn't have a care in the world. He'd taken off his hat and hung it on a branch, and a light breeze picked up a strand of his black hair and blew it sideways.

He was so gorgeous. Looking at him made it hard for her to breathe.

She wanted him so much. Wanted so much for all of this to be real.

She'd had too much wine, and she was feeling way too good. Which was usually right around the time she got herself into trouble.

"Thanks for bringing me here. It's wonderful," she said, slurring the last word just the slightest bit.

"I knew you would like it."

I like you. A lot.

She wanted to say it, but she couldn't. "Do you bring all your 'girls' up here?"

He shook his head. "Nope. I haven't ever brought anyone up here. I mean, I've been here with my family, but I've never brought a woman here."

I'm the first woman he's brought here. That has to mean something.

"I guess that makes me special." She let out a tiny hiccup.

"Yeah, it definitely makes you special. This is one of my favorite places, and I wanted to share it with you. I guess because you're becoming one of my favorite people." He brushed at a bit of dust that had settled on the knee of his jeans. "Sorry, that sounded stupid."

"I think it sounded sweet."

"You're sweet." He jerked a thumb at the lake. "The water's a little cold, but I was thinking maybe we could go skinny-dipping."

She nudged his shoulder. "I swear it seems like every time I'm with you, we're doing something that gets me wet." She felt her eyes widen.

Oh. My. Gosh. She couldn't believe she'd said that.

A naughty grin played across his lips.

She held up her hands, fighting the giggle bubbling up inside her. "I didn't mean it like that…" She stopped. Maybe she did. Swallowing the giggle, she took a breath, gathering her courage, then climbed over him.

Straddling his lap, she offered him a coy smile. "Actually, I *did* mean it like that."

His face split into a sexy smile.

"And furthermore, I think we should forgo the dipping, and get straight to the skinny." She grabbed the hem of her shirt and tugged it over her head, then tossed it to the ground next to the blanket.

Chapter 17

TESS WAS BLAMING IT ON THE WINE.

It had to be the mixture of the alcohol and her newfound brazenness that had her straddling Mason, whipping her shirt off, and practically demanding he take her now.

"You make a convincing argument," Mason said, gazing down at her lacy bra. "I have to agree. The skinny is always the best part anyway."

Her hair was pulled back in a ponytail, and she reached for the elastic, sliding it out and letting her hair fall free. Using her fingers, she combed through her hair, shaking her head to let the curls fall loosely around her shoulders.

He reached up, running his hands through the strands, all the while holding her gaze. His fingers trailed down her neck, then slid under her bra strap and drew it slowly down her shoulder.

She caught her breath, heat swirling in her stomach, as he sat forward and placed a kiss on the soft dent in her shoulder where her strap had been. His hands smoothed up her back, easily unsnapping her bra and pulling it free of her body.

His fingers tickled her skin as he skimmed them along her ribs before cupping one of her breasts in his palm. He dipped his head and ran his tongue along the top curve. Her nipples tightened with the combination of being exposed and anticipation of his touch.

Moving his head lower, he breathed on the taut, hard nub, then sucked it between his lips.

She let out a gasp, feeling the pull of it down to her toes as sparks of sensation surged through her body.

He slipped his hands around her waist, holding her captive as his mouth did delicious things to her breasts, sucking and licking, nibbling at the tender nubs and sending waves of heat to her already sensitive core. She moved her hips, rubbing against him, and loved the small moan he released against her breast.

Lifting his head, he dragged her chest to his and took her mouth in a deep, hungry kiss. She gripped his shoulders, riding his hips to create a delicious friction.

His fingers fumbled with the button of her shorts, finally freeing it and sliding down the zipper. "I want you naked," he demanded against her mouth, then lifted her and easily turned her over so she was lying on the blanket under him. He tugged her shorts and panties down her legs, leaving her fully naked and panting on the blanket as he yanked his shirt over his head. His boots came off next, then he stood to shimmy out of his jeans.

Her gaze traveled the length of him, taking in every muscle, every solid plane, every hard inch of him. And he had plenty of muscles and plenty of inches.

"I hope that saddlebag also has some condoms in it," she said, her voice husky with need.

"It doesn't."

"What?" she cried.

An impish grin spread across his face as he pulled several packets from his jeans pocket. "But I did bring some. You know, just in case."

"Thank goodness." She returned his naughty grin. "I hope you brought enough."

He let out a chuckle. "Damn woman, I *do* like you." Dropping most of the packets to the blankets, he kept one in his hand, quickly ripping it open and covering himself before he settled between her knees.

He brushed his fingertips along her stomach, a caress so light and tender she shivered with the need for more. "Your skin is so soft," he whispered, his voice achingly sweet. He slid his hand lower, slowly skimming his fingertips along her thighs, then into the crevice between her legs.

She arched her hips, already anticipating, craving his touch. A gasp escaped her, and she closed her eyes, focusing on the circular motions of his hand. Heat centered and pooled between her legs, and her chest rose and fell as she struggled to fill her lungs. She wanted this man so much. Wanted to feel him, to touch him, to know every part of him.

Another gasp as he took his hand away and filled her instead, completing the ultimate connection between them.

Intertwining his fingers with hers, he lifted her hand above her head and laid a trail of hot, greedy kisses along her neck before taking her mouth in a deep, hungry kiss. His tongue thrust deeply, his hunger consuming her, as their bodies moved in rhythm, already seeming to know what the other one needed.

She threw back her head, lifting her hips as circles of liquid bliss grew tighter, swirling with growing intensity in the quivering spot of sensation between her thighs and bringing pure deliciousness to every cell in her body.

With her free hand, she gripped his shoulder, holding on as he moaned into her mouth, the vibration echoing through her body.

Every sensation built upon the last, until the tension had her ready to explode.

Panting, desperate for breath, hungry for release, she finally cried out as the warm waves of satisfaction rolled through her.

He tightened his grip on her hand, then tensed and shuddered, matching her release as a low growl escaped him.

He collapsed on top of her, clutching her body to his as he buried his face in her neck and sighed into her skin.

A contented smile curved her lips as she wrapped herself around him, reveling in the weight of his body on hers and the warm, intimate connection.

It was just getting dark by the time they made it back to the bunkhouse, and the night had started to cool.

Mason took off his boots and built a fire while Tess fed the dogs and made herself and Mason each a cup of hot tea.

It all felt very cozy and domestic as they sat together on the sofa, the fire crackling and popping and the two dogs curled together at their feet. Mason's arm rested along the back of the sofa, while his long legs stretched out across the coffee table.

Tessa cradled the warm mug in her hands, her feet tucked under her as she sat next to him. "I was thinking about how this whole thing has happened so fast and that maybe we should slow things down a little and just spend some time talking. You know, try to get to know a little more about each other."

"I feel like I've gotten to know you pretty well." He waggled his eyebrows at her.

She laughed. "Not in the Biblical sense."

"The Biblical sense, huh? Are you going to take me to church now?"

"Stop it. You know what I mean. Get to know each other more *intimately*. Like figuring out things that we like or don't like." *Like a real couple*. She caught herself before she said it. But that's what she wanted them to be. Not just having a couple of dates, but starting a real relationship. They certainly felt like a "real" couple to her already. That thing he'd done to her up at the lake was real enough anyway. But that was sex, and sex could feel real without having real feelings involved.

He ran his finger lightly down the side of her arm. "So how about I pick a new place to kiss you, and you tell me if you like it or not."

She rolled her eyes. "So maybe *intimately* was not the best choice of words. Let's make it easy. How about we start with you telling me three things that you love."

"Okay, that's easy. God, my country, and my mom."

Hmm. "That was easy."

He shrugged.

"But I already knew all of those. I was thinking of maybe three things that you love that I don't already know about. Things that I would only know if we had actually spent a lot of time together."

"Hmm. Well, I love listening to Johnny Cash and Merle Haggard, and I love my mom's fried chicken and pretty much anything with maple frosting smeared on it." He wiggled his eyebrows again. "And I do mean *anything*."

Oh. My. Quick, where can we find some maple frosting?

She nudged his arm. "Stay focused." She was telling herself as well. Although it was hard to remain intent on anything other than the sexy cowboy sitting next to her who was gazing at her as if he wanted to eat her up—maple frosting or not. "Tell me what else you love."

"I don't know. I love a cold beer after a hot day, and old John Wayne movies, and I'm partial to peanut butter cups. Is that good?"

"That's a start."

"What about you? I already know you love creamer with a little coffee in it, and you like to order a side of mayo to dip your burger in. What else do you love?"

She wrinkled her nose and moved her mouth from side to side. "Well, I love to have my back scratched, and I *love* crunchy Cheetos. Like, I could eat them every day of my life. And I love to read. I could get lost in a book and spend all day reading." She shook her head. "I'm terrible at this game because I love tons of stuff. I love soft-serve ice cream and flannel sheets and feather pillows. I love a summer day spent at the pool and going to the movies. And I love, love, love macaroni and cheese. I could eat it until my sides bust."

"I knew about the mac and cheese from the first night I met you."

She grinned. "Oh yeah. Then I should probably also add that I love barbecue. That was way more than three, but I'm loving this, so give me more."

"Fair enough. I love grilled cheese sandwiches and

warm pecan pie with a scoop of vanilla ice cream melting on top of it. I'm a rancher, so I love the rain, especially a good ground-soaking rain. My livelihood can at times depend on it, but I also just love the sound and the smell of it. And I love getting caught in it with a gorgeous woman."

She laughed. "Okay, now tell me three things you hate. And they can't be things everyone hates, like the smell of a dead skunk or stepping in dog poo. But something that only someone that knows you well would know that you hate."

"Let me think on that. You go first."

"For starters, I *hate* onions. *Loathe* them. And I really hate when people say they're so small you won't even notice. I notice."

"My brother is like that too. He can pick the smallest onion out of any bite of food. So, no onions. Got it. What else?"

"You already know I hate public speaking. Not just hate, but am terrified of it. And I also hate rude people, and oh, I absolutely hate snakes. Now you."

"All right. I hate rap. I hate it so much, I refuse to call it music. And I hate stupid drivers, and shopping malls, and bank fees. I hate bullies, and mosquito bites, and anyone who knows me well knows that I hate needles. Getting a shot gives me the willies."

"That one surprises me. Big, tough cowboy like you hates getting a little shot?"

He shrugged, then narrowed his eyes, his lighthearted expression turning serious. "Something else I hate is the idea of you sleeping in your car again tonight." He reached for her and pulled her into his lap. "So you have three choices. You can either stay over at my mom's in one of the guest rooms or, if you feel like you must sleep in your car, you can do it here in front of my house, so at least I know you're safe."

"Gah... I don't like my car that much. What's the third choice?"

"The third choice is you can stay here...with me."

"This doesn't seem like that tough of a choice."

"So...?"

"So...I'll stay."

"With me?"

"Yes. I'll stay with you."

"Good." He dipped his head and pressed a sweet kiss to her lips, then nuzzled the side of her neck. "I also love the smell of your hair. Especially when it smells like my shampoo, because that means you've been in my shower."

She liked playing this game, liked learning things about him.

He narrowed his eyes at her, his expression turning serious. "Will you tell me something about you? Something a little more serious than how much you love Cheetos."

She swallowed. "Sure. What do you want to know?"

"You said earlier that you hadn't been out on a date in a year."

"Yeah. So?"

"So why not?"

She shrugged, the blanket of insecurity and self-doubt settling around her shoulders. "I'd rather not say. It's humiliating."

His brows knit together. "Did someone hurt you?"

She let out a shuddering sigh, surprised at the prick of tears that could still come so quickly to her eyes. "You could say that."

"Tell me," he said, picking up her hand and holding it in his.

Could she? Could she really tell him?

I have to. If I want this to be real.

She had to trust him, to tell him the truth. If she wanted this to be the real deal, then she had to tell him the truth about herself. Not about Rock and the stupid story, but about her. About *her* story—about what happened to her. And if he didn't want to see her anymore, then so be it. At least she'd tried.

She leaned against his sturdy chest and squeezed his hand. "You know how I told you that my parents died when I was younger?"

"Yeah. You said they were in a car accident."

"Well, what I didn't tell you was that it was my fault."

Chapter 18

"Your fault?" Mason asked. "That's ridiculous. You were a kid. It couldn't have been your fault."

Tess squeezed her eyes together and sucked in a deep breath, then let it out slowly. "I can assure you it was. I mean, I wasn't driving the car, but it was my fault that we were in the accident."

"We? You were in the car?"

She nodded. "The back seat. We were going on a trip to visit my other grandparents, my mom's folks. It was a four-hour drive, and at the time, I had this little set of dolls that I used to play with all the time. They came in their own special case and had a bunch of different outfits and accessories. I could play with them for hours and had planned to set up a whole adventure for them in the back seat during the trip. Except I forgot to bring them. My dad had reminded me three times to put anything I wanted to bring by the door, and I forgot. I'd been playing with them in my room and got distracted and left them on my bed."

Her shoulders hunched forward, and she brought her knees closer to her chest, as if curling into herself might guard her from the truth of the story. "We'd only been gone about fifteen minutes. We'd just gotten on the highway when I realized that I'd forgotten them. And I started crying, begging my father to go back, acting like those dolls were the key to heaven instead of some stupid plastic toys. He refused at first, said that I would learn for next time, which is what any good parent would do. And they were good parents." She choked on her words, then whispered, "The best."

Mason nodded but didn't say anything. His expression remained calm, caring, and he acted like he understood. But he couldn't understand. No one could.

Talking about it brought the memories back, as sharp and as clear as if she were sitting in the back seat again, the gray fabric of the seat belt digging into her chest as she leaned forward to plead with her father.

A shiver ran over her skin, and Mason tightened his arm around her shoulders.

"Normally my dad wouldn't be swayed, and normally I wouldn't have pressed it, but I'd had my heart set on playing with those dolls during the whole car trip, and I burst into tears, crying and sobbing and pleading with my dad to go back. I cried so hard I almost made myself sick. And he finally relented. I had thrown a big-enough fit, been enough of a brat, and he finally agreed to turn around and go back. He was angry and frustrated and must not have been paying enough attention when he turned the car around, because that's when we got hit."

She heard Mason's sharp intake of breath, but couldn't look at him. "Broadsided by another car that sent us off the road. We hit the shoulder and the car slid off the embankment, rolling several times and finally coming to a stop against the side of a tree. The car was tipped forward, and I was hanging from my seat belt. I can still remember the screech of the metal and the sounds of my mom's terrified screams. Then everything went silent. No engine, no other cars around us, no sounds of breathing from anyone but me."

She shook her head and swallowed at the thickness in her throat.

Mason brushed away the tears that wet her cheeks. She hadn't even realized she'd been crying. She sniffed and let out a shuddering breath. "Anyway, after that I went to live with my grandma...my dad's mom, Mimi. And she is the most incredible woman. She took in this traumatized little girl without a second thought. And I swear, she has the patience of a saint.

"I didn't talk for a year. Was inconsolable. Mimi tried. She was pretty much the only person I could stand to be around. And she never pressured me. Never tried to make me to talk. She just loved me. And she brought me journals and markers and reams of notebooks to express myself, but she always told people, 'She'll talk when she's ready.'"

"And obviously you must have finally started talking again at some point."

"I did. Finally. But I wasn't really ever the same. I had been a little timid before, but after the accident, I was painfully shy. And suddenly I was scared of everything, scared of my own shadow. And when I eventually started talking again, I had developed a slight stutter when I spoke. I went to therapy for years—speech therapy, physical therapy because I'd broken my leg—and I saw a child therapist for PTSD. I don't know if they called it that back then, but that's what it was."

"But surely if you saw a therapist, they would have told you that the accident wasn't your fault. You were just a kid." Mason's eyes were full of compassion, and he pulled her closer.

She shook her head. She didn't want him feeling sorry for her. "It doesn't matter how old I was. I was acting like a brat, and if I hadn't thrown such a fit, or if I had just remembered my dolls in the first place, we never would have turned the car around and my family would still be here today."

"You don't know that. Accidents happen every day. And that's what happened to your family. An accident."

He wasn't going to convince her, but the fact that she'd told him, and he hadn't seemed to judge or condemn her, loosened a small amount of the tightness in her chest.

"I don't know why I told you all of that. I could have started with the fact that I used to have a problem with stuttering."

He brushed a loose strand of hair from her cheek. "I'm glad you told me."

She pushed her shoulders back and blew out a breath. "I did eventually grow out of the stuttering. Except for when I get really nervous, then it can come back. Which leads me to the answer to your question of why I haven't dated in a year.

"I was working for this company, in a leadership type role, I guess." She'd been with another magazine, one that appreciated stories about kitten rescuers, and had worked her way up to being an associate. "I met a guy who had just started, and he must have thought dating me would somehow help his chances of moving up in the company. It wouldn't have. I had zero pull. But anyway, I didn't know that's what he was doing at the time, and I really liked him. He seemed cute and funny and acted like he liked me too. But then I had to give this big presentation to a bunch of people…"

She paused and looked at Mason. "You can see where this is going, can't you? Me, speaking in front of a bunch of people. It doesn't matter what it was about. All that matters is that I got through it. I was nervous as hell, and my stutter came out a few times, but I thought I'd done okay. After it was over, I went to find Rob, the guy I was dating. He'd been in the room, and I guess I was looking to celebrate a little, or for some confirmation that I'd done okay.

"I found him in the break room with a group of our colleagues. He didn't know I'd come in, because he was too busy telling a story." She took a deep breath. "A story that involved an imitation of a part of my presentation where I'd really stuttered."

A small hangnail had formed on her thumb, and she picked at the loose piece of her cuticle. She couldn't look at Mason. It was too humiliating. "He was apparently mocking me and the thing about myself that I was the most self-conscious of. And everyone was laughing, like he was hilarious and I was a big joke."

Mason's hands clenched into fists. "What an asshole. I would have punched the guy in the throat."

She blinked at the tears pricking her eyes and let out a light chuckle, surprised that she could laugh at all. She tried to keep going, but couldn't seem to find her voice. "It was the single most humiliating moment of my life," she finally whispered. "I was mortified."

"Why? You shouldn't have been embarrassed. That idiot Rob is the one who should have been embarrassed.

And all the jackasses standing around listening to him make fun of you. One of them should have stepped up and knocked out a couple of that jerk's teeth. See how good a storyteller he'd be then."

A small smile pulled at her lips. She liked the way Mason's body tensed, the way his brows knit together in obvious anger, the way he stood up for her and wanted to belt the guy instead of awkwardly listening, then changing the subject as fast as he could. Which was what she'd expected him to do.

Another piece of the hard shell sealed around her heart cracked and fell away.

She leaned forward and pressed a kiss to Mason's whiskered cheek.

"What was that for?"

"For wanting to punch Rob in the throat."

"I want to do more than that. I'd like to hook him by the leg to the back of my tractor and haul him around the pasture for an hour or so. Do you have his address? I could find this guy."

She shook her head, a real grin forming on her face. "No. I deleted his contact from my phone. In fact, I quit my job. That day. I never saw or talked to him again."

"Why did *you* quit? He should have been fired. You could have called HR, got him and the rest of them sacked."

"I didn't want to. I didn't ever want to face those people again. He eventually realized that I was standing there and everyone tried to apologize, but it was too late. I couldn't stand to be there another second. So I left. I eventually found another job, but I didn't go out with another guy, until…well, you, I guess."

"Wow. I can see why. But Tess, you gotta know, most men—hell, most human beings—aren't like that."

"I know. And I know there are good guys out there." She offered him a shy smile. "Present company included. But it wasn't worth the risk. It was just easier to stay home." She looked down at Dewey, who was curled between Theo and the side of the sofa next to Mason's legs. "I can see why some women prefer the company of dogs."

He chuckled, then rested the back of his fingers against her cheek. "Thank you."

"For what? For bringing down the mood with my sad story and depressing life."

"No. For sharing your story with me. It means a lot."

She tried to swallow around the swelling in her throat, then cleared it instead. "Well, enough of this gloomy stuff." She offered him a brave smile. "Let's go back to talking about pecan pie and soft-serve ice cream and your favorite country-and-western singers."

His eyes narrowed, and he looked like he was about to say something else, but instead, he smiled back, letting out the tension in his shoulders. "Okay. Who are your favorite country singers?"

"No way. I'm done talking about me. I've already said more words in the last twenty minutes that I usually do in a whole day." It was true. She'd shared more with Mason than she had with most of her girlfriends. She wanted to move on, talk about something lighter, something that would make him smile again, make him laugh. "Tell me more about some things that you love. Besides maple frosting, I know you love your mom and your brothers—"

"And my horse and my dog."

"That goes without saying. Of course, your horse and your dog." She tapped her lip, searching for another question to ask. "How about this... Have you ever been *in* love?"

His eyes widened, and he studied her face as if trying to decide if she wanted a serious answer or a light one.

"I thought I was," he finally said. "Once. But I was mistaken."

"Mistaken? What do you mean?"

"It was a long time ago. I was a kid. I had all these big feelings, and I thought they were love." He picked up a strand of her hair and wrapped it around his fingers. "But just recently, I met someone who is challenging everything I thought I knew about love. Who makes my heart pound in my chest so hard that I think it might break through my skin."

He stared at her mouth and ran the edge of his thumb along her bottom lip. "Who flashes me a smile and makes me feel like I'm a superhero. Who trusted me enough to share the deepest story of her heart." He brushed the back of his fingers along her side. "And who keeps me awake at night thinking about the feel of her skin and the taste of her lips."

"Just how recently did you meet this person?" she whispered, her own heart beating a quick staccato rhythm.

"Just a few days ago."

"A few days ago, huh? How did you meet?"

A grin tugged at the corners of his lips. "She flashed me her bra, and I was lost."

"Wow. That must've been some bra."

"It was. In fact, I'm hoping to get another look at it soon."

She let out a small chuckle, then pulled her jersey over her head and tossed it behind the sofa. What was it about this man that had her whipping her shirt off every time she was around him? "Is this soon enough?"

He glanced down. "Mmm-hmm. And it still looks pretty good. But I know how it could look better."

"How's that?"

"If it were lying on the floor."

Tessa sat at the kitchen table the next morning and watched Mason pull on his boots. Her hair was loose, and all she had on was the hockey jersey from the day before and a pair of panties.

He'd made her breakfast, and the scent of bacon and maple syrup still lingered in the air. "I'm sorry to leave you like this," he said. "But it can't be helped. This is the only morning I can get to auction, and I need to take care of some ranch business."

"Are you kidding? You made me bacon and fed my dog. As far as I'm concerned, my day has already been made." It was funny how she was already thinking of Dewey as hers.

"You're easy to please."

She offered him a naughty smile. "I think that's already been established."

He let out a chuckle. "I still feel bad leaving you alone."

"I'll be fine. Really. I know you're a busy man and you have things to do." She had things to do too. Like write an article about his famous brother.

She'd lain awake the night before trying to come up with a way to get them all out of this mess. And she might have come up with a halfway decent idea. An idea that involved neither her naked body nor selling illegal drugs.

If she could get all the pieces to fall into place, she might be able to save her grandmother's house and still salvage a relationship with Mason and his family. And after everything they'd talked about the night before, she felt like a relationship, a real relationship, was actually in the realm of possibility.

"I was thinking I'd like to take the dogs for a walk around the ranch, but I can go into town and hang out at the library as well," she told him.

He gave her a look, suggesting his thoughts had gone to the night he'd found her at the library. "Don't be ridiculous. It's fine for you to stay here. You can walk all over the ranch. And if you're looking for reading material, I have plenty. My shelves are stacked with books. And if you can't find something there, I'm sure you could borrow something from my mom."

"I can find plenty of things to amuse myself. Plus I have a zillion books on my to-be-read list on my Kindle."

"You sure?"

"I'm sure."

He crossed the room, leaned down, and captured her mouth in a kiss. "Maybe I should blow off the auction and get you naked and back into bed." He ran his hand up her thigh and under the hem of the jersey as he eyed the kitchen table. "Or right here would do nicely as well."

The idea of Mason getting her naked and having his way with her on the kitchen table had surges of heat licking up her spine. And his hand between her legs had her mind spinning with dark, delicious thoughts of indecent behavior.

He groaned and pulled his hand away. "But I can't. I've got to go."

She sighed, already missing the heat of his large palm as she patted the wooden surface. "Don't worry. The table will still be here when you get back."

He chuckled and gave her one last kiss, then whistled for Theo, and the two of them headed out the door.

Tess spent the next hour taking a luxurious bath and reading a book.

Digging through her bag, she pulled out a pair of jeans and her last clean shirt, a light-pink cotton V-neck that hugged her body. Thank goodness she'd thrown in so many choices for alternative outfits. Sometimes it helped to be a shameful over-packer.

She had applied her makeup and fluffed out her hair, letting it air-dry as she settled on the sofa with the notepad and pen. The idea that had come to her was about a different kind of story to write. She prayed the magazine would still want it because of all the details she would layer into it, details that the public—especially the single women of Colorado—would want to know about their favorite hot hockey-playing cowboy.

The magazine wanted a story about the bad-boy bachelor and his sudden wedding, and that's what she would give them. It would still be a story about Rock and would star him and Quinn, but it would highlight their love story instead of smearing it.

She worked on the article for several hours, scribbling and scratching and perfecting the wording. She could type it up later.

But for now, she just needed to get the story out and on paper.

Finally finished, she let out a sigh and closed the notepad, happy with the results and hoping this would be the answer.

Now came the hard part. She had to talk to Rock and Quinn—had to come clean with them about who she was and what she was really doing there. Or what she'd been doing there in the beginning. She prayed they would see her sincerity and believe she really cared about Mason, cared about the whole family.

But they might not. Rock hated reporters. Her palms began to sweat, and she started to hyperventilate just thinking about admitting to him that she was one. Dread consumed her as she imagined their response.

What if they kicked her off the ranch before she ever had a chance to talk to Mason? What if they exposed her before she could even defend herself? And could she defend herself? What would she even say?

And what the heck was she going to do if they did reject her idea and refuse to let her write the article? She'd be back to the idea of selling drugs or running the spiked-lemonade stand with Mimi. Although hawking curbside margaritas sounded a lot easier than facing down Rockford and Mason James and telling them the truth.

But she'd face that hurdle when she came to it—one James brother at a time. Right now, she needed to muster her courage, hike up her big-girl panties, and come clean with one of Denver's most notorious hockey players and his fiancée.

She stuffed her feet into her tennis shoes, and taking

the notebook and Dewey with her, she headed up to the house in search of Rock and Quinn.

Mason sang along with the radio later that afternoon as he drove down the driveway of the Triple J.

He'd finished his business early and was excited to get back to Tess. He couldn't remember the last time he'd been this excited about seeing a woman. Any woman.

But something about *this* woman had his palms sweating and his heart racing as if he were a teenager in love. And there was no denying that that's what was happening.

He'd fallen head over heels in love with Tess. With a woman he'd just met and barely knew. Yet he felt like he did know her. Like he knew her heart. Especially after the things she'd shared with him the night before. Plus, they'd laughed and joked and gotten on as if they'd known each other a lot longer than just a few days.

They'd spent the majority of their time together over those few days, but instead of getting tired of her, he only wanted to spend more time with her. And get to know her better.

He'd gone out on dates before, and as much as he'd enjoyed the company of the women he'd taken to dinner or the movies, he'd never felt the deep desire or hunger for any of them that he felt with Tess. And he'd never been compelled to want them to stay for one night, let alone for several.

He pulled his truck into the Quonset hut and parked next to Tess's car. They kept most of the ranch vehicles and tools in the large building that served as a garage and workshop.

He'd sent a ranch hand to retrieve Tess's car the day before, but neither he nor Tess had been in the car since it had arrived. He peered through the windows as he passed and shook his head at the mess inside. The interior had to be stuffy. He should probably at least roll down the windows to air the car out. He opened the door and slid into the driver seat. The car smelled like stale bedding, wet dog, and the faint scent of vomit.

He glanced around the messy car. Tess had done the breakfast dishes this morning while he'd been in the shower. It might be a nice surprise if he cleaned her car.

It wouldn't take him long, and he'd cleaned up much worse messes when he mucked out the stalls or assisted in the birth of a farm animal. Ranching was a messy business. Cleaning out this car would be a piece of cake and would hopefully bring a smile to Tess's face.

And he was all about making her smile lately.

It only took him a few minutes to open all the doors and shake out the meager blanket. He pulled over the wet-dry vac and vacuumed the seat and the floor. The center console was full of crumbs, so he ran the vacuum hose over the plastic and inside the cup holders.

"Damn," he cursed as the suction from the hose grabbed a length of lanyard that had been sticking up between the seats. He snatched the lanyard before the vacuum sucked it down. A laminated card was attached to the ribbon, and he caught his breath as he read the writing on the card. Bewildered, he turned it over in his hand.

It appeared to be a press pass.

And it belonged to Tess. Her name was clearly printed on the card.

Tessa Kane. Reporter. Colorado In-Depth *magazine.*

Tess was a reporter?

What the hell?

He peered between the seats, looking for something else, anything else, to prove that this was a mistake. Maybe the pass was old, from a former job.

A steno pad was stuffed between the console and the seat, and he pulled it free and flipped it open, quickly scanning the notes written there.

Bad Boy Bachelor Becomes a Bridegroom.

All the dirt I know on Rockford James.

He couldn't believe it. His heart sank as he read each new word, each new damning piece of evidence that Tess was just like all the rest. That she'd been lying to him this whole damn time. Lying to him and using him. Using him to get to Rock.

He slammed his fist against the steering wheel. *Why?*

Seriously? How the hell had he been fooled again? How had he let himself believe that Tessa cared about him, loved him even, just for himself? Why would she?

How could anyone be interested in him when Rock was around?

This was on her for using him, but it was also on him for letting her. He should never have let his guard down, never trusted her.

Because apparently he couldn't trust anyone. Couldn't just let himself believe that a woman could be into him and care less about who his brother was.

Letting out another string of curses, he grabbed the heartbreaking evidence and slammed the car doors shut. Leaving the wet vac where it lay, he marched toward the bunkhouse, his heart in shreds and his head pissed as hell.

Chapter 19

MASON SLAMMED OPEN THE FRONT DOOR OF THE BUNKHOUSE.

Tessa was curled into the corner of the sofa, and Dewey lay sprawled on the cushion by her feet. She looked up from the book she was reading, a welcoming smile on her face.

Her smile fell as her gaze traveled from his expression to the lanyard and notebook he held in his hand.

The look of utter devastation on her face almost caused him to back down. But was she devastated because he'd found out she was a reporter or because she was about to lose her connection to his brother?

He held up the items in his hand. "I thought I'd clean out your car as a surprise, but apparently the surprise is on me. You want to tell me about these?"

"Mason, I can explain."

"Can you?"

Lord, please let her be able to explain all this away, he prayed. *Let this all be a big mistake.*

"I was going to tell you," she said.

"That sounds like an excuse, not an explanation."

She cringed.

He knew his words were sharp, but he didn't care. "What were you going to tell me, Tess? That you've been lying to me since the moment I met you?"

"I haven't lied about everything."

"Really? Because it seems to me that you have. In

fact, it seems like every single word out of your mouth has been a lie."

"Let me explain."

"I'm listening."

"It's not what you think."

"It's not? Because what I think is…" he said, as he threw the lanyard and notebook onto the coffee table in front of her, "that these are evidence that you were not fired from your job, but are still employed at *Colorado In-Depth* magazine, as a *reporter*. And if I recall correctly, you told me you were a writer."

"I am a writer," she whispered.

"Yes, you are a writer, just not one who's working on a book. No, apparently you are working on a story about my brother. And you are currently looking for—How did you put it in your notes there?—all the dirt on Rockford James. And his gold-digging fiancée."

"It's not what you think."

"You said that before. And it appears nothing with you is what I thought it was. I thought you were a nice girl who got stood up at my brother's prewedding celebration, but that wasn't true. I thought you were fun and sweet, that we had a real connection, and that you were sincere when you said you wanted to be my date for the weekend. But that wasn't true either. Was that whole thing just another ploy to get closer to my brother?"

"No."

He stared at her, drilling her with a steely glare.

She hung her head. "Sort of, I guess. Maybe a little, at first. But I also really liked you. I *do* like you."

He held up a hand, acid churning in his stomach.

"Save it. I don't believe you. I don't believe a single word you have to say."

"Mason, I'm sorry. I wanted to tell you."

"So, tell me now."

"It's complicated. And I didn't lie to you about everything. I *did* get fired from my job. I *was* a reporter for *Colorado In-Depth*, but I didn't write the stories that they wanted to publish." She averted her eyes and stared down at her tightly clasped hands. "I wasn't good enough."

Mason let out a huff. "So, you're saying *you're* the victim here?"

"No. I didn't say that. I just meant that the magazine wanted tough, hard-hitting stories, and I wasn't making the grade. My stories were apparently too nice, and my boss let me go. He fired me the same day I met you, right after I found out that I'd been stood up. I was still in the parking lot of the lodge, and I was getting ready to head back to Denver when he called me. Then it came out whose party I was attending, and he said I could keep my job if I got him the story on Rock and the dirt on why he was getting married so quickly."

"So, what? You sought me out? Thought I would be a good patsy? Was that whole thing with the closet just a big setup?"

"No, of course not. That was all an accident. I didn't even know who you were at first. And everything's changed since then. What I have with you now doesn't have anything to do with the story on Rock."

"You don't *have* anything with me," Mason snapped, the words causing his throat to tighten. "But whatever *is* going on here seems to have everything to do with Rock."

Tess scrubbed her hand over her face. "Could you please sit down? And stop interrupting me. Just let me tell you what happened. *Please*."

He grudgingly sat on the edge of the sofa, but angled his body away from hers.

She blew out a sigh. "I told you that I live with my grandmother."

"What does that have to do—?"

She held up her hand. "Let me finish. I've lived with my grandmother most of my life, and I love her dearly, but sometimes she doesn't make the smartest decisions."

He raised an eyebrow but kept silent.

"She really *was* a victim. She got involved in an online scam and thought she was helping a nice family in Nigeria, but really a fraud ring was helping themselves to all her money. They convinced her to send them cashier's checks, then gained access to her bank accounts and wiped out her entire savings. Not only were her accounts wiped clean, but they'd given her fake checks to deposit so she was also then in debt to the bank. She was embarrassed and ashamed and didn't tell me until she was so far behind in our bills and on the mortgage that she was in danger of losing the house. I came home early one day to find collection notices and unpaid bills spread across the kitchen table. She finally came clean with me, but it was too late. She was in too deep. I gave her everything I had. And I mean everything, every red cent. But it wasn't enough."

She blew out a shaky breath. "I've been looking for a second job, but jobs are scarce in the city right now. We were doing everything we could think of to raise money. I was working overtime and turning in extra articles, but like I said, they weren't the kind of thing the magazine was looking for. But when my boss found out about the wedding, he said he'd give me one shot to save my job and would even throw in a bonus if I could get the real truth—which meant the dirt—on Rock and Quinn's wedding. I told him this isn't the type of story I write, but he was adamant, and the bonus alone would cover an entire delinquent mortgage payment. We need the money, and I can't let my grandmother down. And at the time, I didn't know Rock from a hole in the ground. What was I supposed to do?"

"You were supposed to tell me the truth. Not lie through your teeth and use me to get to my brother."

"Yeah, right. My boss told me that Rock loathes reporters. The only way I was getting a story was if I could get him to talk to me without knowing I was one."

"So, you used me to get to him. From the very first minute that I met you." Mason rubbed a hand across his neck and tried to unclench his tightened jaw.

"I'm sorry. I didn't know you. I didn't care about you like I do now. I was wrong."

"No, I was wrong. I was wrong for thinking that for once, I'd met someone who didn't care anything about my famous brother. Who saw me just for me and didn't give two shits about Rockford."

"I do see you," she whispered.

"Don't," he said through gritted teeth, feeling the vein pulsing in his forehead. "Don't lie. Not anymore. You got what you wanted. You can go now." His muscles jumped under his skin, and his stomach cramped at the thought of her leaving, but what else could he do? There was no way that he could ever trust her again.

"I don't want to go."

His nails bit into his skin as he tightened his hands into fists. He drew in a slow, steady breath, keeping his voice in a carefully controlled tone. "Well, I don't want you to stay."

"Mason, please. Can't we talk about this?"

"What is there to talk about? You've been around Rock and Quinn enough times now that surely you've got enough *dirt* to write yourself a story. You got what you came for. You don't need to pretend to care about me anymore." The words burned his throat and left a sour taste in his mouth.

"I'm not pretending. I *do* care about you."

"Last night you asked me to tell you about things that I hate, and I said things like bad drivers and itchy socks, but the thing I hate the most is being lied to. And I hate being used."

"You also told me some things that you loved, or things you thought you were starting to love."

He felt his heart thud painfully in his chest and was surprised to feel it beating it all. He'd thought it was completely broken. "I was wrong about that too."

"I did lie about some stuff—about the article—but I wasn't *trying* to use you. Especially not after I got to know you. And I've never lied about how I feel about you. We have something here. I don't want to lose that. I don't want to lose you."

"Too late."

She stared at her feet, then let out a long, low sigh. "I'm sorry."

"I want to believe you. I want so badly to believe this is all a big misunderstanding, one awful mistake, and that you didn't mean to lie. But it isn't. You did lie, and you purposely wound your way into my life, into our lives, not because you cared about us, but because you wanted something from us. You wanted to use us, use me, to get what you needed. Well, you've got it now. So you can go. I want you to go."

"I never meant to hurt you. I never meant to hurt anyone." Her voice was thick, and her chin trembled as if she was going to cry. But she didn't. She just nodded her head and stood up.

She took a shaky step away from him, then turned back as if she was going to say something else.

He couldn't look at her, couldn't take a chance he would get taken in again by the hurt in her eyes. No, it was better this way. Make a clean break.

She'd go back to Denver, and he'd go back to his life and try to forget about her. Try to pretend he'd never met her. *Yeah right*.

The dog gave his leg a tentative sniff, then jumped from the sofa and followed Tess as she turned and walked into his bedroom. The room where just the night before—hell, just that morning—they'd lain naked and tangled in the sheets, and he'd almost told her he loved her.

He'd thought they had a chance at something good and honest. Something real.

But that chance was gone.

He sat where he was, his limbs too heavy to move, as he listened to her gather her things. She didn't have much. Hell, most everything she'd been using, and wearing, was his. His shirts, his socks, his toothpaste, his shampoo, his favorite mug.

Even though she'd only been with him for a few

days, she was already in every part of his life. And he knew that as much as he would try to forget, memories of her would haunt him even in the simplest things—like taking a shower or making coffee in the morning.

She came out of the bedroom, her shoes on and her bags slung over her shoulder. She stopped at the door and tried one more time to talk to him. "Mason—"

He cut her off with a shake of his head and a hard, glinty stare. He couldn't speak, couldn't get words to come out around the thick lump in his throat.

But she got the message. Her shoulders sagged as she turned away.

His body felt numb, disconnected, his heart in shreds, as he watched her walk out the door.

Tess pushed through the screen door, her legs leaden and her heart heavy with sorrow and regret. Dewey trotted along at her ankles.

Her car sat in the middle of the driveway. Mason must have had someone pull it around for her. She trudged toward it, her heart breaking further with each step she took away from Mason.

Her phone buzzed in her purse. She pulled it from her bag, her breath catching in her throat as she glimpsed the screen.

Fifteen missed calls from Mimi.

Fifteen!

How could she have missed them?

She missed them because all her attention had been on Mason, trying to get him to talk to her and to persuade him not to hate her.

Her phone had been in her purse. She hadn't bothered with it since she turned in the article. She hadn't wanted the real world to intrude on the happiness she felt.

She'd talked to Rock and Quinn, told them the truth, and let them read the article she'd written. They'd both been angry at first—Rock especially was pissed. She knew they would be, but they'd spent a long time talking it through, and she'd repeatedly told them how sorry she was and how she wanted to make it up to them.

Quinn was pretty great. She'd reminded Rock that they'd all made mistakes, done things they were ashamed of, and she said she admired Tess for coming clean and telling them the truth. She actually loved the article and had convinced Rock to let her turn it in. He had admitted that it was pretty good, and they had finally forgiven her for not being up front and honest with them.

But Rock had warned her that Mason would be a lot less likely to. He told her his brother was stubborn and wouldn't take being deceived lightly. He was right.

She'd been planning to tell Mason the truth as soon as he came home. She'd spent the last hour sweating and rehearsing exactly what she'd say, how she would word it so he would understand. Her hands had been shaking all afternoon, and her back ached from tensing her muscles against his imagined reactions. But whatever the outcome, she wanted him to know the truth about what she did, what had happened with her grandmother, the article, all of it. But most of all, she wanted to tell him the truth about how she felt about him.

She'd fallen in love with him and wanted them to have a future together. A future that wasn't tainted by lies and deception.

But it was too late now. He'd made up his mind and didn't want to hear anything she had to say. Any chance she'd had with him had just slipped through her fingers.

Nausea spiraled through her stomach and her knees threatened to buckle, because now not only had her beautiful world with Mason fallen apart, but something terrible must have happened with her grandmother. With the only person she had left.

Her pulse raced as she threw her bag in the car, then pressed the screen to return the call. *Come on. Pick up.*

The phone hadn't even finished the first ring when Tess heard an engine racing toward her. She looked up to see a small cherry-red car come screaming down the driveway, followed by a cloud of dust.

A small cherry-red car that looked suspiciously like her grandmother's.

What in the hell?

What was her grandmother doing *here*?

Pain shot through her chest, like a hand squeezing her heart. Now she *knew* something terrible must have happened.

But what? If something had happened to Mimi, she would be in the hospital, not blowing up her granddaughter's phone and driving up the pass. Tess shook her head.

She hadn't been able to believe it when Mimi had first brought the flashy red Mini Cooper home. It made her nervous the way her grandmother zipped around in the little thing, but Tess didn't think she'd ever taken the car much farther than their neighborhood, let alone driven it up the mountain.

The Mini Cooper pulled to a stop, dust flying as the

driver hit the brakes. The door opened, and her grandmother stumbled from the car. Her normally tidy hair was sticking up in some places and hanging in loose strands in others. Her clothes were in disarray—part of her shirt was loose and untucked, and a big tear ran down the front of one of her pant legs.

And she appeared to be missing a shoe.

Holy crap! What was going on?

Tess raced to her grandmother. "Mimi! What happened? Are you okay?" She reached her just as the older woman collapsed into her arms.

"Oh, Tess. I'm so glad you're here," Mimi said, hanging onto her arms as her body sagged against Tess.

The screen door of the main house slammed, and Vivi came rushing down the stairs, Rock and Quinn on her heels.

"What's happened?" Vivi asked.

"I'm not sure," Tess told her. "This is my grandmother, Mimi. I mean, Miriam Kane."

"Let's get her inside," Mason's deep voice said from behind her. He must have heard the commotion and followed her out, but in the craziness of rushing to her grandmother, Tess hadn't noticed him.

She wanted to lean back against him, to take comfort in his arms. But those days were over. That time was done.

Besides, she needed to focus on Mimi right now. She helped her grandmother up the stairs and into the kitchen of the farmhouse.

"Can we get you something?" Vivi asked, pulling out a chair and helping to ease the older woman into it. "A glass of tea or some water?"

"Some water would be nice. Thank you."

Tess was thankful Mimi hadn't asked for a beer. She wouldn't put it past the woman. But the fact she was asking for water, looked so disheveled, and wasn't cracking any of her trademark jokes told her something serious was going on.

Quinn hurried to the kitchen and filled a glass with water, then set it in on the table.

Mimi picked it up and took a long swig. "I'm sorry to be such a bother. I didn't want to intrude on you folks. I just needed to find my granddaughter."

"Well, you found her," Tess said. "Now tell me what's going on. You raced in here like someone was chasing you."

Mimi's cast her eyes down and pulled the edges of the tear in her pant leg together. "Oh look. I've torn my pants. And this is one of my good pairs."

Tess arched an eyebrow. She was well acquainted with the evasive tactics of Miriam Kane. "Mimi, what is going on? *Are* you being chased by someone?"

Her grandmother still refused to meet her eye. "In a way, I guess. I mean, maybe someone could perceive that…"

Maybe someone could perceive that? What was she talking about?

"Mimi, is someone chasing you or not?"

She blinked, tipping her chin up in a peevish way and pursing her lips. "I don't think you need to take that tone with me, young lady."

Tess made a growling sound in her throat.

"Okay, fine. Yes. Someone is chasing me. Are you happy?"

"No, I'm not happy. Of course I'm not happy that

someone is after you. I just don't understand what's going on. Why would *anyone* be chasing you?" Tess's thoughts went to the money scammers who had swindled all her grandmother's money from her. Had they somehow found Mimi and tried to get more cash from her?

"Are you in danger?" Mason asked. He'd been leaning against the side of the counter, apparently letting his mom and Quinn fuss over Mimi while he stood back. "Should we call the police?"

Mimi vigorously shook her head, sending the mussed white shocks of hair into more disarray. "No police." She narrowed her eyes at Mason. "You must be Mason, the guy Tess can't stop talking about."

"I am. Mason, I mean." His brow furrowed as he dodged Tess's gaze. "I wouldn't know about that other stuff."

Tess's lungs constricted, and a painful tightness squeezed her chest. He *would* know about that other stuff if she'd only had a chance to talk to him before he'd found her press pass and notes in her car. If she'd only had a chance to tell him the truth.

Or if I'd been honest with him from the start.

She didn't have time to dwell on that right now. Something had happened, and the way her grandmother was dodging and sidestepping her questions told her that it was something serious.

"Mimi," she said, her tone stern as she tried to recapture the woman's attention, "can you please tell me what is going on?"

They had all settled around the table, except for Mason, who continued to lean on the edge of the kitchen counter.

"Well, I may have gotten myself in over my head," Mimi said, her voice a little shaky as she held up her hand, her thumb and forefinger not quite pinched together. "Just a little bit. And really, it seemed like a good idea at the time."

"What seemed like a good idea?" Tess asked. "And how big of a 'little bit' are we talking about?"

"Oh, Tessa, you always worry too much."

"Mimi, you drove halfway up the mountain in a car the size of a tin can and must have used the GPS in it for the first time ever in an effort to find me, so I'm assuming that my worry level right now should be somewhere between a major catastrophe and DEFCON 5."

Her grandmother gave a small shrug of her shoulders as she pursed her lips together. "All right. My plan might have gotten a little out of my control. It's just that I was talking to a couple of men down at the senior center, and they told me about these guys who would loan money to people who needed quick cash and had a few blemishes on their credit records."

A few blemishes? With the recent scandal, Mimi's credit had taken a nose dive into a full-blown acne attack.

"And these men... Apparently a few of them do a little gambling on the side and have some connections. They gave me a couple of names, and Arthur... You remember Arthur, Tess? He's the one with the messy pompadour. He's really quite handsome, for being in his eighties. He's still got his hair and all of his own teeth, you know."

"Not for long," Tess muttered.

"Don't be fresh." Her grandmother gave her a quick stink eye.

Seriously? Mimi was the one cavorting with criminals, and she was giving Tess the stink eye?

"So anyway, I guess I was a little desperate." She turned to Rock, Quinn, and Vivi, who had been silently watching the conversational exchange. "I'm sure Tess told you I got taken in by a fraud ring posing as Nigerian royalty, and they swindled me out of thousands of dollars. We're now in peril of losing our home."

The three of them didn't say anything, just collectively shook their heads and blinked at the older woman.

"No, Mimi. I did *not* tell them all that. I try not to tell *anyone* that." She offered the others an apologetic glance. All except Mason. She was avoiding looking at him altogether. She lowered her voice as she turned back to her grandmother. "And besides, I told you I was taking care of it."

"I know, honey. But you were having such a rough time at your job, and I didn't want you to have to solve my problems. And this seemed like the answer. So I called Arthur, and he took me to see this guy, Vinnie the Rake."

"Vinnie the Rake?" Tess's voice rose two octaves, and her blood pressure skyrocketed. She could feel a pulse beating on the side of her forehead. "Why in the heck would you borrow money from a guy named Vinnie the Rake?"

"It was either him or Tommy the Fist, and I thought a rake sounded a little more pleasant. More like a regular household item."

"There is nothing pleasant about a man who has a gangster name that includes some type of weapon, household or otherwise."

Mimi pursed her lips again. "Do you want me to tell you what happened, or do you just want to lecture me?"

Tess rubbed her forehead. "Fine. Go on. Please tell us what happened when you visited Vinnie the Rake."

"Well, it was really quite simple the first time."

The first time?

Tess pressed her lips together and squeezed her hands into fists underneath the table.

"He seemed perfectly nice and loaned me two thousand dollars, no questions asked. But when I took that down to the bank, they said it wasn't enough."

"What do you mean, it wasn't enough? I thought two thousand was all we needed."

"*Well*, I might have underestimated the amount."

"Underestimated?"

"I *might* owe a little more."

"Might?"

"Okay. Fine. A *lot* more. Apparently the two thousand barely made a dent in the money that was overdue. Between the overdraft fees and the late charges on the mortgage and the rest of the bills, I needed a couple thousand more."

"A couple thousand?" Tess's heart sank. She didn't know if Gordon would come through with even two thousand dollars for her article—especially since she'd changed it so much from the kind of story he'd originally asked for. But there was no way she could find *another* two thousand dollars.

"So I had to go back to Vinnie," Mimi said, her voice lowering as she wiped at a smudge of dirt on her arm. "And this time he wasn't as nice."

"Did he hurt you?" Mason interrupted, his voice as cold as steel.

"No, honey. Not physically at least. But he did make a few overt remarks about how I could pay the money back. I assumed he meant with my body in some kinky sex acts, and I emphatically told him I was not into whatever weird, sexual old-lady fetishes he had in mind. And I may have mentioned something about a rake."

Rock let out a chuckle, then covered his mouth with his hand and tried to pass it off as a cough.

Tess was not amused.

Mimi shrugged. "Apparently, he had been talking about me giving him my car. But at that point, the comment about the rake was evidently a sore spot with him, and he got all pissy and demanded I immediately pay him back the money I owed him plus a ridiculous amount of interest. So now I still owe the bank two thousand dollars, and I owe Vinnie three thousand dollars, both due immediately."

Tess sucked in her breath. "Wait. You owe Vinnie *three* thousand dollars now? That's fifty percent interest. That's straight-out robbery."

"Did you miss the part about Vinnie being a criminal?"

"Well, there's criminal and then there's outrageous. Surely, he'll listen to reason. Maybe I can talk to him… try to reason with him."

"There's no reasoning with him. Especially now."

"What do mean, especially now?"

"Because now he's mad, and he's hell-bent on me paying the money back. That's why he sent his two goons to collect the cash today."

"What do you mean, 'sent'?"

"What do you think I mean? Two guys showed up at the house a few hours ago—interrupted my soaps and about scared the life out of me. I didn't know who they were at first. They didn't look so bad. Both of them had on dark suits. I thought maybe they were a couple of those religious types and just wanted to give me a leaflet. Then they pushed their way into the house and started busting things up. The short one... He had a crew cut. Who even wears a crew cut anymore? He tipped over the coffee table and started pulling the cushions off the couch. Like maybe instead of some stale Cheetos and dust bunnies, he thought he was actually going to find two thousand dollars in the sofa cushions."

Tess knew he wasn't. They'd already raided the couch, the kitchen drawers, and the dryer to collect any spare change that may have been hidden in the house.

"The tall one... He didn't have *any* hair. His head was shaved," Mimi continued. "But he's the one who had a gun."

Chapter 20

Tess gasped. "A gun?"

Her grandmother nodded. "He didn't wave it around or point it at me. He just calmly took it out and set it on the kitchen table. Like he wanted me to know it was there. He was the smarter dressed of the two. He was wearing this purple shirt... You know, the kind all the Mafia guys wear on television, the kind that probably cost more than my car. So obviously they didn't need the money that I'd borrowed that badly."

Tessa rolled her eyes so hard she was surprised she didn't see her brain. She didn't care how the guy's hair was cut or how expensive his stupid shirt was. She cared about the fact that two men had been in their house, and one of them had a gun. "So what did you do?"

"They said they wanted the money, and they weren't leaving until I gave it to them. They said they would take cash or my car. Well, I clearly didn't have any cash, and I can tell you I wasn't about to give them my car. I love that car. So, I told them all the excitement had set my bladder off, and if they didn't let me pee, I'd have an accident. Then I snuck out the bedroom window. I think that's when I ripped my pants. Thank goodness I'd been planning to go to the grocery store, so I had my phone and my car keys in my pocket."

"Yeah, thank goodness," Tess muttered.

Mimi offered her an impish grin. "I also had my

smarts with me. They'd driven up in this big, black Cadillac and had my car blocked in. But that Mini Cooper is small, and I knew I had enough room to squeak it out of the driveway if I cut through the lawn. I also knew that I didn't want them to be able to follow me, but didn't have much at my disposal to slow them down. My purse was still inside, and of course that's where I keep my pepper spray. I had to think fast and use what was handy, so I may have broken a couple of those cute ceramic garden gnomes—you know, the ones with the metal stakes up their heinies—and propped them under their tire. But I'm not copping to anything for sure."

Not copping to anything? Who was this woman?

"Mimi, this is not an episode of *Law & Order*. These are *actual* bad men. Men who will not think twice about hurting an old woman."

"Who are you calling old?"

Oh. My. Gosh.

Tess held up her hands. "I'm sorry. Of course you're not old."

"No, I'm not. But I *am* smart." She tapped the side of her head. "And I will admit I wanted to drive those stakes into their whitewalls to flatten them, but I wasn't strong enough. So I just hope the glass and the stakes were enough to puncture a tire and slow them down. Otherwise, those garden gnomes sacrificed themselves for nothing."

Tess cradled her head in her hands. "How could this have happened? I've only been gone for four days."

Mimi patted her arm. "A *lot* can happen in four days, honey."

True. *Her* last four days had certainly been eventful.

She'd made new friends, helped save some cows, been caught in a rainstorm, found a dog, watched a hockey game, survived sleeping the night in her car, and fallen in love.

And lied to the guy she'd fallen in love with—don't forget about that. Lied, deceived, and broken both of their hearts in the process.

So yeah, a lot *could* happen in four days.

The sound of an engine drew their attention to the open front window. The hair on Tess's arms stood on end as she glimpsed the black car speeding down the driveway in a cloud of dust.

Chairs scraped the hardwood floor as the group stood.

"They're here," Mimi cried, clinging to Tess's side. "How did they find me?"

"I have no idea."

Mimi reached for Vivi's hand. "I'm so sorry. I never meant to bring trouble to your family."

"Nobody ever *means* to bring trouble or cause damage..." Mason muttered. "But they hurt you just the same." He gave Tess a sideways glance, just a second's look, but enough to cut her to the bone.

She hadn't meant to hurt Mason, but she'd done it anyway. And now she didn't know how to fix it. She didn't know how to fix any of this.

She jumped as the screen door banged open.

Colt rushed into the house. "I don't know what's going on, but two guys just pulled up in a black Caddy, and something about them is real scary. They looked like extras from the set of *The Sopranos*."

They backed toward the kitchen. Rock spread his arms, pressing the women behind him. Mason moved to the front window, standing to the side as he peered around the curtains.

"What are they doing?" Tess whispered.

"Nothing. They're just standing next to the car looking around."

"Do you think they're the same guys who were at Mimi's house?"

"I would assume so." Mason tipped his chin toward Mimi. "One is tall and bald, and the other is shorter and has a crew cut. They both look like they could be linebackers for the Denver Broncos. Except they're dressed in black suits."

"Is the tall one wearing a purple shirt?" Mimi asked. "And do they both look like they've eaten way too much pasta?"

Mason pulled back the curtain and peered out the window again. "Yep."

"That's them, all right."

"What's happening?" Colt asked. "Are these guys really dangerous?"

Tess quickly filled him in. "Colt, this is my grandmother, Mimi. She got caught up in a financial fraud scam and lost all her money. So she borrowed money to pay the mortgage from a loan shark named Vinnie the Rake, and these are his two goons here to collect the debt. Oh, and she also spiked their tire and made them chase her all the way up the mountain so they're probably pretty pissed off."

Colt's eyes widened as he looked from Tess to her grandmother.

Mimi shrugged. "That about covers it. Nice to meet you, Colt." She leaned toward Tess. "Are all the cowboys in this town as handsome as these boys? No wonder you haven't come home in days."

"Could we just focus on the matter at hand?" Mason asked. "Like the two gangsters standing in our driveway. By the way, the garden gnomes must have worked because they've got one of those tiny doughnut-wheel spares on instead of a regular back tire."

Her grandmother gave a tiny fist pump, then shoved her hand into her pocket when Tess gave her a disapproving glare.

"Will you just try to behave?" Tess hissed.

"They're heading toward the porch," Colt said. He'd joined his brother at the front window.

Mason dropped the curtain. "They're *not* coming inside. Let me at least try to reason with them and get them to leave." He put his hand on the screen door, then glanced from Rock to Colt. "If they won't go, you know what we have to do."

Both brothers nodded.

A grin tugged at the corner of Rock's lip. "Operation Gunslinger."

Mason dipped his chin. "Hopefully it won't come to that." He pushed through the screen door and stepped out on the porch. "Can I help you fellows with something? You appear to be lost."

"We're not lost," Purple Shirt said. "We know exactly where we are. The Triple J Ranch owned by Vivienne James and her sons. You one of those sons?"

"I am."

"How do they already know that?" Tess asked her grandmother. She, Mimi, and Quinn had taken Mason's place at the front window while Rock, Colt, and Vivi stood by the door. "Did you tell them about Mason and his family?"

"No, of course not. Vinnie just knows things. He knew stuff about me. And you. He knew the name of the magazine where you worked and that you were in the mountains working on a story. He makes it his business to know stuff."

Crew Cut pointed a finger at the Mini Cooper. "We're not here to cause any trouble. We're looking for the lady who owns that car. Our business is with her."

"Well, she's my guest at the moment," Mason said. "So, apparently your business is now with me."

Purple Shirt narrowed his eyes. "I don't think this is the kind of business you want to get involved in." He pulled back his jacket, flashing Mason the revolver stuffed in his waistband.

Tess gasped, and Rock and Colt hastened into action, rushing through the house to collect weapons.

"There's no reason for things to get ugly, fellas," Mason told them.

Tess was amazed at how calm his voice sounded and how steady he looked as he casually leaned on the post of the front porch. Her hands were shaking and her stomach was queasy, and she was standing inside.

"There are about three thousand reasons to get ugly." Purple Shirt pointed at the small spare tire. "Over three thousand now, since somebody's going to have to pay for that."

"Yeah, over three thousand," Crew Cut repeated. "And we've come to collect them. So why don't you just send Ms. Mimi out here, and we'll be on our way."

"I don't think Ms. Mimi currently has that kind of cash on her," Mason said.

"Then I guess things are going to have to get ugly." Purple Shirt pulled the gun from his waistband and pointed it at Mason.

Mason narrowed his eyes, staring at the gangster and the loaded gun with more bravado than he felt.

His brothers needed to get out here. *Now*.

The screen door banged open, and Rock stepped out, two shotguns cradled in his arms. He passed one to Mason. "You all right there, Brother?"

"Yep." He hoisted the shotgun to his shoulder, his heart pounding as he pointed it toward Purple Shirt. "I think it's about time for you fellas to be on your way."

"We're not leaving without what we came for," Crew Cut stated, drawing his weapon as well. "We want the money, or we're taking the old lady back to our boss."

"Who are you calling 'old'?" Mimi's voice shouted from inside the house.

Mason heard Tess shushing her. "That's not going to happen."

"It appears we're at a standoff then. It's your two guns against ours," Purple Shirt said. "You comfortable with those odds?"

"Three guns against yours," Colt said, stepping out on the porch with the antique revolver lighter.

Ahh hell. Leave it to Colt to bring a lighter to a gunfight.

"Make that four," his mom said, coming out behind him, holding one of his dad's old hunting rifles at her shoulder.

"Make that five." Tessa stepped out on the porch, a

hockey stick in her hands. *Seriously?* Why didn't she just stay inside where she was safe? And what was she going to do with the hockey stick? Shoot a puck at the bad guys?

Purple Shirt studied the group of them, as if trying to decide how far this family would go to protect one little old lady they didn't even know.

How far *would* they go?

How far would *Mason* go?

Mimi was Tess's grandmother—*her* family, not his. And he'd just told her he didn't want anything else to do with her. So why was he even involved with this?

Why was he putting his own family at risk to help the family of a woman who'd lied and deceived him and who he'd just broken things off with?

Because it was the right thing to do.

Purple Shirt waved his gun at the front porch. "You pretty confident in your little army?"

"This isn't my whole army," Mason said.

One of the barn doors banged open and a ranch hand stepped out, a shotgun pressed to his shoulder. Another man came around the side of the house, cocking the barrel of his gun as he appeared.

Colt must have notified the cavalry. Two more hands appeared, each with either a rifle or a shotgun.

"Still think you have business here?" Mason asked.

The two men looked at each other, then lowered their weapons. "You're making a mistake, you know. You might have more guys right now, but we'll be back. With more men and bigger guns. We can make things a lot uglier than you and your little band of cowboys and your mom can. Hope that little old lady is worth it." He reached for the car door.

"Wait." The screen door banged open again, and Mimi rushed out. "I'll go with you."

"No, you won't," Tess cried, grabbing her grandmother's hand. "You can't."

Mimi glanced around at Mason's family standing guard over her. "I appreciate what you're doing. I really do. But I'm not going to let you nice people put yourselves in danger for me. This is my battle. And I'm the one who needs to fight it. But don't worry. I'll be giving Vinnie the Rake a good piece of my mind when I see him."

Mason had to admire the woman. She was all of five foot nothing, but she had the gumption of a giant. He could see where Tessa got her fighting spirit.

He could admire her, but no way in hell was he letting her get in that car with those criminals. He lowered his shotgun. "Tess is right. You can't go with them. But there's also no way that we can let them leave like this. Because they *will* be back. I believe them."

Mimi's eyes widened. "Are you suggesting we kill them?"

He shook his head. "No. No one's killing anyone." He gestured to the lighter in Colt's hand. "Especially with that. I'm suggesting we *pay* them."

"With what?" Mimi asked.

"With cash."

"I don't have any."

"I do."

"Mason, we can't take your money," Tessa said.

"I'm not giving it to you. I'm giving it to her," he told her. "And I'm doing it because it's the right thing to do." He called out to Purple Shirt and Crew Cut. "Stay where you are. I'll get you the money. Three thousand, right?

Then you'll leave, and leave us *and* Ms. Mimi alone. For good."

Purple Shirt squinted at the back tire of the car. "Three thousand plus an extra two hundred for the tire."

"Fair enough. But I want your word that this will be the end of it."

"You have it. We'll be happy if we never have to see that woman again."

Mason turned to his brothers. "Keep an eye on them. I've got some cash in the safe in the office."

Rock put a hand on his arm. "You don't have to do this. I can pay them. I've spent that much on a night out downtown. It's no big deal to me."

That's why Mason wasn't going to let Rock step in and be the hero. Not this time.

He knew his brother had the money. Rock could easily cover the debts and not even flinch. But it wasn't his battle. And Mason wasn't going to let his brother come out as the victor.

"No. I'll take care of this. I've got the money." He peered at Tess. "I'm not going to let you pay for *my* girl's mistake."

Except she *wasn't* his girl.

She was just a girl. A girl who had pretended to like him. Pretended to care. When all she was really interested in was getting to his brother.

He looked away as Tess's eyes filled with tears. "I'll be right back." He hurried into the house and into the study, setting the shotgun on the desk. They did the majority of the ranch business out of this office and kept some cash in the safe.

He had the money to give. He had plenty in his

savings. Not plenty like Rock, but plenty for a normal non-rock-star, nonathlete kind of person.

He was frugal and a saver. Once he'd finished the renovations to the bunkhouse, he hadn't had much else to spend his money on, so he just dumped everything into his savings. He could give the money to Tess and her grandmother. Then he'd tell her goodbye and never have to see her again.

The safe held several thousand dollars as well as important documents and some family heirlooms. Mimi had said she owed the loan sharks three thousand and the bank another two. He grabbed five thousand and swung the door shut. After stuffing two into his front pocket, he picked up the shotgun and walked swiftly back outside and down the front porch steps.

He held out the three small stacks of bills to Purple Shirt. "I have your word this will be the end of it."

"You have my word."

He let go of the bills, then reached for his wallet. He'd been to the bank a few days before and gotten cash for all the wedding hoopla. He was pretty sure he had a couple hundred left. Pulling out four fifties, he handed them over as well, then stuffed his wallet back into his pocket. "How good is the word of a criminal?"

"It's the best thing we've got." The man folded the bills and tucked them into his breast pocket. "Nice doing business with you."

"Just make sure you tell Vinnie that our business is concluded."

He nodded and climbed into the car. "I'll let him know."

"Smell you later," Crew Cut sneered before sliding

into the passenger side and slamming the door. The car engine roared to life.

Mason let out his breath as the Cadillac with the two criminals sped down the driveway. He waved at the ranch hands still standing guard around the yard. "It's done. Thanks, men."

The hands dispersed, and Mason walked back up the steps to the porch. His mom, Quinn, and his brothers went back into the house, leaving him standing outside with Tess and her grandmother. He pulled out the other two thousand dollars and handed it to Mimi. "Take this."

She held up her hands. "No way. I can't take your money."

"You took money from a schmuck like those guys, but you won't take it from me?"

"Good point." She took the cash and stuffed it down her shirt and into her bra. "I'll pay you back. I can leave my car. You know, as collateral."

"I don't want your car. And you don't have to pay me back."

"Yes, we do." Mimi reached for his hand. "This was my mistake. My debt to pay. And everything I've done and everything my granddaughter has done have been my fault. Don't take it out on her."

Her hand looked so small clasped in his. "I appreciate that. But I think we're all responsible for our own actions."

"Grandma, we can't take that money," Tess said.

"Yes, you can," Mason told her, letting go of Mimi's hand and drilling Tess with a hard glare. "And you will."

"But not after…"

"Especially after." He leaned in and lowered his voice.

"Take the money. Consider it payment for the article. Then you don't have to turn in the one you're writing."

The color drained from her face. "I already turned the story in," she whispered.

"What? How the hell could you have already turned it in? Have you been working on it this whole time?"

"No. I just wrote it this morning, but we needed the money as soon as we could get it. And you weren't here. But I was going to talk to you about it as soon as you got back."

"Of course you were."

"I was. You've got to believe me."

"No, Tess. I don't *have* to believe you. And I don't believe you. Not a single word out of your mouth."

"I was just doing it to save my grandmother and her house."

"I understand that, but it doesn't change anything."

She took a step toward him. "Can I call you? Maybe in a few days? After you've had a chance to think about it. Can we at least talk about this?"

He took a step back. He had to. He had to make a clean break. "No. It's over. We don't have anything left to talk about."

Mason's chest hurt as he watched Tess and her grandmother walk down the porch steps and get into their cars.

Mimi pulled away first, speeding down the driveway in her little red car. Tess followed, pulling away slowly. She kept her eyes forward and her chin up, but Mason could see the white-knuckle grip she had on the steering wheel of the car. Dewey's nose was sticking out of the passenger-side window.

Four days and five thousand dollars. He wasn't getting either of them back.

Apparently five thousand dollars was the cost of a broken heart.

Tess tried to focus on the road, her heart breaking with every mile she drove farther away from Mason.

She drove slowly through town, one arm clutched around her middle as if trying to hold herself together. Mimi had sped off, and she was sure her grandmother was probably halfway to Denver by now.

Her phone rang, and a flutter raced through her belly. She pulled it from her bag, praying that it was Mason.

It wasn't.

The caller ID showed an unfamiliar number. She tapped the screen and held the phone to her ear. "Hello?"

"Yes, hello. This is Anita. I'm a dispatcher for the sheriff's office. Are you the one who put up the flyers about the lost dog?"

Tess gripped the steering wheel, her throat going dry, and she tried to keep the tremble from her voice. "Y-yes."

"Well, I've got good news. The owners just showed up to claim it."

Chapter 21

A WAVE OF DIZZINESS SPIRALED THROUGH HER, AND TESS pulled off to the side of the road. Her throat was painfully tight as she tried to swallow. "Are you sure?"

"Yes, ma'am," the dispatcher assured her. "They brought the flyer in and had a picture of the dog as well. They're here now. Any chance you can bring it down to the sheriff's office?"

She looked over at the little dog standing in the seat next to her, his brown eyes staring up at her with such devotion. How was she going to give this dog back?

She couldn't. She wouldn't.

All she had to do was say she didn't have him anymore. She didn't know anyone in this town, and she wasn't ever coming back. She could take Dewey and run, and no one would ever know.

Except that she would know.

And she could never actually do that. It wasn't fair to the dog's owners, and it wasn't fair to Dewey. Or whatever his name was.

If they loved him half as much as she did, they had to be going out of their minds trying to find him. She had to give the dog back. Besides, she'd already screwed up enough people's day today. It would be kind of nice to actually make someone's better.

"Yes," she told the dispatcher. "I'll be right there."

"Thanks, hon. I'll tell them to wait for you in reception."

Tess had seen the sheriff's office on her way into town, and it only took her five minutes to backtrack and pull into the lot. She turned off the engine and slumped in the seat. Dewey crawled across the console and into her lap.

Blinking back tears, she put her arms around him, cuddling him to her chest. "I love you, you little mutt. But I'm sure your real owners love you just as much. I'll bet they've been out of their minds wondering what happened to you." She imagined a cute, little old couple like Lee and Helen, the Kansas folks with the RV who she'd met at the KOA campground.

Holding the dog in her arms, she grabbed her purse and slung it over her shoulder as she trudged into the sheriff's office.

Pushing through the door, she glanced around for a cute couple or even a distraught family, but all she saw were two scruffy guys whose similarly disheveled brown hair and freckled faces distinguished them as brothers.

They looked to be in their mid-twenties, and both wore ratty T-shirts and faded jeans with dirty knees. One nudged the other when he spotted the dog, and they both clamored to their feet.

"There he is," the taller of the two said, reaching out his hand for the dog.

Dewey trembled in her arms, and Tess clutched him to her chest, horrified at the thought of turning him over to these two. "Are you sure this is your dog?"

"Sure as shit we are," the shorter brother said. He gave her a condescending smile. His teeth were stained yellow, and bits of chewing tobacco clung to his dry and cracked bottom lip. "The dumb mongrel must have jumped out of our truck when we were in town the other day. We've been looking all over for him."

The taller one held up a length of rope. "We know to tie him in now. He won't get away again."

Cold fingers of dread snaked their way through Tess's chest. Where was the nice family with the weeping little children who had been missing their dog? Where was the sweet little old lady who was going to cuddle him and feed him extra treats now that she'd found him?

There was no way she was going to hand her dog over to these two.

Except that he wasn't *her* dog. He belonged to them.

She glanced at the clerk sitting at the reception desk, praying he would see her predicament and offer his help, but the man only shrugged. "Sorry, lady. If he's their dog, you've got to give him back."

Why had she listened to her stupid conscience? She should have kept driving and told the dispatcher she had the wrong number.

She couldn't bring herself to let go of the dog. Maybe they would listen to reason. She had to try, at least. "You know, I'm happy to keep him," she told them. "I've grown quite attached to him and would be glad to take him off your hands. Since he's so much trouble and all."

A knowing glance passed between the brothers.

"Nah," the short one said. "We want him back. And he belongs to us."

The taller one sneered down at her. "Yeah, he belongs to us, so hand him over, lady."

She had no choice. She was in the sheriff's office, for goodness sake. She couldn't just make a run for it. She loved the dog, but she didn't really want to get arrested for him.

Tipping her head, she kissed Dewey on his furry head and gave him one last squeeze. Her hands shook as she held him out.

The shorter brother roughly grabbed him, and a shiver of disgust ran through her as his filthy hand brushed against hers. Dewey let out a heartbreaking whine, his feet scrambling in midair as he tried to climb back to her.

Oh gosh. She couldn't do this.

Her throat burned, and tears stung her eyes. She turned away, hurrying toward the door. She couldn't bear to see the little dog with them, couldn't handle the sound of his pitiful cries.

She stumbled toward her car, fighting for control as despair threatened to overwhelm her. She'd lost everything she loved today. Mason. Dewey.

Well, not everything. She still had Mimi. And the thought of how close those two thugs had come to hurting her grandmother stole the breath from Tess's lungs.

How had things gotten to this point? She'd let them all down, and her heart felt as if it had shattered to pieces. Her chest burned with the pain of it. She just wanted to get in her car and fall apart.

A shadow fell across her car, and the scent of unwashed skin surrounded her as she felt a presence behind her. She jumped as one of the scruffy brothers stuck an arm out, pressing his hand against her car door, blocking her from getting away.

"Hey, lady," he said, "my brother and I were thinking about what you said. How you were so attached to this here dog and all. And we were thinking that you might want to buy him back from us."

Buy him back? Was that what this whole thing was about? Was this all a scam to get money?

She turned around and took a step back, hoping they wouldn't actually get rough with her in front of the sheriff's office.

The taller one had Dewey tucked into his arm, the rope wound tightly around his neck. These guys didn't give one fig about the dog. The little shits.

Well, she did. She loved him, and she'd give them whatever she had to get him back.

"How much do you want for him?" She tried to keep her tone casual, as if she didn't really care about the dog.

Although these two bastards already knew she did.

The shorter one narrowed his eyes, studying her. "Two hundred dollars."

"Two hundred dollars? Are you kidding me? I don't have that kind of money." She gestured to the Ford Taurus. "Look at the car I'm driving. Do I look rich to you?"

"Yeah. You do." He spat a long stream of tobacco on the ground next to her feet.

Disgusting pig.

But she didn't flinch. She knew they were trying to bully her.

"And you also look like you want this dog pretty bad."

You sound like you could use a lesson in grammar. Ignoring his poor sentence structure, she racked her brain for how she could possibly come up with two hundred dollars or *any* dollars for that matter.

She suddenly remembered the bag of tip money

Quinn had given her. She'd looked inside it the night before, expecting it to hold an assortment of ones and maybe a five, but had been surprised to see several tens and twenties mixed in as well.

"Listen, I just worked the snack bar at the hockey game, and I have my tips from that night." She pulled the crumpled paper sack from her bag and held it out. "There's got to be close to eighty dollars in there. You can have it, but that's all I've got."

"We didn't expect you to have it on you. We can wait while you go to the ATM."

"Then you'll be waiting a long damn time. I just got fired from my job, and my bank account is completely drained. I can't even buy a cup of coffee. Literally, what is in this bag is all the money I have to my name."

The shorter one eyed her with suspicion. "I don't believe you."

"It doesn't matter if you believe me or not. It's the truth. I've been sleeping in my car for the last few nights because I'm so broke."

The taller brother peered into the back seat of her car. "We might take something in trade. You got anything in there you can give us? Anything valuable like a car stereo or an iPad? What about a laptop?"

She shook her head. "I wish I did. You can have the radio, if you want. I don't care."

"That radio is a piece of crap. It's not worth anything."

She racked her brain again for anything she had that was worth any value at all. All she had were a few toiletries, several fast-food condiment packets, an emergency blanket, and the clothes on her back. She mentally ran through the items in her bag. Her makeup was mostly drugstore brands, and somehow she didn't think these guys were interested in a few tampons and her seventeen tubes of lip gloss.

She did have one thing though. One thing of value.

"Listen, fellas, we both have an objective here. I want the dog, and you want money or something you can sell." She pointed to her bag. "This purse is the most expensive thing that I own. I'll trade you it for the dog."

The taller one scoffed. "What the hell are we gonna do with a purse? You think we're some kind of cross-dressers?"

"No, of course not." Not the least reason being they had zero sense of style and didn't recognize a good designer bag when they saw it. "It's just that this is an expensive bag. It's designer, and you can easily pawn it for a couple hundred dollars."

The shorter one nudged his brother. "You could give it to Angie. Then she might forget about the two hundred bucks you owe her."

The taller one seemed to be thinking it over. "You sure that's all you got?"

"I'm sure."

"Yeah. Okay. We'll take the bag of money *and* the purse."

Tess unlocked and opened the back door of the car and dumped the contents of her purse into the seat. She quickly brushed a hand lovingly over the row of leather daisies, but knew her mother would totally approve of the swap.

Straightening, she pushed the back door closed with her rump, then handed the paper sack and the purse to one brother as the other unceremoniously dumped the dog into her arms.

Dewey's body wriggled with joy as he licked her neck and chin.

"Nice doing business with you," she said, clutching the dog to her chest as she slid into the driver's seat and slammed her car door.

Not.

She turned over the engine and fled the parking lot before either brother changed his mind.

Dewey sat in her lap for the whole drive home. His fur smelled a little like the brothers had, but she'd give him a bath when they got to Mimi's. Until then, she was content to stroke his back and know that while she might have lost her most valuable possession, she'd gained a prize worth more than any treasure.

Mason picked at his food, his appetite apparently having left with Tess when she'd pulled out of the driveway earlier that day.

Had it really been only a few hours since she'd left?

He looked around the table at his family and the small wedding party and tried not to think about the fact that Tess was supposed to be here at the rehearsal dinner. With him.

The rest of the afternoon had gone by in a flurry of activity as he showered and dressed, then piled into the trucks with his family and went into town to the church. They'd spent well over an hour rehearsing the fifteen-minute ceremony, and Mason had done his best to pay attention and be happy for his brother. His job as the best man wasn't all that difficult—stand next to Rock, hand him the rings, then smile and walk down the aisle with Leanne Perkins on his arm.

He wouldn't have to give the toast until the reception tomorrow, but luckily, he'd written it weeks ago. Of course he had. He was the levelheaded brother, the one who took care of things, who got things done. Who planned for the best and prepared for the worst.

Well, he'd planned for the best with Tess, and the worst had happened.

He was still in shock—pretty sure that he'd just missed the last ten minutes of the story Colt had been telling him. The food on his plate, normally his favorite, had his stomach churning and nausea building in his throat. He just wanted this night to be over. He wanted to go home, to crawl into bed and lick his wounds.

The whole point of asking Tess to be his date was so he wouldn't have to show up at all of these events as a single. So he wouldn't have to explain why he still wasn't married or why he hadn't found a nice girl to settle down with yet. It was supposed to make the wedding festivities easier on him. Instead, he felt even more humiliated, even more self-conscious of the fact that he was alone.

Because he'd had someone. For one fleeting second, he'd had a girl. And not just any girl, but *the* girl. The one he'd thought would stay.

But he'd been wrong.

―――

Tessa padded barefoot into the kitchen. She couldn't sleep.

The clock read close to midnight, and she hoped some warm hot chocolate would help her sleep. But no amount of chocolate was enough to soothe the pain in her heart.

She slumped into the chair and laid her head on the kitchen table, her energy drained just from walking down the stairs. She didn't care about the stupid hot chocolate anymore, didn't have enough strength even to get up and find a cup.

She'd royally stepped in it, and this was one mess she didn't know how to fix.

She'd tried to text Mason a couple of times that night—short messages that said how sorry she was and that she hoped maybe they could talk again in a couple of days. He hadn't responded to either text, and she knew it was over. That she'd ruined everything this time.

Dewey stood by her chair, the one thing she'd done right in the last four days. She reached down and picked him up, cuddling the little dog against her chest. He nuzzled his head into her neck.

It was hard to believe she could love something so desperately after only having it in her life for a few days, but it had only taken her five minutes to fall madly in love with this dog.

And the same went for Mason.

Although it might have taken ten minutes to fall in love with him.

It didn't seem possible that she could feel so much for a man she'd just met, didn't seem feasible that her heart could ache this awfully bad after having spent only four days with him. But the pain in her chest was real. The desolate ache of her bones was genuine. And the despair she suffered from knowing that this pain was all her own doing was as authentic as any emotion she'd ever felt.

Forgetting the hot chocolate, she stumbled back to bed, fell onto the mattress, and pulled the covers over her head. Pressing her face into the pillow, she bit back the screams she wanted to roar into the fabric.

The pain in her chest built until she feared her skin would tear and split from the force of it. Her throat burned, filled with thick emotion.

Drawing in a long, shuddering breath, she finally broke. Finally allowed the desperation to take her and let the sobs loose. Deep, racking sobs that came from a cavernous place of heartache and heartbreak.

Dewey curled up on the pillow next to her head, standing guard over her as she cried herself out and finally fell asleep.

Mason sat on his front porch, his feet propped up on the railing in front of him. Theo lay on the floor next to his chair, and he absently scratched the dog's back as he rocked back and forth.

It was late, had to be past midnight. He knew he should get some rest, but he didn't want to go inside. Didn't want to climb into his bed and smell the scent of Tess on his sheets. Instead, he'd spent the last hour staring into the darkness, listening to the crickets and the night sounds.

The soft thud of footsteps had Theo lifting his head and letting out a sniff. A dark shadow approached from the house, and Mason was surprised to see his older brother climb the few steps to his porch.

"Hey, Rock. What are you still doing up? Aren't you supposed to be tucked in bed getting your beauty rest for the big day tomorrow?"

"Beauty rest is overrated," Rock said, passing Mason one of the two opened bottles of beer he held before sinking into the rocking chair next to him. "How you holding up, Brother?"

Mason shrugged and tipped the bottle to his mouth, letting the cold beer soothe his dry and achy throat. "I'm not ashamed to admit that I've been better."

"I bet."

They sat in silence for a few minutes, each staring out over the pasture.

"That was a good thing you did today," Rock finally said. "You know, giving them the money. You didn't have to. Especially after Tess…"

"Lied to me? Used me?"

"Yeah, that."

"I know I didn't have to. But it was the right thing to do. I couldn't let them lose their house. Or let those goons rough up that little old lady. Although, I think they would have had their hands full on the drive back to Denver. That old gal has some spunk."

"Just like her granddaughter."

Mason sighed. "Yeah, just like her granddaughter."

"I know she lied to you, lied to all of us, and that was wrong. But I think she did it for the right reasons."

"That doesn't matter."

"Doesn't it?" Rock tipped his beer back and took another swallow. "Seems to me you really liked this girl."

"I did. That's what makes it sting so much."

"I know how you feel about people lying to you, so I know this has got to be tearing you up, but are you going to at least talk to her? Try to work things out?"

"What's the point? She wasn't interested in me anyway. All she wanted was to get close to you. Just like every other woman I've let into my life."

"That's bullshit, and you know it. Tess didn't give a crap about me. She didn't even know I was in the room if you were around."

"Oh, she knew. Everyone always knows."

"Hoss, you have got to get over this thing about women using you to get to me. It happened a couple of times, and once was when we were in high school. So what? If that was the kind of women they were, you didn't want them anyway. And that was a long time ago. We're grown men now. And believe me, you're a hell of a lot better catch than I am anyway."

"Oh yeah, right. You're just a rich guy who's a professional hockey star."

"So what? You're just a rich guy who runs a successful ranch."

"Those are completely different kinds of rich."

"Doesn't matter. There's no reason for any woman to pick me over you. We've both got money, and we're both successful. Plus we've both got the James family's devilishly good looks."

Mason let out a light chuckle.

"My point is that you've got plenty of things going for you, Mace. And Tess saw those things in you. She couldn't care less about me. Even today, when she came to talk to Quinn and me, all she could talk about was you and how she didn't want to hurt you."

Mason's hand stilled on the dog's back. "What do you mean when she came to you and Quinn? Came to you about what?"

"To tell us the truth about who she was and why she was here."

"I didn't know she did that. Did she admit that the only reason she was here was to dig up dirt on you and write some trashy article for a rag magazine?"

"Not in so many words, but yes. She told us the truth about the story and why it was so important. But she apologized and said she wouldn't turn it in until we read it and gave her our blessing."

"But she's already turned it in."

"I know. We told her she could."

"But why? Why would you let her turn in a story like that? Why would you let her print a bunch of trash about you being a bad boy who couldn't settle down and Quinn being a gold digger?"

Rock let out a chuckle. "Because that wasn't what the story was about. She told us her boss wanted some kind of 'hit piece' that covered all the dirt of our wedding and smeared my name, but that's not the story Tess wrote. She wrote this beautiful article about redemption and forgiveness and how we found each other again after all these years. It was really freaking beautiful, man. I acted pissed, but it almost brought me to tears. Hell, it did make Q cry."

Mason shook his head. He couldn't believe what he was hearing. His brother was actually sticking up for Tess—for the woman who had tricked them. For a reporter, for frick's sake.

"You usually hate news stories about you."

"I know. But that's because they usually report on what a schmuck they think I am. This was different. And it wasn't all about me. Or Quinn. I mean, it was. But it was also about second chances. I'm telling you, it was good. And it impressed me that she came to us first and talked to us about it. She was all torn up, and she was freaking out about how she was going to tell you about it when you got back. It's obvious that woman really cares about you."

"It doesn't change the fact that she lied."

"True. But we've all made mistakes and done things we wish we could take back. I know I've done tons of stupid shit, said loads of things I wish I could forget or erase. And so have you. That's what makes us human. And the fact that we've all screwed up is what gives us the strength to offer forgiveness to others."

Mason shrugged. Could he forgive Tess?

"Letting yourself care about someone is almost a guarantee that you *will* get hurt. No relationship is perfect, and sometimes you hurt each other. But then you forgive each other and move on. Because the good stuff far outweighs the bad. So you just have to decide if she's worth the risk of getting hurt. If she's worth fighting for."

Mason rubbed a hand across his neck and offered his brother a wry smile. "You say some pretty smart stuff for being a dumb jock."

"That's because I'm a dumb jock who knows what he's talking about. Remember, I almost let my pride get in the way of winning back the best thing that ever happened to me. I made stupid mistakes with Quinn, and it almost cost me everything. I don't want to see the same thing happen to you."

"Thanks."

"That's what big brothers are for. To watch out for their little brothers and knock some sense into them when they need it." Rock finished the last swallow of his beer and stood up from his chair. "Now, quit your moping and go to bed. I need you sharp tomorrow. I'm getting married, you know."

Mason chuckled. "Yeah, I know."

Chapter 22

Tessa stumbled into the kitchen the next morning, her eyes dry and gritty from her crying jag the night before.

"Good morning, sunshine," her grandmother said, holding up the pot of coffee. "Pour you a cup?"

Tess nodded and sagged into a kitchen chair.

Mimi set a steaming cup of coffee and the container of creamer in front of her. "You planning to mope around here all day?"

"That was the plan. You got a better idea?"

"In fact, I do."

Before her grandmother could share her idea, Tess's phone rang. Hope sprang in her chest that it was Mason, but it was only her boss.

She considered for a moment letting the phone ring. He could leave a message if it was important.

But in the middle of her pity party the night before, she'd made a decision. A big one.

She was tired of being asked to write hit pieces that aired dirty laundry and shared the secrets and gossip in Colorado. Writing Rock and Quinn's love story had filled something in her. She was proud of what she'd created. It wasn't just a story about two people; it was a story about all people. A story about second chances and forgiveness and grace.

It was the kind of story she wanted to write again. And that's what she was going to tell her boss.

She picked up the phone. "Hello."

"Hi, Tess," her boss's voice boomed.

"Listen, Gordon, before you say anything, there is something I need to tell you. I spent a lot of time with Rock and Quinn, and they're good people. I wrote a great story—one I'm proud of—and I'm not going to change it."

"Good."

"Good?"

"Yeah, good. Because I loved it. We're going to run it in the next edition. It's not our normal style, but the article *was* in-depth, and you captured a lot of details while drawing the reader into the story. You delivered on your side of the deal, and I've already cut you a check for the full bonus—two thousand dollars. You can pick it up in payroll on Monday."

Well, she hadn't expected that.

She paused and considered turning down the money. Just to prove to Mason he was more important than any story.

But maybe she should have considered that the day before. Heck, maybe she should have considered not turning in the story at all. Or trying to retract it after she'd sent it.

Rock and Quinn had been so great. Yeah, they'd been mad at first, when she'd admitted to being a reporter, but both gave their blessing for the article after she'd explained everything and they'd both read it.

She'd been so happy, so glad to be able to turn in the story and get the money to help her grandmother, that she'd dictated it into her phone and sent the first draft to her boss as soon as she'd gone back to Mason's.

In hindsight, she probably should have waited to talk to Mason. But what was it they said about hindsight—that it was a mother, or a dish best served cold with perfect vision? She couldn't remember the exact metaphor, which made it an even better metaphor for the jumbled-up mess she'd made of her life the past few days.

Which seemed par for the course for her life.

All she'd wanted to do was help her grandmother save their house. She hadn't planned on hurting anyone and sure as heck hadn't expected to fall in love. But that's what she'd done. On both accounts.

And in the end, Mason was the one who'd ended up saving their house. Her grandmother had stopped at the bank on the way home from Denver and already paid off the late mortgage payments. So Tess would take the money from the magazine and use it to pay Mason back.

"That sounds fine," she finally told Gordon. "But what about my job?"

"It's yours again if you want it."

Did she want it?

"Sorry, Gordon, but I loved writing this story…loved writing about something good, something that inspires people. I'm tired of being asked to report on news that showcases the worst in them. And I want a chance at some of the bigger features. I want to write articles that help people or offer some kind of hope. And if I can't do that with you, I'll find another magazine."

She really meant it. She was tired of messing things up, making bad decisions that just screwed everything up.

"You don't have to find another magazine. I was really impressed with this article. It's the best writing I've seen from you, and I was thinking the magazine might benefit from something in this style anyway. Maybe we could come up with a monthly feature for you to work on. Why don't you come in and see me this week, and we can talk more about it?"

"That sounds good."

"All right. See you then."

"See you then." She hung up the phone with a satisfied grin. "Well, I told him."

"You sure did," Mimi said, raising her coffee cup in a toast. "I'm proud of you, girl."

Tess clinked her cup to her grandmother's and took a sip of coffee. Then she set down her cup and let out a sigh. "Now if I could only fix the other thing I screwed up. The most important one."

"Why can't you? Have you tried talking to him?"

"That's part of the problem. He won't talk to me. He said he didn't want anything to do with me. And I tried texting him a couple of times last night, but he didn't reply."

"I'm not talking about this stupid texting nonsense. I'm talking about *actually* talking to him. And if he doesn't want to talk to you, you need to find a way to make him listen."

"How am I supposed to do that?"

"I don't know, by doing something different that'll show him he's worth the effort and that you want a second chance. Hire a skywriter, serenade him with a boom box, flash him your boobs, it doesn't matter. Just *do something*. Do something that shows him he matters to you…that he's important."

"And you think flashing him my boobs is going to accomplish that? My boobs aren't that great."

Although, it had been the way they'd met, so it might be worth a try.

"Don't blame me. You got those from your mother's side." Her grandmother gave her chest a shimmy.

Tess rolled her eyes. "Not helping."

"Okay, maybe that wasn't one of my best ideas. You're the creative one. I'm sure you can think of something big that will prove to him you're truly sorry and deserve a second chance." Mimi picked up her cup and took another sip of coffee. "Or you can sit around here all day in your pajamas and feel sorry for yourself. It's your choice. But if it were me, and I had a chance at fixing things with a hotsie-totsie piece of cowboy beefcake, I'd sure as hell try."

She made a good case.

And Tess couldn't fix anything by sitting around moping.

She took a deep breath. She didn't have to just let things happen to her. Not anymore.

The last few days had taught her that she was stronger than she thought, that she could be funny and self-assured and part of something bigger than herself. She'd already stepped out of her box with Mason. She'd shown him the real Tess—the Tess she truly was, and the one she wanted to be—and he'd liked her, maybe even fallen in love with her.

All this time, she'd felt unworthy of being loved, been crippled by the feeling that she didn't deserve happiness because of what had happened with her parents. She'd been viewing herself through the eyes of some jerk and a few coworkers and had only seen the parts where she wasn't enough, the parts they'd mocked and joked about.

But Mason hadn't seen her like that at all. For the first time in a long time, she'd let her guard down. She'd lowered her defenses and let him see the real her. The woman who was helpful and useful, who teased and joked around instead of being a joke.

She'd shared with him her deepest secrets, her most humiliating moments, and he hadn't laughed or pulled away or run for the hills. Instead, he'd gotten sad and mad, and was ready to dig in and go to battle for, and with, her.

For a few short days, she hadn't seen herself as a slightly overweight, socially awkward, too-tall girl. Instead, she'd seen herself through Mason's eyes. He'd made her feel like a confident, curvy woman who could be sexy and alluring, who could make a hot-as-hell cowboy fall to pieces with the touch of her hand on his skin.

When she'd been with Mason, she'd felt a new part of her blossom and grow. And not just the sexier part of her—the stronger part, the more confident part. The part of her that'd stepped out onto a porch to fight a couple of goons with a hockey stick. The part that'd wrangled cows and helped fixed a fence, that'd ridden a horse and stood up to her boss and fought for what she wanted. The part of her that'd sacrificed whatever it took to hold on to a little dog that she loved.

Pain tore at her heart as she realized she'd fought harder for the dog than she had for Mason.

So why was she letting the best thing that ever happened to her slip away without even putting up a fight? She wasn't. Not now.

Not the new Tess.

The new Tess was going to put on some lipstick and a

knockout dress and march into battle. Because what she had with Mason was worth fighting for.

And she would do whatever it took to prove that to him.

All the rehearsing must have paid off, because the wedding ceremony went off without a hitch.

Mason did his part—handed off the rings and smiled at Leanne, smiled at everyone, as he escorted her down the aisle after his brother and Quinn. He was still smiling—his cheeks hurt from smiling so much—but he was dying on the inside.

The happy couple sat at the head table, holding court as throngs of people flocked to give them best wishes and offer congratulations.

Mason needed a break. He didn't think he could take one more well-wisher who smiled at Rock, then offered a pitying glance at him. Apparently, word had traveled fast that Mason had met someone new and that he and Tess were indeed an item. Unfortunately, the news of their breakup had traveled faster, spreading through the grapevine and the gossips in the reception hall.

He wasn't sure which was worse: their earlier callous remarks about his sad state of singlehood or their pity for the fact that he'd almost had something, then lost it.

He pulled at his collar and made his way out of the reception hall. He needed some air.

A dark-haired woman stepped out of the kitchen and into the hallway in front of him. He recognized her as Angie Miller. She worked as a checker at the grocery store in town.

With a start, he also recognized the leather bag slung across her shoulder.

He quickened his step, trying to get a better look. Yes, he was sure—the brown leather and the little blue flowers along the top edge. That was Tess's purse. It had to be.

But what was Angie Miller doing with Tess's purse?

Maybe she had one that was similar. *Yeah right*.

Tess had said that bag was a designer brand and had cost her a pretty penny. There was no way Angie could afford a designer bag with one of her paychecks at the supermarket.

"Hey, Angie," he said, catching up to her and holding the door. "You leaving already?"

"Hey, Mason. Yeah, I got a shift at the market tonight. I was just helping my mom in the kitchen. She made Rock's cake, ya know?"

"Oh yeah. It was great. Delicious." He peered down at her purse and noted the silver daisy charm and the one flower that was hanging by a thread off the side. It was definitely Tess's bag. But how did one go about starting a conversation with a woman about her purse? "Um, so that's a nice bag you've got there."

Real smooth.

She glanced down at the purse, then held it out with a note of pride in her voice. "Thanks. It's not really my style. But it's a designer bag—*very* expensive. It was a gift from my boyfriend."

"Wow. Nice gift. Don't you date one of the Harris boys?"

"Yeah. Why?"

"Well, no offense intended, but where do you think he got the money to buy a nice purse like that?"

She shrugged. "He said he suckered it out of a rich city girl who traded it for some stupid farm dog that jumped out of their truck a couple days ago."

Her words hit Mason like a punch to the gut. She had to be talking about Dewey. Tess must have traded her purse in order to keep the dog.

He pretended to study the bag. "I used to date a gal who had a thing for designer bags, and to tell you the truth, this one kind of looks like a knockoff to me. In fact, I'm almost sure it's a fake. You can get those in Denver for, like, fifty bucks."

She glanced down at the bag. "That son of a bitch. He told me this purse was worth five hundred dollars, and he gave it to me to square up the two hundred he owes me."

Mason played it cool. He didn't want to show his hand.

"He does sound like a jerk. And that's a dang shame that now you're carrying a cheap purse *and* you're out the money that he owed you." He rubbed a hand across his chin. "Tell you what… I've got a friend who would probably like that and wouldn't know or care it was a fake. I'd give you a hundred for it."

She eyed him suspiciously. "If it's a knockoff, why are you willing to give me a hundred bucks for it?"

"Yeah, you're right. And it does have this one flower thing that's coming off. I was just trying to help you out because I felt bad, and I thought my friend would like it. But let's just forget it." He turned to walk away.

"No, wait." She grabbed his arm. "You're right. I'll take the hundred."

"I don't want to start trouble. Seeing as how your boyfriend gave it to you and all."

Her mouth pulled into a tight line. "I'm gonna give him something..."

Mason didn't even feel bad for the guy. Served him right for swindling Tess out of her bag. He was sure she'd traded it for Dewey. And he didn't give a crap what kind of trouble the Harris kid got into with his girlfriend.

He pulled two fifties from his wallet and held them out to her.

She grabbed the bills and stuffed them in her pocket. "Let me just empty my stuff out."

"Sure." He followed her to her car and waited while she dumped the meager contents into the front seat, then shoved the bag into his hands as if it offended her.

He needed to make a quick exit before she changed her mind. "You take care now, Angie. It was good to see you."

"You too." Her expression turned flirty as her gaze traveled over him.

Uh-oh.

"Hope you get your money back from your boyfriend. I'd sure give him the business if I were you." He took a few steps back.

The pissed-off look returned. *Thank goodness.*

"See you around." He made a quick exit, detouring around the cars in the parking lot to his truck. He tossed the bag into the cab, then headed back into the reception hall.

He didn't know what to think now. He was still angry—and hurt—from Tess lying to him.

But how could he stay mad at a woman who traded her most valuable possession for an ugly, scruffy dog?

The reception was still in full swing as Mason stepped back into the room. It had been warm outside, and he grabbed a bottle of water from the buffet table. He took a long swig, then dropped into the empty chair next to his aunt. "How's it going, Sassy?"

"It's going. My bunion is killing me, my arthritis is acting up, and my bra strap is too tight. But other than a few aches and pains, I'm thankful I woke up and could get out of bed this morning." She studied his face. "How are you doing?"

"Other than the whole arthritis and bra-strap thing, about the same as you." His hands might not hurt, but his heart sure did. He offered her a wry smile.

"I'm guessing there's trouble in paradise."

"Yeah? What makes you say that?"

"Besides the rumors flying around about you and Tess, you've been moping around here all day, and now you're back at the singles table with me."

"You can't believe everything you hear. And maybe I just like sitting here with you."

"Uh-huh." She folded her arms across her chest. "Plus, your mom told me all about it."

"Of course she did." He took another drink of water. "It doesn't matter. You're my best gal anyway."

She chuckled. "Don't let Vivi hear you say that."

"Why? I say it to her all the time."

"You always were a fresh talker."

"So I've been told."

She took a sip of coffee, then squinted at him over her cup. "So, how are you doing, really?"

"I'm fine."

"This is me you're talking to."

He shrugged. "I *am* fine. Except that I feel like hell, like I've just been hit by a truck. Then the truck reversed and ran over me, then dragged me along behind it for a mile or two. Other than that, I'm doing pretty well."

"Sounds about right."

He stared at her. "About right for what?"

"For what a broken heart feels like."

"Well, if you knew that, I wish you would have warned me, and I would have tried to avoid getting one."

"No, you wouldn't have."

He sighed. "No, I wouldn't have."

"So what are you going to do about it?"

"You mean, besides wallow in self-pity and drown my sorrows in this bottle of water?" Now he'd wished he'd grabbed a beer instead.

"Yes, besides that."

"What do you mean? What am I supposed to do about it?"

"How are you going to get her back?"

His eyes widened. "What are you talking about? Why would I want her back? She lied to me. And used me."

"And?"

"And I hate being lied to and used."

"Well, I hate prune juice, but I drink it anyway because I know it's good for me. And I know that little gal was good for you. I've never seen you as happy as you've been the last few days, and your mom agrees. She told me this girl was something special, and the two of you seemed to really care about each other."

"We did. Or at least I did. I'm not sure what she was feeling." Although he *was* sure. He knew all the things he and Tess had shared hadn't been fake. He knew she had to care for him, at least a little.

"So? Have you called her?"

"No."

"Have you talked to her at all?"

"No."

"Well, hell's bells, boy, how do you expect to work anything out if you don't even talk to each other?"

He'd wanted to call Tess, to talk to her. He'd even picked up his phone several times, then stopped himself. It was no use. How could he ever trust her? How could he ever know if she was telling him the truth? How could he forgive her for using him and trashing his brother?

Except that she hadn't trashed Rock. He'd said her article was flattering and shed him in a good light. And then there was the whole thing with Dewey and her bag.

He didn't know what to do. His head hurt almost as much as his heart. "You make a very good argument. But I think it's too late for talking."

"It's never too late for talking."

Was it too late?

Could he and Tess have a chance at working things out? Did he *want* to try?

"It seems like there was something special about this one."

"There was. There is. Tessa *was* different. She was great. We had a lot of fun together, and she just seemed to *get* me. We talked about everything, and I always felt good when I was around her. Like I was a better person, a better man. And when I wasn't with her, I couldn't wait to get back to her."

"Sounds to me like you're in love."

"Can you fall in love with someone in four days?"

She shrugged. "I once fell in love within fifteen minutes of meeting a man."

"You did? What did you do?"

"I married him, of course. He was your uncle."

"How did you know that you were in love so quickly?"

"You just do. Everything in the world seems different. Everything in your body goes on alert when you are around them. Your hands sweat and your skin heats, and you feel like you're either going to throw up or spin out of control."

Yeah, that about summed up how he felt about Tess.

She nudged his arm. "From the look on your face, it would appear that you recognize the feeling. So, I'll ask you again. What are you going to do about it?"

What was he going to do about it?

Not sit around here and mope anymore. That wasn't getting him anywhere. And it wasn't getting him any closer to working things out with Tess.

"Thank you, Aunt Sassy." He leaned over and kissed her cheek, then pushed back his chair. "I gotta go. Apparently, I've got to find the girl I love and try to win her back."

Before he could stand, the squeal of the microphone rang out in the reception hall. The mic was up front, on a little stage they'd set up for the DJ stand, and the crowd quieted as they looked toward the platform.

What was happening now? They'd already done the toasts and tossed the bouquet and the garter.

Great, he finally makes the decision that he's going to go after Tess, and now he was going to get stuck here for more wedding games.

"Is this on? Can you hear me?" A voice spoke into the mic. A voice that Mason recognized.

What the hell?

He whipped his head around and blinked. He couldn't believe it.

Tess was standing at the microphone, her hands clutching the stand in a white-knuckled grip. Her eyes were big and round and had that deer-in-the-headlights glazed look of pure terror.

She had on a teal-blue dress that hugged her curves, and her hair was curled and hung loose around her shoulders, shiny in the bright lights.

His heart leapt to his throat, and his mouth went dry at seeing her again.

She looked gorgeous. Amazing. Except for that whole terrified, wish-she-could-melt-into-the-floor state of panic she had going on.

Chapter 23

Tess took a deep breath.

What am I doing here? This was the dumbest idea she'd ever had.

She should forget it. She hadn't said anything—hadn't made a fool of herself yet. It wasn't too late to run.

But her legs wouldn't move. In fact, her whole body seemed to be frozen in place.

Everyone in the room was looking at her, staring at her with expectation, and she suddenly forgot everything she'd spent the last hour in the car preparing to say.

Oh heck. Who cared if she made a fool of herself? She'd come here to talk to Mason. To try to win him back. To show him she'd do anything to get him to talk to her, to give her another chance, even the thing she hated the most. The thing that terrified her to her very toes.

But there was one thing that terrified her even worse. And that was not taking the chance, not even trying, and losing him forever.

She'd come here to speak, so it was now or never.

Open your mouth, she silently commanded herself.

Just say something.

Anything.

"Hi. I'm...uh...Tessa Kane. Tess. If you don't know me. I'm a f-f-friend of the best man. Of Mason's. Well, I *was* a friend of his. More than a friend, really. Until

I s-s-screwed everything up." The mic squealed again, and another drop of sweat rolled down her back.

She took a deep breath and tried not to look out at the sea of faces staring at her. At the huge room full of people who were most likely thinking about what a supreme idiot she was. Because that didn't matter. What mattered was Mason. And telling him the truth.

"Because, you see, that's what I do with my life. I screw things up. I've been doing it for years. Good things have come my way, or chances at good things, and I blow them. Usually because I don't think I d-d-deserve them or I'm too afraid to go after what I really want. So I don't really try, or I give up too easily. But here's the thing... Mason James is the best thing that's happened to me in a l-l-long time. And I blew it with him. Big-time. Like colossally big."

She could hear the tremor in her voice, the occasional stutter of her words, but it was too late to stop now. She was on a roll. And she didn't care if she stuttered—didn't care if the whole room heard her and mocked her for it—as long as he heard what she had to say.

"Mason is a good man, and we had a really great thing going. We got along well, we could talk about anything, he made me laugh, and he even thought I was funny. Yeah, we laughed a lot. But more than that, he f-f-filled something in me, something that had been missing. You know that feeling you get when you go home after a long day and you change into your pajamas and wrap yourself in a blanket and sink into your favorite spot on the sofa? Like you're finally home and can relax and be yourself? That's how it felt to be with Mason. Like I was finally home.

"Which sounds great, r-r-right? I mean, I'm with this man who makes everything in my world seem better. And let's face it, he's crazy hot too. Have you seen this guy? All dark hair and brooding eyes, and those muscles." She bit into her bottom lip and let out a little sigh.

"I should have grabbed on to this man and never let him go. But that's not what I did. I didn't exactly *let* him go, but I sabotaged any chance we had at the real thing. And not just a tiny sabotage, but a full-on explosion with burn-the-house-down kind of damage. And I did it to myself. I lit the match and torched our relationship. Because I lied to him.

"I actually lied to all of you. Well, not all of you. Some of you I've never met.

"The truth is, we all lie. We exaggerate and mislead. We delude, and fabricate, and prevaricate. But it all comes down to the fact that we lie…about big things and insignificant things. I totally lie about my appearance. I don't have twenty-twenty vision. I'm wearing contacts. And I'm not the weight my driver's license says I am. Not even close. I haven't been for years." She touched her hand to her head. "And this isn't even my natural hair color.

"I've lied about a lot of things this week. I lied to a guy I really care about and a family that has come to mean a great deal to me. I told myself that I had a good reason, and I did. But in the end, it doesn't matter. Because it was too late. I'd already inflicted the damage and lost the one guy who could have changed everything.

"Because the b-b-biggest lie that I told this week was to myself, when I thought that I could walk away."

She put her hand above her eyes, shielding them from the glare of the lights of the DJ stand. Searching the crowd, her heart raced as she scoured the faces, looking for the only one that she cared about. The only one that mattered.

There. In the corner, sitting next to Aunt Sassy.

Her heart broke at the sight of him. He was so damn handsome in his tuxedo.

She couldn't read his expression, but he didn't budge, didn't get up or move toward her. He just sat there.

Her body told her to run, that this whole idea was backfiring. But she'd come here to try, to salvage the destruction that she'd created.

She dropped her hand and tried to block out everyone else in the room. There was only one person who she really cared about anyway. Only one person who needed to hear what she had to say. She focused on his face.

"The biggest lie I told this week, Mason, was when I told myself that I didn't love you and that it didn't matter that you d-d-didn't want to see me anymore. Because it does matter. You matter. You are worth fighting for.

"So this is me, Tessa Kane, panicked and petrified public speaker, doing the thing that I hate, facing my biggest fear, standing up here to tell you that I am in love with you. It doesn't matter that it happened fast. It only matters that it happened.

"And this whole public-speaking thing—the thing I thought was my greatest fear—isn't really the thing I'm the most afraid of.

"My biggest fear is losing you."

There. She'd said it.

She swallowed, trying to catch her breath. The air rushed in her ears as she waited for Mason to move.

What did she expect him to do? Race to the stage and sweep her into his arms and declare his undying love? Yeah, that would work. Heck, anything would work. Anything but having him just sit there and stare at her. And do nothing.

Nervous titters flitted through the crowd. And her paralysis finally broke. Her legs finally moved and carried her from the stage, through the side door, and down the hall.

Glancing around, she looked for a place to hide, to disappear.

The reception was in the Masonic Lodge, the same venue where the prewedding party had been, and she spied the door to the closet where she'd first met Mason. The closet where this whole charade had started with a half-baked plan and a too-small shirt.

She ducked into the closet, turned on the light, and sank onto the floor, leaning her back against the wall as she clutched her knees to her chest.

This could work. She could stay in here until the reception was over, and then she could slip out and sneak out of town under the cover of darkness. It was a perfect plan. Okay, maybe not perfect, but it was a plan anyway. And a plan that allowed her to stay hidden and not have to face Mason or anyone in his family or this town again.

She rested her forehead on her knees, taking a deep breath and willing herself not to cry.

Mason was sure he'd seen Tessa run down this hall. He hadn't heard the main doors open so she must not have left the building. Peering down the hall, he knew there was only one place that made sense for her to hide. He knocked on the closet door, then pushed it open and looked inside.

Flashes of memories flooded his mind, images of her laughing as she held the edges of her shirt together, the black lace of her bra peeking from between them.

"Tess?"

She was there, huddled on the floor, her arms wrapped around her knees.

"Can I come in?"

"Sure." Her voice was soft.

He closed the door behind him, then crossed the room and sank to the floor next to her. He stretched his legs out in front of him. "That was some speech. Especially from a—what did you call it?—a panicked and petrified public speaker. That took guts to get up there and admit that you lied… I mean, *prevaricated*."

He thought he could tease a smile out of her. She looked so miserable. She was breaking his heart.

"I did it for you," she whispered.

"I know." He wanted to touch her, to pull her into his arms. "And I know what it took for you to get up there and do that. It was crazy brave."

"It doesn't matter if it was brave, or bold, or just plain stupid. It didn't work."

"What do you mean?"

"You didn't move."

"That's because I was stunned. I couldn't believe that you were standing on the stage. I was in shock." He leaned against her side. "And I did move. I'm here."

"Why?"

"Because your words meant something to me. Because I wanted to talk to you."

"You haven't answered my texts or called me."

"I know. I'm sorry. I was hurt and pissed off. I needed some time to cool off and think."

"And…?"

"And to tell you the truth, I was just getting ready to come find you."

She raised an eyebrow.

"I swear. I had just told Aunt Sassy I was leaving when I heard your voice boom out into the room. That's why I was in such shock… I mean, besides the obvious that you were standing up in front of a whole room of people at a microphone. But I really had just made up my mind to come find you. I was going to drive to Denver. And then there you were."

"Why were you going to come find me?"

"To talk to you. To try to work things out. To tell you that I love you."

Her eyes widened and pooled with tears. "You do?"

"Yeah, I do. I think I have from the moment I met you. The last four days have been incredible. I mean, I feel like my heart's been thrown in a washing machine and set to spin. I've run the gamut of every emotion. I've been happy as a pig in mud and mad as a hornet. I've wanted you like nothing I've ever wanted in my life, but I've also felt sorrow deeper than a mountain canyon. Sometimes when I'm with you, I feel like I'm high or drunk, like my head is whirling and I can't breathe. And other times I feel the purest sense of calm, like I'm right exactly where I'm supposed to be.

"I had a hard time accepting that I could actually fall

in love with someone in such a short time, but if I had any doubt about it, seeing you standing on that stage pouring your heart out while your hands shook and your voice trembled, that cinched it for me. That's when I knew for sure."

He rested his hand lightly on top of hers. "Your hands are still shaking."

"That's because I'm still scared," she whispered.

"Of what?"

"Of losing you. Of screwing up again. I swear, I never wanted to hurt you. I never wanted to hurt any of you. And I tried to make it right...with the article. I swear I did."

"I know. Rock told me. He said that what you wrote was really great. I think he even said it was so beautiful, it might have brought tears to his eyes." He understood that feeling. He was having it right now as he looked down into Tess's blue eyes. She was so beautiful that it hurt to breathe, and his throat filled with the emotion building there.

He offered her a small smile.

"Thank you. That was nice of him to say. Your brother really is a good guy."

"I know." He sighed, prepared for the feelings of inadequacy to wash over him. But they didn't. "I feel like I've spent my whole life in a race against my brother, and I've always felt like I came in second place."

He turned his body toward her and lifted his hand to her cheek. "Until I met you. And for the first time, I felt like someone saw me, and liked me, just for me."

"I did. I didn't even know Rock. But even after I met him, he didn't hold a candle to you. I didn't like you because you could play some sport really well or were famous or a celebrity." She touched her hand to his chest. "I liked you for what was inside of you. I liked the chivalrous guy who loaned me a shirt and gave me a piggyback ride in the rain. I liked the guy who went out of his way to make sure everyone else was doing okay before he ever worried about himself. And I fell in love with the guy who made me laugh and listened when I talked, and fed me pie and sugar cubes, and treated my little stray scruffy dog like he was one of his own."

Her words touched something inside him, and he knew all that other stuff didn't matter. He hated that she'd lied, but he believed her now—believed that what she was telling him was the truth from her heart.

"I know what happened with Dewey. That you traded your favorite purse—the one that reminded you of your mom—for him."

Her eyes widened. "How did you know?"

"I saw a local girl walking out of the reception with it slung over her shoulder. I asked her about it, and she said her boyfriend gave it to her, that some woman had given it to him in trade for one of his farm mutts. I knew it had to be you."

"I would have given just about anything I had to get that dog back. Actually, I did. I gave them everything except the clothes on my back. And I would do it again." She shrugged. "I loved that purse. But I love the dog more. And if the last few days have taught me anything, it's to go after and fight for what you love. Even if you think you're unworthy or that you screwed it up so bad that it can never be fixed. Fight for it anyway."

She peered at him from under her lashes. "That's why

I came up here and commandeered the microphone at your brother's wedding reception. To fight for you. To do something I never thought I could do, to prove to you I would do anything to win you back."

He dipped his head and pressed his lips to hers.

She tasted like spearmint and vanilla. And home.

"It worked," he said.

She wrapped her arms around him. "Mason, I have made so many poor judgment calls and plenty of bad decisions, but coming up here and putting my fears behind me to fight for you is the best decision I've ever made."

"Letting go of my pride and forgiving you is the best decision I've ever made." He kissed her again. "That, and the spontaneous decision to invite a woman I just met—but who had already shown me her bra—to be my plus-one for an entire weekend of wedding festivities *with* my family. I was sure you wouldn't last a day. I thought you'd make a run for it as soon as you could."

She let out a soft chuckle. "You thought wrong."

He offered her a roguish grin. "That was only one of the thoughts I had about you. I had plenty more, starting with the moment I met you in this closet and your shirt busted open. I had this crazy fantasy of tearing it the rest of the way off and getting you naked and pressed up against the wall, then having my way with you in this closet."

"That's a fantasy I could turn into a reality." She flashed him a flirty grin.

His heart pounded against his chest. "Tess, as much as I love that idea, I don't want this to be a fantasy. I want this to be real. I *am* in love with you, and I want to have a future with you and build a life with you. I want to have a relationship with you that lasts longer than the one you had with your favorite purse."

"Keep talking like that, and my dress is going to tear itself off." She laughed and crawled over him, straddling his lap. Taking his chin in her hands, she gazed into his eyes. "Seriously, I want all of that too. I love you, Mason James."

His chest felt light, and he could breathe again. As if all the pain and hurt that had been stuck in his chest had just been released and replaced with pure happiness.

But he kept his face grim and his tone somber. "I don't know if it's gonna happen though."

"What? Why?"

"Because I bought that purse back from Angie for a hundred bucks, so it's still got a good five years on me."

"You bought it back? Are you serious?"

He laughed. "It's in my truck right now."

The biggest grin cut across her face. "You really are my hero. In my eyes, you've never come in second place to anyone." She cupped her palm around his cheek. "Your brother might be the one getting married, but you really are the best man. The best man for me."

"I love you, Tess." Unable to hold back his smile, his heart full to bursting, he pressed a kiss to the spot just below her ear, the spot that drove her crazy, then whispered, "Now, what was that you said about your dress?"

Keep reading for a sneak peek of the next book in Jennie Marts's Cowboys of Creedence series

IT STARTED WITH A COWBOY

Fluffy flakes of snow swirled against the window as Chloe Bishop raced into the kitchen and grabbed the travel mug of coffee she'd set to auto-brew at exactly 7:00 a.m. Several inches had already accumulated, even though it had only started an hour ago, and too late for the district to call a snow day. A few of her students would most likely be absent or late today, but dealing with snow and cold was a normal part of life in the small mountain town of Creedence, Colorado.

"Fudge nuggets," she swore as some coffee splashed over the edge of the mug and splattered across the counter. She didn't have time for this, but she grabbed a paper towel and quickly swabbed at the mess anyway. Nothing in her DNA would allow her to leave the house in disarray—even if she was running late.

Which she also did *not* do. Not usually. And this morning, she *should* have had plenty of time, had she not stepped out of bed and into a squishy pile of cat vomit. Hauling out the steam cleaner and dealing with the disaster had eaten away twenty minutes of valuable currency in the measured moments of her morning routine.

She tossed the soiled paper towel into the trash, then

poured a perfectly measured scoop of kibble into a bowl for Agatha, the carpet-contaminating culprit. Stuffing her feet into her snow boots, she caught a glimpse of red out the window.

Rubbing at the thin layer of frost, she peered through the pane and sighed, her heart breaking as she saw Madison Johnson, one of her third grade students, standing ankle-deep in the snow and awkwardly brandishing a broom as she tried to clean the snow off her mother's car. Her scuffed sneakers had to be soaked through, and Chloe recognized the thin winter coat as the same one Maddie's brother had worn a few years before. Her blond hair was pulled up on either side of her head in uneven ponytails.

Chloe leaned out the front door, her cheeks tingling with the bracing cold as she called to the girl, "Just leave it, Maddie. I'll give you a ride to school."

"I got it, Teach," Tina Johnson, her neighbor and Maddie's mom yelled, her voice carrying the slightest slur, as she stumbled out onto her front porch. She wasn't dressed much warmer than her daughter in a denim jean jacket over a pair of mismatched flannel pajamas. At least she had on a tattered pair of snow boots. And maybe it wasn't a slur, maybe Tina had just woken up and her tone was still tinged with sleepiness. Chloe hated to judge, but she wasn't taking a chance on Maddie getting in the car with her mom if she'd been drinking.

"It's okay, Tina," Chloe called back. "It's no bother for me to take her. I'm going to the school anyway."

The woman swayed from one foot to the other, then nodded. "Okay, if you're sure. If not, I can take her," she said, but she was already turning and heading back into the house.

"I'm sure," she said to Tina's retreating back, then she waved Madison up to her porch. "Come on in, honey. I just need to grab my bag, then we can go."

The girl dropped the broom, then scrambled through the snow-covered front lawn, a smile spread across her rosy-cheeked face. "Thanks, Miss Bishop," she said, stomping her feet on the mat before clambering inside.

"Where's your scarf?" Chloe made a point to knit each of her students a scarf every year, knowing that for some, it would be the only winter gear they would have. She pushed the door closed against the cold, then grabbed her down parka from the hook on the wall and quickly pulled it on.

Maddie's smile fell as her shoulders shrank inward. "I think I left it at school," she mumbled as she bent down to pet Agatha, who had meandered out from under the sofa to grace them with her presence.

Chloe sighed as she pulled her pink scarf from her pocket and wrapped it around the small girl's neck. "You can borrow mine for now." She tugged the matching hat and mittens onto the girls head and hands. There was nothing she could do about her feet for now. There was no way her boots would fit the girl's feet, but she added "snow boots for Maddie" to her mental lists of things to look for the next time she was in the local thrift store.

A quick glance at the wall clock told her she didn't have time to rummage for another set of hat and gloves for herself, but she had an extra set at school. She'd make do until she got there. Her school bag sat prepared on the bench by the door, and she hoisted it and her purse onto her shoulder.

"Let's go," she said, pulling the door shut behind her and shepherding Maddie toward her car. The silver sedan had belonged to her dad—it and the house full of stuff the only things of value she'd inherited when he'd passed away a few years back.

She clomped through the snow, then helped Maddie climb into the passenger seat and buckle her seat belt. She grabbed the snow scraper from the back seat and gave the car a quick brushing as she plodded back around to her side.

She dropped the scraper in the back as she got in and then rubbed her hands together before starting the car. The radio blared out a heavy metal song, the thump of the bass rumbling through the car.

Maddie's eyes went wide, then she cracked up. "This song is on my brother's video game," she said, completely oblivious to the irony of a bashful teacher jamming out to metal as she lifted her hands and did a decent air guitar impression.

Chloe laughed with her, doing her own headbanging impression as she switched on the wipers and defroster. She knew she should get out and completely clear the windows of ice and snow, but the wipers swished most of it off, and she could see well enough. Besides the fact that now they were going to be even later.

With the radio blaring and the defroster whirring at full blast, she put the car into gear, looked over her shoulder as she pulled out into the road, and crashed right into the snowplow that had just turned onto the street behind her.

Colton James swore as the silver car pulled out in front of him. He hit the brake, but there was nothing he could do. The car crashed right into the thick snowplow blade affixed to the front of his truck with a sickening thud.

Well, shit. He wasn't even supposed to be on this street. He'd been called out early this morning to help plow the school parking lot. But spending time at the school had him thinking about a certain cute curly-haired third grade teacher, and he'd figured as long as he was out, he could swing by her street and make sure it was plowed as well. It seemed like the neighborly thing to do.

Not that they were neighbors. She lived in a house in town, and he lived in a cabin in the country on ranch land that his family owned. The Triple J Ranch had been in his family for years and he, his mom, his brothers, and a slew of ranch hands ran it.

Speaking of his brothers, Rock and Mason were going to give him a ration of crap for this debacle. Even if it wasn't his fault. He'd been helping out the city by plowing roads for years now and hadn't ever had an accident.

But his mind hadn't usually been preoccupied by a woman. A woman who'd so far only offered him bashful smiles and a few kind words.

He swore again as he peered through the side window of the car that had hit him and saw that same woman behind the wheel. And from the frustrated look on her face, it didn't look like she was saying any kind words now.

He cut the engine and grabbed his gloves as he climbed from the truck. The frigid air stung his cheeks, and he pulled up the front of his scarf and dipped his cowboy hat to protect his face from the biting wind.

The edge of the plow was smashed into the driver's side door, so he scrambled to the other side and yanked open the passenger door. "You guys okay?"

A small girl blinked up at him from the passenger seat. He recognized her as a girl in his nephew Max's class. "We're okay, but Miss Bishop said a curse word."

"I most certainly did not," Chloe said, leaning her head on her hands, which still clutched the steering wheel.

"You said son of a beach chair."

"Which is not *technically* a swear word." Her face was still buried against her fingers.

"Then can I say it?"

"No, you probably shouldn't." She pushed her bangs from her eyes as she leaned over the girl. "I'm so sorry. I didn't even see you."

"It's okay. No harm done to me. But your car isn't going anywhere." He pulled the scarf down from his mouth. "I'd be happy to give you all a ride to school."

Her eyes went wide as she looked up at him. "Oh, son of a nutcracker. It's you."

"You did it again," the girl pointed out helpfully.

He tried to keep the grin from cracking his face, somehow knowing that breaking into laughter would not help the current situation. "Let's get you out of there and into my truck. I've got the heat on and it's colder than a witch's t—teeth out here."

She arched an eyebrow. "Good save." She nodded to the girl. "This is Maddie, she lives next door and is in my class. I was giving her a ride to school."

"Nice to meet you, Maddie. I'm Colt. I'm a friend of

your teacher." He looked down at her sneakered feet, then at the new accumulation of snow. "You're going to get your feet even more soaked trying to walk to my truck. Why don't you put your arms around my neck, and I'll carry you?"

The girl raised her arms, and Colt carried her to his truck. She weighed less than a bale of hay. "Stay right here, and don't touch anything," he instructed the girl. "I'll be right back with your teacher."

He trekked back through the snow to where Chloe was trying to climb over the center console and into the passenger seat.

"Son of a bacon bit. My foot is stuck," she gasped, her body spread halfway across the seat.

Colt leaned into the car, intent on helping, but was instead struck dizzy by the nearness of her and the honeysuckle scent of her hair. She had on black pants that were tucked into her boots, and her coat and pink sweater had ridden up to her waist. He had the sudden urge to reach out and run his hand along the perfect curve of her butt.

Dang. What was wrong with him? Was he looking to get slapped? He shook his head and tried to focus. He could see the problem—the heel of her boot was wedged between the crumpled door and her seat. He reached his arm out, acutely aware of how close he was to her body, and tried to tug on the top of the boot.

"Ouch."

He snatched his hand back as if he'd touched a hot surface. Double dang. Now he was thinking about her body as a hot surface. "Sorry. You okay?"

"Yeah, I'm fine, I just can't twist my foot in the boot."

"No, I think your boot's good and stuck. Can you just pull your foot out?"

She yanked her leg up, then fell against him, her head knocking into his chin as her foot popped free of the trapped boot.

His arms automatically went around her, the slight bump to his chin ignored with the warm press of her body. "I got ya."

She held on to him for a second, then straightened up in the seat. "Oh my gosh, I'm so sorry. Did I hurt you?" Her cheeks went as pink as her sweater.

"No, darlin'. You did *not* hurt me," he said with a light chuckle. "I'm a lot tougher than that. But you look half froze." He guessed by the oversized accessories Maddie had on that Chloe had given the girl her scarf, hat, and mittens. His cowboy hat might not warm her head, but he could at least offer something to warm up her face and hands. He pulled his scarf free from under his coat and wrapped it around her neck. "There, that should help a little. Now you better put your arms around my neck like Maddie did so I can get you to school."

She sat frozen, blinking at him, her cheeks partially covered as the color drained from her face. "Oh no. I couldn't."

"Sure you can. I won't drop you."

She shook her head, her eyes wide and round.

He arched an eyebrow. "Now, Chloe, we can sit here and debate this for another ten minutes but you've met my mother, and you know Vivienne James would tan my hide if I let you walk through foot-deep snow in your stocking feet, or foot, or sock, or whatever." Now he felt his cheeks heating. His efforts at sounding cool and convincing were coming out as full-on dorkster. But he still wasn't about to let her walk through the snow without a boot. He needed to appeal to her more rational side. "Besides that, the longer we fret about it, the later you're going to be to school, so come on, woman, just let me carry you to the truck."

"Valid point." She sighed, then slid her arms around his neck, and let him lift her from the car. "Sorry about all the potty mouth talk before. I don't usually use such inappropriate language, and especially not around kids."

A grin tugged at the corner of his mouth. "It was pretty bad, but I can take it," he teased. And he was pretty sure that growing up with three older brothers, Maddie had heard much worse as well.

"I was just so frazzled. I never run late. But with the snow this morning, and Agatha being sick, and seeing poor Madison out in the storm with no boots, then running into you—" She clasped a hand to her mouth. "Oh no. Should we be calling the police? Exchanging insurance information? Is this going to raise my rates? I've never been in an accident."

He could barely keep up with the way she jumped from subject to subject, but he liked to hear her talk. "Don't worry about it. We're on cold reporting this morning anyway, so they only want you calling the police if someone is hurt. And no one was hurt."

"Thank goodness." She shook her head, sending another wave of honeysuckle scent swirling through the air. "I wouldn't be able to live with myself if anything had happened to Maddie." She looked up at him from under dark snow-flake dotted lashes, her eyes round and sincere, as she whispered, "Or you."

A hard pull of protectiveness and need spun through his gut. This woman got to him. He wanted to pull her close, to hold her against himself and protect her, while at the same time he wanted to capture her pretty pink bow-shaped lips with his and kiss her proper and thoroughly.

It had been a long time since a woman had gotten to him—a long time since he'd *let* a woman get to him. He'd learned years ago that it was easier not to take a chance at all rather than risk taking a chance and having his hopes destroyed. He lived his life like that now—freewheeling through his days, taking life as it came, but never letting himself hope for something more. Until he'd met Chloe.

Something about Chloe Bishop was poking the edges of his heart, as if looking for a soft place to sneak in. And he could feel those rough edges giving in, not breaking, but bending a little each time she offered him a bashful smile.

He knew better than to hope though—the Colton Curse had hit too many times. Best to stick to the details, the everyday minutiae, and keep things like feelings and possibilities at bay.

"Don't worry. No one did get hurt. And the damage isn't even that bad. We can worry about filing a report later." He had no intention of reporting the accident. He was sure it hadn't done any damage to his truck, and he didn't want her to incur any kind of loss with her insurance. "I've got a buddy who runs the autobody shop in town, and he owes me a favor." Justin really owed him about seventeen, but they'd quit counting a long time ago. "If you want to leave me your keys, I'll have him come over and take a look at your car. He can tow it in to his shop if he thinks it needs it."

"You don't have to do that."

"Would you quit arguing with me, woman, and just let me help you out. I'm trying to be the hero here, and you're seriously messing with my man card."

She grinned and pushed the keys into his hand. "Fine. I already crashed into the front of your truck, I don't want to be responsible for wrecking your man card, too. But make sure your buddy sends me the bill."

"Will do." Not really. He doubted Justin would charge him for anything more than parts.

He shielded the side of the car from her view as he opened the truck door and got her settled in the cab. He knew the car was going to need some major repairs—the driver's side door was completely crumpled in.

Chloe and Maddie were buckled in by the time he got back around to his side and climbed into the truck. He'd left the engine running, and the cab was plenty warm. Although he imagined he was feeling warm for another reason—a petite, curly-haired brunette crushed against his chest reason.

He put the truck in reverse, and they all cringed at the screech of metal as the plow implement separated from the smashed-in side of the sedan.

"Son of a beach chair—that's loud," Maddie cried, pressing her hands to her ears, the too-big mittens flopping over the tops of her fingers.

Chloe looked down at her, a stern teacher expression on her face.

"Sorry." Maddie shrank back against the seat, the

impish grin on her face implying that she wasn't really that sorry.

Colt pressed his lips together to keep from laughing as he pulled out and drove toward the school.

Acknowledgments

As always, my love and thanks go out to my family! Todd, thanks for always believing in me and for being the real-life role model of a romantic hero. You cherish me and make me laugh every day, and the words it would take to truly thank you would fill a book on their own. I love you. Always.

Thank you to my sons, Tyler and Nick, for always supporting me and listening to a zillion plotting ideas. And for all of your technical help when I call you with crazy, oddball questions. I love you both more than my heart could ever imagine.

I can't thank my editor, Deb Werksman, enough for believing in me and this project, for your amazing editing talents, and for always making me feel like a rock star. Thanks to Dawn Adams for this incredible cover that captures the awesome broodiness of Mason James. I love being part of the Sourcebooks Sisterhood, and I offer buckets of thanks to the whole Sourcebooks Casablanca team for all of your efforts and hard work in making this book happen.

Huge shout-out thanks to my agent, Nicole Resciniti at the Seymour Agency, for your advice and your guidance. You are the best, and I'm so thankful you are part of my tribe.

Special acknowledgment goes out to the women who walk this writing journey with me every day. The ones who make me laugh, who encourage and support, who offer great advice and sometimes just listen. Thank you, Michelle Major, Lana Williams, Anne Eliot, Kristin Miller, Ginger Scott, Selena Laurence, Cindy Skaggs, and Beth Rhodes. XO

Big thanks go out to my street team, Jennie's Page Turners, and to all my readers: the people who have been with me from the start, my loyal readers, my dedicated fans, the ones who have read my stories, who have laughed and cried with me, who have fallen in love with my heroes and have clamored for more! Whether you have been with me since the first book or just discovered me with this one, know that I write these stories for you, and I can't thank you enough for reading them. Sending love, laughter, and big Colorado hugs to you all!

About the Author

Jennie Marts is the *USA Today* bestselling author of award-winning books filled with love, laughter, and always a happily-ever-after. Readers call her books "laugh out loud" funny and the "perfect mix of romance, humor, and steam." Fic Central claimed one of her books was "the most fun I've had reading in years."

She is living her own happily-ever-after in the mountains of Colorado with her husband, two dogs, and a parakeet that loves to tweet to the oldies. She's addicted to Diet Coke, adores Cheetos, and believes you can't have too many books, shoes, or friends.

Her books include the contemporary Western romances of the Cowboys of Creedence and Hearts of Montana series, the romantic comedy/cozy mysteries of the Page Turners series, the hunky hockey-playing men in the Bannister family in the Bannister Brothers books, and the small-town romantic comedies in the Lovestruck series of Cotton Creek Romances.

Jennie loves to hear from readers. Follow her on Facebook at Jennie Marts Books, or Twitter at @JennieMarts. Visit her at jenniemarts.com, and sign up for her newsletter to keep up with the latest news and releases.

COWBOY TROUBLE

Fall in love with Joanne Kennedy's cowboys all over again with this exciting reissue of her first saucy, sexy contemporary romance

Her latest love-life disaster behind her, Libby Brown flees to the Wyoming countryside. But it turns out that starting her own farm is way harder than she ever imagined. If it weren't for the sexy, sturdy cowboy next door, Libby couldn't survive...

Rancher Luke Rawlins is impressed by the sassy, independent city girl, and he's ready to prove that he's with her for the long haul. But the past soon threatens their new bond and tests their love in ways they never could have imagined...

"Kennedy's characters are sexy, smart, flawed—real. If you are a fan of Western romances, Joanne Kennedy should be at the top of your list."

—*Fresh Fiction* for *How to Kiss a Cowboy*

For more info about Sourcebooks's books and authors, visit:

sourcebooks.com

MISTLETOE IN TEXAS

Bestselling author Kari Lynn Dell invites us to a Texas Rodeo Christmas like no other!

Hank Brookman had all the makings of a top rodeo bullfighter until one accident left him badly injured. Now, after years of self-imposed exile, Hank's back and ready to make amends... starting with the girl his heart can't live without.

Grace McKenna fell for Hank the day they met, but they never saw eye to eye. That's part of why she never told him that their night together resulted in one heck of a surprise. Now that Hank's back, it's time for them to face what's ahead and celebrate the Christmas season rodeo style—together despite the odds.

"This talented writer knows rodeo and sexy cowboys!"

—B.J Daniels, *New York Times* bestselling author

For more Kari Lynn Dell, visit:
sourcebooks.com

Also by Jennie Marts

COWBOYS OF CREEDENCE

Caught Up in a Cowboy